Gatherings & Celebrations

GATHERINGS &

History, Folklore, Rituals and Recipes for the

CELEBRATIONS

Occasions that Bring People Together

BURT WOLF

DOUBLEDAY

NEW YORK   LONDON   TORONTO   SYDNEY   AUCKLAND

PUBLISHED BY DOUBLEDAY

a division of Bantam Doubleday Dell Publishing Group, Inc.

1540 Broadway, New York, New York 10036

DOUBLEDAY and the portrayal of an anchor with a dolphin are trademarks of Doubleday, a division of Bantam Doubleday Dell Publishing Group, Inc.

Library of Congress Cataloging-in-Publication Data

Wolf, Burton.
    Gatherings and celebrations:history, folklore, rituals, and recipes for the occasions that bring people together/ Burt Wolf.
    p.   cm.
    Includes index.
    ISBN 0-385-48265-5
    1. Holiday cookery.   2. Cookery, International.   3. Food habits
1. Title
TX739.W64 1996   96-32401
641.5'68—dc20   CIP

Printed in the United States

November 1996
First Edition
10 9 8 7 6 5 4 3 2 1

This book is dedicated to my father,
Edward E.Wolf,

and to my sons,
Stephen, Andrew and James

Acknowledgments

EMILY ARONSON was the Executive Producer for the television series and this book. CAROLINE MCCOOL was the Senior Producer. DAVID DEAN was the Executive Editor for all of the television series and assisted with the editing for much of the book. NATALIA ILYIN directed the book project and wrote the final draft of the text. MARGARET VISSER put together the research that became the basis for both the television series and this book. RAY SOKOLOV talked me through the original plan for the project. JENNY MCPHEE took my scripts and prepared the first draft of the book text. KATHERINE ALFORD adapted the recipes that we taped on location and created the additional recipes to round out each section of the book. LISE BATTAGLIA was responsible for the second round of recipe testing. MARGERY CANTOR designed the pages of the book. RAYMOND W. MERRITT of Willkie, Farr and Gallagher completed his 27th year as our legal adviser and most uncompromising critic. MORT JANKLOW and CULLEN STANLEY are technically our literary agents, but in fact they were responsible for turning the work into a book about ideas as well as recipes. TED TURNER at Cable News Network put me to work for CNN when it first went on the air, which made all of this possible. KEVIN SENIE, DALTON DELAN, and PATTI NEWI at The Travel Channel encouraged and funded much of my world travel. GENE NICHOLS and JOHN PORTER at American Program Service in Boston and MIKE LA BONIA and his staff at WKNO in Memphis have been bringing my series to public television since 1992.

I would also like to thank the individual public television stations across the country that have accepted my series and featured them prominently in their schedules. This partnership has granted me the opportunity to share my love of good food, travel, and cultural history with viewers throughout the United States.

AND:

Fred Brady	Kenneth Jackier	Janet Pappas
Ron Brown	Judith Kern	John Peaslee
Ken DellaPenta	Joel Kleiman	Steven J. Ross
Philip Di Belardino	Kip Knight	Zahid Sardar
Luisa Francavilla	Calliope Lappas	Robert Slimbach
John Fulvio	May Mendez	Tanya Sparer
Thomas Gurtner	Anita Michael	Bruce Stark
Julie Harris	Debra Netkin	Susan Van Velson
Nora Horan	Larry Ossias	

Table of Contents

Introduction

Many people in my generation grew up with a very limited understanding of the rituals that mark the passages of our lives. We knew that a bunny would show up at Easter, but we didn't know why. We knew that there was a stuffed turkey at Thanksgiving, but we didn't know what the turkey or the stuffing symbolized. We saw annual gatherings and celebrations in our own culture and cultures around the world, but we understood very little of their real meanings and did not realize what they could tell us about ourselves and the world we live in.

During the summer of 1994, I set out to discover the history and folklore behind twenty of our most important gatherings and celebrations. Some were major public events, like Easter in Florence, Holy Week in Seville, and Christmas in Germany. Some were much smaller, like a Sunday dinner with a winemaking family in Italy and a romantic supper for two in Verona (the hometown of Romeo and Juliet).

I spent two years searching out the answers to my questions. Along the way I co-produced a television series called *Gatherings & Celebrations* and wrote this book, which is based on the series.

My first days of work on the series were spent with Father Timothy Verdon of the Catholic Archdiocese of Florence. He brought me to a monastery that had a painting of The Last Supper in its dining hall, and showed me how the painting was used to remind people of the importance of a *daily* commitment to the things they believed and the people they loved.

A few weeks later I was in Finland learning how a number of ancient rituals showed many Finns how to find their true love on June 21st, the longest day of their year.

I learned a great deal about the importance of eating and drinking at each of these gatherings and celebrations. I found out why there is champagne in my glass at New Year's Eve, why men think they should do the cooking at a barbecue, how young children learn to use language at a family meal to increase their power, and how grandparents use that same meal to maintain their power. I was taught why I should never leave a napkin on a chair after a meal, what the meaning is of red and green at Christmas, and why coins are thrown at Mardi Gras.

I came to realize that these gatherings and celebrations, some of which have been going on for tens of thousands of years, evolved to help people bring balance and order to their lives.

I also found out that these gatherings and celebrations and their very specific rituals and recipes still have the ability to put us in touch with our true feelings about families, nature, and the world around us. I tried to present this information in both the television series and this book.

I should, however, point out that our selection of gatherings and celebrations was limited by the demands of the television season and by the number of pages that a publisher is willing to put into one book. For these reasons you will not find the great gatherings that are part of the Jewish, Islamic, or tribal cultures of the world. No weddings, no confirmations, and no funeral traditions have been included in this text. But they will be part of our work when we next address these subjects in a new series.

BURT WOLF

New York City
July 1996

Gatherings & Celebrations

A t the moment that the old year ends and the new begins, people all over the world pause to reflect on the experiences they had in the passing year and the dreams they have for the new. They stay up until the clock strikes, they have parties, they wear dumb hats and pour champagne. All in an effort to negotiate those uncertain seconds of change.

NEW YEAR'S EVE

IN VERSAILLES

Celebrating at Versailles

The palace of Versailles stands about fourteen miles west of Paris. It was built in the 1600s by order of Louis XIV, who was then King of France. Louis XIV loved elegance and luxury above almost all else. And when it came to throwing a party, Louis was, to say the least, opulent. He left no peasant unturned in the pursuit of pleasure. He was the party animal of his century.

Louis hated Paris. It was hard for him to control the nobility there, and he felt a bit insecure. This insecurity was not unwarranted, since they had tried to kill him on a number of occasions. So he eventually decided to get out of town and build himself a place in the country. And while he was planning this retreat, he decided to build a place that was so big, and so luxurious, and so magnificent, that its sheer size would overpower the minds of the nobles that came to visit, and render them speechless, insecure, and vulnerable. And you know what? It worked.

Versailles was just a little country village when Louis started drawing up his plans. But when he finished construction, it was one of the architectural wonders of the

world. It has eleven square miles of gardens to be weeded; 44,000 windows to be washed; 6,000 mirrors to be polished—and it takes a team of four people more than thirty days just to do the dusting. Ownership had its rigors. But it sure was a great place to visit. Especially if you had been invited to one of Louis' little parties, thrown for five or six thousand of his nearest and dearest. And it was just the place to celebrate New Year's Eve.

A Brief History of New Year's Eve

Some historians believe that one of our very first rituals was the one we created to celebrate the start of a new year. It makes sense to start at the beginning. But how do you decide when the beginning begins? Interesting problem— and it was solved in many different ways from society to society, from century to century, and from place to place.

Often, something happening in nature spurs a society to choose the date for its New Year. A change in the weather, the beginning or the end of a growing season, or the return to the neighborhood of an animal or vegetable often made a people decide to start the festivities right then and there.

Some cultures chose autumn for the start of their New Year. We still feel that influence. The school year starts in the fall. Many corporations begin their fiscal year in the fall. And, lest we forget, the new TV season begins in the fall.

Originally, the French linked the start of their New Year to the arrival of Easter Sunday. They celebrated the rebirth of the year along with that of Christ, combining two important festivals of regeneration in one. That the spring was also a time of good eating didn't hurt. The food was younger, the wine older. The French have always understood the importance of coordinating their gatherings and celebrations with what's good to eat.

The ancient Romans were the people who decided that they would celebrate the New Year on a day when nothing much was happening in nature. They had a calendar that divided the year into ten months. The first month was March and the last was December. At the end of December, everyone just stopped counting for sixty days until March came back. Since this policy was confusing, the Egyptians of the time decided to add in two months where previously there had been a blank space, and the Roman Senate just loved the idea. In 153 B.C. they named the two months January and February, and made January 1 the official opening day of the New Year. This was quite a change. Suddenly we had the ideas of Man taking charge in Nature's arena.

After the fall of the Roman empire, Europe was thrown into confusion about which day to start the New Year. Britain celebrated New Year's Day on December 25th until William the Conqueror had himself crowned on January 1, 1066, and thought it would be nice to move New Year's to that date. Later, Britain shifted again, celebrating New Year's Day on March 25th, as did Renaissance Florence. The French chose Easter Sunday. Italy liked Christmas Day, and Spain preferred January 1. In 1582, Pope Gregory XIII decreed that the Church follow a new system (humbly named the Gregorian calendar), which chose January 1 as its starting date. But England held on to March 25th as its New Year's date until 1752, when it finally capitulated.

The ancient Romans gave each other presents to celebrate the New Year. These were usually either terra-cotta plaques or lamps, each with a molded inscription. The rough translation of the greeting on the plaque is "Everyone at our place wishes everyone at your place a healthy and happy New Year." Archaeologists have uncovered thousands of the plaques, which were a very early form of greeting card. The lamps were lit and hung outside on New Year's Day, then taken down and kept in the house for good luck until the next year.

Superstitions and Rituals

The transition from the old to the new year is filled with superstitions and elaborate rituals. Many people feel that what you do on New Year's Day you'll do the whole year long. Some people say that if you like your work and want to continue it in the coming year, you should carry a symbol of your profession throughout the day. If you wear something new, it will help you to get new things. You should also make an effort to get up early in the day, not lend anything, and avoid crying.

A baby in diapers is often used as an image. This symbol illustrates the old Germanic idea of welcoming in the New Year "child" as we chase out the "old man" of

last year. At my age, I'm not thrilled with that imagery, but in the interest of journalism I thought I should pass it along.

Money plays its role in the celebration of the New Year. Many people make an effort to pay off all their bills at the turn of the year. But remember (if you plan to follow this custom) you need to pay them off before New Year's Eve! You certainly don't want to start the New Year laying out money. The pattern could start a trend, and you could end up writing hefty checks all year long. There's also a belief that you should keep some money in your pocket on New Year's Eve and on New Year's Day. And if you have children, put some money in their pockets, to diversify. Hide some money outside your house on New Year's Eve, and take it back in on New Year's Day. Might send a signal.

In Scotland, people believe that the first person to come into your house in the New Year will set the tone for the coming months. That person is referred to as the "first footer," and is sometimes chosen by the family in an attempt to control its own luck. In case you'd like to try out for the job, the person should be tall and dark-haired, but not be flat-footed or have eyebrows that meet in the middle. This "first footer" is often called "the lucky bird." He may bring a present to the household, but it should be something that will be used up, and it should not be taken out of the house again.

In France, there was a time that people used New Year's Day as an excuse to go calling, paying visits to their associates or to the people with whom they hoped to be associated. Very often, the people they went out to see weren't home because *they* were out trying to visit people *they* wished were *their* associates. The result of all this visiting was a general lack of reception: almost no one was at home! But you left your visiting card, to show you had been there. Eventually, what with the wear and tear on the horses and whatnot, people gave up leaving cards in person and began popping them in the mail. That's how our present custom of mailing New Year's cards got started.

We make a great effort to differentiate Christmas celebrations from New Year's festivities. Christmas, to this day, is a private, family affair, which often focuses on the children. New Year's Eve celebrations, on the other hand, are public, and focus on adult pastimes.

The moment when the old year becomes the new is always very important. You are supposed to stay up and be clear-headed and happy as the bells start to toll. It is a turning point, and you want to be able to consciously direct your fate at this very significant moment. The whole idea of the New Year's Eve party is to establish a happy setting as the new year begins. You want to get off on the right foot.

In farm communities it was important to keep crops and animals protected from evil spirits at the moment of change from the old to the New Year. The tried-and-true technique for keeping these spirits on the move appears to be the blowing of horns combined with the banging of drums. We're still keeping them away by shouting, blowing whistles, tooting horns, ringing bells and generally making nuisances of ourselves during those few moments when the old year changes to the new. Making noise has often been part of the rituals that are associated with beginning something new. We bang on a door to have it open; we bang on a pan to start the New Year.

The Foods of the New Year

Many people believe that the food and drink of New Year's Eve will influence life during the coming year. The Romans, for instance, covered their tables with all the foods they loved. They thought that the table held the Luck of the Coming Year, and that piling all the food on its surface assured abundance in the future months.

The foods we traditionally serve at New Year occasions often show both sides of our personalities. One group of foods is always simple, inexpensive, easy to make. These foods show that we are not wasteful, and that we deserve good things in the coming year. The other group of foods are expensive and extravagant. These foods send a signal that says, "Excuse me! Could I have more of this good stuff in the new year?" Both groups of foods are served at the same time in most cultures, and they balance each other out.

The shape of the foods is also important. Breads should be well-rounded—the way you want your year to be. No long loaves, because they have ends where good luck might escape. The same goes for pasta: round, not straight. New Year's celebrations are also the time to eat something unusual, in the hope that something or someone new will enter your life. In some cultures, the festivities are also a time for gift-giving. The Romans, as we have noted, gave plaques and lamps. But they also gave presents of foodstuffs—nuts and dates, dried figs, honey, and sweet cakes of all kinds. Nuts, aside from marking the turn of the year, were often given at the start of any new enterprise. The French still give jars of cooked chestnuts in sweet syrup on New Year's Day. It's that old Roman idea in action—and very nice with ice cream.

Chocolate plays its part at the New Year, symbolizing the rich and sweet hopes that the giver has for the recipient's year. I guess if you have other kinds of hopes for that special recipient, you can always send a bar of "unsweetened bitter."

A Bit Of Bubbly

Champagne is the traditional beverage for a New Year's celebration. The first introduction of the sparkling wine was at one of those small parties for the nobility that Louis XIV was always throwing at Versailles. It was golden, it was bubbly, and it tickled your nose. It was festive; its cork tended to pop (if handled roughly), spraying foam and making a general commotion. It was a luxurious product that you'd like to drink more of throughout the year.

Champagne is actually the name of a winemaking region in France. Many places now make wines by the "champagne method," but, if you notice, they don't (or shouldn't) say "Champagne" on their labels. True champagne comes only from Champagne. One of the most notable champagnes of Champagne comes from the house of Laurent -Perrier. It is owned and operated by the family of the Duke de Nonancourt; they make their champagnes by the most traditional and authentic methods in a small town in the middle of the region. The grapes are

selected from the production of over a thousand different growers in the area. The trick is to find just the right balance.

Each champagne maker tries to develop a "house style" for the taste of its non-vintage wines, and goes to great effort to maintain that style from year to year. The person who has the job of developing and maintaining that special taste is called the champagne blender, and he uses wines from many years and from over 200 villages to make that special flavor.

After blending, the wine is bottled along with a small amount of yeast and a little cane sugar. The bottles go into the cellar for the next three to five years. When the bottles are put down in the cellar, the yeast begins a second fermentation. (The first fermentation took place when the original grapes were crushed and held in tanks before blending.) Gas is formed again, but this time it is trapped in the wine—and that's how champagne gets its very famous bubbles.

The next step in the process is called riddling. The bottles lie on their sides, with their necks slightly lower than their bases. Every day, the riddler comes by and turns the bottle a little to one side and slightly up. The solids that have formed in the bottle as a result of this second fermentation slowly slide down into the neck of the bottle. A good riddler turns and tips 60,000 bottles a day.

When all the sediment has settled in the neck, the bottle is placed in an icy solution of brine. The liquid in the neck freezes, and when the cap is taken off a block of sediment shoots out. A little cane sugar is added to balance the acidity, and a bit more wine goes in to top off the bottle. Then the cork goes on, covered by a wire cage to keep it in place. The wire is important, since the bottle is under considerable pressure. Three more months of rest in the cellar, and the champagne is ready to come to the party.

Laurent-Perrier also makes a rosé champagne by a method called vatting, which is a more difficult process than the simple, everyday practice many vintners use of merely adding a bit of red wine to a large amount of white wine. Vatting requires the grape juice to rest together with the grape skins for about two days at the very beginning of the process. The skins give a delicate color to the champagne.

What makes one great champagne house different from another is the style that it uses in making its non-vintage champagne. But every once in a while, the grapes of a specific year are so extraordinary that the blender decides to make a champagne just from the grapes of that year. When the house makes such an unusual blend, it is called a vintage champagne. Yet a vintage champagne tells you more about the attributes of a specific year's grapes than it does about the style of the house.

When all the elements of the process are absolutely perfect—perfect sunshine, perfect temperature, perfect blending—Laurent-Perrier makes a *Grand Siecle,* which means the "Great Century," a reference to the grandeur of the time of Louis XIV, when great champagne was first introduced.

Recipes for New Year's Eve
Versailles

Herbed Spiced Nuts

Puff Pastry Cheese Straws

Chicken Provençale

Wild Rice Pancakes with Salmon Roe

Warm Chickpea & Basil Salad

Sautéed Salmon with Orange & Asparagus

Individual Chocolate Cakes

Herbed Spiced Nuts

Makes 3 cups

1 cup macadamia or hazelnuts

1 cup shelled pistachios

1 cup raw cashews

1 tablespoon unsalted butter

1 clove garlic, crushed

1 teaspoon dried rosemary, crushed

½ teaspoon dried thyme, crushed

¼ teaspoon cayenne or less to taste

¾ teaspoon kosher salt

1   PREHEAT THE OVEN TO 350°F. Spread the nuts on a roasting pan and toast in the oven until they are golden brown, about 10 minutes. While the nuts are toasting, heat the butter in a pan with the crushed garlic, herbs, and cayenne.

2   REMOVE THE GARLIC from the butter and discard. Toss the toasted nuts in a bowl with the flavored butter and the salt. Cool and serve.

Puff Pastry Cheese Straws

Makes approximately 18 long straws

½ pound frozen puff pastry, defrosted

1 tablespoon Dijon-style mustard

3 tablespoons finely grated fresh Parmesan cheese

½ teaspoon sweet paprika

1 ON A LIGHTLY FLOURED work space, roll out the puff pastry to approximately 12 x 14 inches. Paint the lower half of the pastry with the mustard, and sprinkle with the cheese and paprika. Fold the top end of the pastry over to cover the bottom, and press the dough together. Roll the dough back to a 12 x 14-inch rectangle and chill for 30 minutes.

2 PREHEAT THE OVEN to 400°F and line a baking pan with parchment paper.

3 WITH A PIZZA WHEEL, cut the dough into strips about ½ inch wide. Twist the strips into long corkscrews, and place the twists on the baking pan. Press the ends to the rim of the pan to help prevent the twists from unraveling during the cooking. Chill for 10 minutes.

4 BAKE THE TWISTS for 15 minutes, or until golden brown. Trim the ends and cool on a rack. Store in a tightly sealed container for up to 2 days.

Chicken Provençale

Makes 4 servings

Sous Chef Vincent Thiessé
Trianon Palace, Versailles

⅓ cup olive oil

4 skinless and boneless chicken breasts, halved

2¼ teaspoons kosher salt

¼ teaspoon freshly ground black pepper

1 large onion, diced

1 medium eggplant, diced

1 large red bell pepper, diced

1 large green bell pepper, diced

1 large yellow bell pepper, diced

2 medium zucchini, diced

½ cup white wine

2 sprigs fresh thyme, or 1 teaspoon dried thyme, crushed

3 bay leaves

5 cloves garlic, unpeeled

6 plum tomatoes, quartered

2 tablespoons tomato paste

¼ cup chopped fresh basil leaves, plus 8 leaves for garnish

1   HEAT 2 TABLESPOONS of the oil in a large stewpot or Dutch oven. Season the chicken breasts with ½ teaspoon of the salt and ⅛ teaspoon of the pepper. Cook the breasts over medium-high heat until golden brown, about 8 minutes depending on the thickness of the chicken. Remove the chicken breasts to a plate and set aside.

2   ADD ALL THE DICED vegetables to the pot and cook over high heat, turning the vegetables with a wooden spoon, to heat through and wilt slightly, 3 or 4 minutes. Pour the wine over the vegetables, add the remaining oil, salt, and pepper, the thyme, and bay leaves. With the broad part of a knife smash the garlic cloves to loosen them in their skins, but do not peel, and add them to the stew. Leaving the skins on the garlic helps keep the cloves intact as they cook. Simmer, covered, over low heat for 5 minutes or until the vegetables release their juices.

3 REMOVE THE COVER, bury the chicken breasts in the vegetables, and cook for 10 minutes, covered, or until the breasts feel firm to the touch. Remove the breasts, and set them aside in a warm spot while you finish the stew.

4 ADD THE PLUM TOMATOES and simmer until soft, about 10 minutes. Stir in the tomato paste and basil, and cook uncovered over high heat to thicken the sauce, about 10 minutes. Return the chicken breasts to the stew to heat through. To serve, remove the bay leaves and thyme sprigs and spoon the vegetables onto a warmed platter or individual plates, place the chicken breasts on top, and garnish with the basil leaves.

Wild Rice Pancakes with Salmon Roe

Makes 16 small pancakes

1 cup cooked wild rice

½ teaspoon salt

1 clove garlic, minced

3 tablespoons all-purpose flour

¼ teaspoon baking powder

1 large egg, lightly beaten

¼ cup milk

2 tablespoons unsalted butter, melted

⅓ cup sour cream

¼ cup salmon roe

1   IN A BLENDER OR FOOD PROCESSOR, combine the cooked wild rice, salt, garlic, flour, baking powder, egg, and milk. Pulse on and off to make a coarse batter. Add 1 tablespoon of melted butter.

2   OVER MEDIUM HEAT in a non-stick skillet, add the remaining butter and spoon in single tablespoons of the batter to form small pancakes about 2 inches wide. Cook over medium heat for 2 to 3 minutes on the first side, until the bottoms are golden brown and the tops are set and slightly bubbly. Flip the pancakes and finish cooking them on the other side for 1 minute. Hold the pancakes in a 200°F oven or serve immediately, with a small dollop of sour cream and salmon roe on top.

Warm Chickpea & Basil Salad

Makes 4-6 servings

For the Vinaigrette:

> 2 tablespoons fresh lemon juice
>
> ¾ teaspoon kosher salt
>
> ½ teaspoon freshly ground black pepper
>
> 1 small clove garlic, finely minced
>
> ⅓ cup extra virgin olive oil

For the Salad:

> ¼ cup minced shallots or red onion
>
> 4 medium carrots, peeled and sliced into thin rounds
>
> 4 cups cooked chickpeas (three 15-ounce cans); rinse before using
>
> 2 tablespoons minced fresh basil or more to taste
>
> Salt and freshly ground black pepper

1 TO MAKE THE VINAIGRETTE: Place all the ingredients in a small jar or plastic container with a tight-fitting lid. Close the top and shake vigorously until the dressing looks creamy. Set aside until ready to use.

2 TO MAKE THE SALAD: When ready to serve, warm the vinaigrette in a medium skillet with the shallots and carrots, for about 5 minutes. Add the chickpeas and heat through. Stir in the basil, adjust salt and pepper to taste, and serve warm.

Sautéed Salmon with Orange & Asparagus

Makes 4 servings

Sous Chef Vincent Thiessé
Trianon Palace, Versailles

12 medium asparagus spears
2 navel oranges or 1 navel orange and ½ cup fresh orange juice
1 teaspoon kosher salt
Four (6-ounce) salmon fillets
¼ teaspoon freshly ground black pepper
3 tablespoons unsalted butter
2 tablespoons black or green olive puree (optional)
1 tablespoon fresh chives, cut into 1-inch lengths

1   TRIM THE ASPARAGUS SPEARS and cut them into 3- to 4-inch lengths. Set aside.

2   PEEL 1 ORANGE so that it is free of all white pith. Slice the orange into thin sections and set aside. Juice the second orange or use ½ cup of fresh orange juice.

3   WHEN READY TO SERVE, bring a small pot of water to a boil with a pinch of the salt. Cook the asparagus for 4 to 5 minutes, until tender but not limp. Or you can steam the asparagus for 2 to 3 minutes.

4   HEAT A LARGE NON-STICK SKILLET. Season the fish with half the salt and pepper. Add half the butter to the pan and sauté the salmon, skin side up first, over high heat until lightly browned, 3 to 4 minutes per side depending on the thickness of the fillets. Remove the fish to a warm spot while you make the sauce.

5   TO MAKE THE SAUCE, pour the orange juice into the skillet, bring it to a boil, and reduce until slightly syrupy. Turn off the heat, whisk in the remaining butter, and season with the rest of the salt and pepper. Add the reserved orange slices to the sauce to warm through.

6   TO PRESENT THE DISH, fan the asparagus tips on a warmed platter or on 4 individual plates and place the cooked salmon in the center. Garnish the salmon with a small dollop of olive puree and the orange slices, and spoon the sauce on top. Sprinkle with chives and serve.

Individual Chocolate Cakes

Sous Chef Vincent Thiessé
Trianon Palace, Versailles

For the Cakes:

6 tablespoons unsalted butter
5 ounces semi-sweet chocolate
½ cup granulated sugar
⅓ cup all-purpose flour
2 large eggs

For the Sauce:

1½ cups raspberries, fresh or frozen defrosted
1½ tablespoons Grand Marnier or
  other orange spirits
2 tablespoons sugar or more to taste

For the Garnish:

Confectioners' sugar
Mint, strawberries, or raspberries (optional)

1   TO MAKE THE CAKE: Preheat the oven to 400°F. Brush four 1-cup ramekins with 1 tablespoon of the butter. Melt the chocolate and remaining butter in a double boiler, or on half power in a microwave oven for 2 minutes, stirring occasionally. Set aside.

2   IN A MEDIUM BOWL, stir together the sugar and flour, and stir in the melted chocolate. In a second bowl, whip the eggs with a hand-held beater, until they're pale yellow and well aerated, about 2 minutes. Whisk a third of the eggs into the chocolate base. Fold in the rest of the eggs, taking care not to deflate the batter. Pour the batter into the prepared ramekins and place the ramekins on a baking sheet. Bake for 18 to 20 minutes, or until the centers of the cakes are slightly soft and fudgy. A toothpick stuck in the center of the cakes should bring up moist batter.

3   WHILE THE CAKES ARE BAKING, make the sauce: Puree the raspberries, Grand Marnier and sugar together. Pour the mixture into a small saucepan and bring to a boil. After the mixture comes to a boil, reduce to a simmer, and cook for two minutes until the sauce is thickened. Press the sauce through a fine strainer to remove the seeds. Serve warm or chilled with the cakes.

4   TO SERVE THE CAKES, pour a small pool of sauce on a plate. Unmold the cake and dust it with confectioners' sugar. Place the cake in the sauce and garnish it with the optional berries or mint.

ROBERT BURNS NIGHT, SCOTLAND

A Grace before Dinner, extempore

> O thou who kindly dost provide
>> For every creature's want
> We bless Thee, God of Nature wide,
>> For all Thy goodness lent:
> And if it may please Thee, heavenly Guide,
>> May never worse be sent;
> But, whether granted or denied,
>> Lord, bless us with content. Amen!

A Grace after Dinner, extempore

> O thou, in whom we live and move—
>> Who made the sea and shore;
> Thy goodness constantly we prove,
>> And grateful would adore;
> And, if it please Thee, Power above!
>> Still grant us, with such store,
> The friend we trust, the fair we love—
>> And we desire no more. Amen!

Scottish Celebrations

The Scots are *very* serious about being Scottish. They have a great sense of their history and the uniqueness of their culture. Being Scottish is very much a part of daily life, but it is particularly pronounced during three annual celebrations.

The Scots felt that Christmas was too much a creation of the Papacy, and proceeded to write it off. Their celebrating became focused on New Year's Eve, which the Scots call Hogmanay. On New Year's Day they go about giving gifts of coal, salt, and whisky. The coal is a symbol promising that the home will be warm throughout the coming year. The salt promises future food. And the whisky just promises.

The second annual gathering of the Scots centers around the feast of St. Andrew, celebrated on the 30th of November. And though St. Andrew's Day is observed in Scotland, it has really become a festive occasion for Scots living *outside* of Scotland. On St. Andrew's Day, people of Scottish ancestry gather in cities throughout the world to celebrate their Scottish heritage.

In Scotland itself, however, the great day for rejoicing in all things Scottish is the birthday of Robert Burns, the national poet of Scotland. Born in 1759, his words have become familiar throughout the world. Every New Year's Eve, millions of people join together and sing the words to Burns' "Auld Lang Syne":

Should auld acquaintance be forgot,
And never brought to mind?
Should auld acquaintance be forgot,
And days o' auld lang syne?

"Auld lang syne" is Scots dialect for "long ago." The poet reminds us to honor the past, and remember the importance of old friendships.

Robert Burns became a national hero because his poetry celebrated the history and beliefs of the Scottish people at a time when all things Scottish were under attack by the English. He celebrated the rights of the common man. He celebrated his nation's battle against the dishonesty of the official government and the Church. And these days, on the night of January 25, all of Scotland celebrates the anniversary of his birth with a Burns Night Dinner.

The Food of Scotland

Scotland is not rich in farmland, and its climate can be less than ideal for growing things. As a result, the history of its cooking demonstrates the Scots' skill at making a lot from a little. The Scots are devoted to recipes that are based on root vegetables like potatoes and turnips. Because of the intensity of the winters, Scots created a cuisine designed to produce a sense of inner warmth —lots of porridge, thick soups, endless rounds of baking scones, oatcakes, and Dundee cakes.

Hundreds of miles of seashore, loch-front, and riverside, however, give Scotland access to an ideal source of seafood. Scotch salmon is world famous, and there is a generous supply of trout and haddock. Aberdeen Angus beef produces excellent steaks, and the hunting season brings in venison, pheasant, hare, and grouse.

Very often the most important dish at a Scottish gathering is based on an ancient recipe that stuffs meat, vegetables, and grain into the stomach of an animal and

then cooks it over a steaming liquid. Christmas pudding was originally a meaty sausage of this kind. In the late 1600s, dried fruit was added and the wrapping shifted to a pudding cloth. Eventually, the fruit replaced the meat entirely.

Robert Burns once wrote a poem entitled "To a Haggis," in which he calls the dish the "great chieftain o' the puddin' race." At a Burns Night Dinner, fittingly, this "haggis" is the featured dish. The word *haggis* comes from the verb "to hack," or mince, as in mince pie. The same root gave us the word *hash*, and haggis has much in common with our modern recipes for hash. Haggis is made from assorted animal parts that have been finely chopped, seasoned, and, nowadays, cooked in cloth.

The Story of Scotch Whisky

The Scots have been distilling spirits for hundreds of years. No one is quite sure when they got started, but there are records in the tax office that go back to 1494. In those days the Scottish monks were making a drink that had a big deal reputation as a cure-all. They drank it, of course, for purely *medicinal* purposes and called the liquid the "water of life." In the Gaelic dialect of Scotland, it was called *usquebaugh*, which sounded like "uishgi" to the English, and was soon mispronounced as "whisky."

These days, the Scots drink two kinds of whiskies—single malt whiskies and blended whiskies. The making of a single malt scotch whisky starts with a process called malting. Barley is moistened with water until it starts to sprout.

After a few days the barley is dried. The traditional system uses a drying fire that is fueled in some part by peat. Peat is a readily available natural soil-like product made up primarily of decomposed plants. The plant matter is so concentrated that it can be cut into blocks and used as a fuel. The burning peat adds a smoky flavor to the malted barley.

The malted barley is then ground and sent off for mashing. It is mixed with warm water in a vessel called a mash tun. After a while a liquid called wort is drained off. Wort is full of the natural sugar that has come out of the barley. Yeast is added to the wort, causing the sugar to convert to alcohol. This process is known as fermentation and it is basically the same chemical reaction that is used to make beer or wine. The fermented liquid, called wash, is then transferred to a still. A still is just a giant teapot used to heat the wash. Alcohol boils at a lower temperature than water, so it turns to a vapor first and rises out of the wash. It passes up through the still, turns down at the top, and recondenses back to liquid alcohol on the other side.

The shape of the still has a considerable effect on the final taste of the whisky. If the maker uses a very tall still, some of the vapor will condense at the top and drip back down to be distilled a second time. The result will be a lighter taste. A short pot can produce a scotch with a creamier body. Every still has its own distinct shape and its own distinct effect on flavor. Makers are very concerned about changing a still. And when they must, they do it by reproducing their old pot down to the last dent.

The whisky is then transferred to its aging casks. In the beginning, the wooden casks were thought of merely as containers to store the whisky. Eventually, however, people discovered that the cask could change the flavor of the scotch. During the 1800s, the English developed a great taste for sherry, which they imported from Spain in oak casks. When the sherry was taken out of the barrels the empty casks were bought by scotch-makers. During the 1900s, they also began to use spent bourbon casks from the United States, which added caramel and vanilla notes to the scotch. The wood the cask is made of also affects the flavor of the whisky.

When the distilled spirit goes into its cask, the law says that the whisky must stay there and mature for at least three years in order to be called scotch. In practice, serious scotch-makers often age their whisky in wood for a considerably longer time.

Single malt whisky is made in one distillery exclusively from barley. It may come from a number of different casks, and different ages, but always comes from the same distillery. During the 1800s, an Irishman named Aeneas Coffey invented a still that did not need the repeated cleaning and refilling that was necessary for the operation of a pot or single batch still. The "Continuous Patent Still" produced a very light, quite palatable whisky that was made from an unmalted grain like corn or wheat. Very soon whisky-makers

began blending single malt whiskies with the alcohol produced from the patent still. One flavor might add a sense of smokiness, another could lighten the overall taste, a third might be selected in order to introduce a touch of honey. That allowed them to combine the flavors they liked in different single malt whiskies with the flavors they liked from the grains. Local merchants began to introduce different blends that they liked and that their customers liked, and they marketed them under their own branded labels.

During the late 1800s, a wine and spirits merchant named Matthew Gloag decided to develop his own scotch whisky. He wanted it to appeal to the tastes of the growing number of ladies and gentlemen who were coming up to Scotland to take part in the local sporting activities. They liked to fish for salmon in the great Highland rivers. They liked to hunt the famous grouse on the moors. They liked to track the magnificent Scottish deer. And to hunt the famous grouse on the moors. They liked to seek out the wild partridge… and hunt the famous grouse on the moors. Matthew Gloag could see the emergence of a pattern and its related opportunity. He devised a blended scotch and called it The Famous Grouse. He got his daughter Philippa to sketch the famous Red

Grouse on the label, and in time The Famous Grouse became the most popular blended scotch whisky in Scotland.

The blenders at Matthew Gloag have a secret formula for The Famous Grouse that includes more than twenty different single malts—one of which is Highland Park from Orkney—and the whisky from the patent still. The master blender balances the flavors so that the final result is superior to its components.

And just for the record, a "wee dram" is a nonspecific unit of measure—it can be a half ounce or a half pint. It's all in the eye of the pourer.

Recipes for Robert Burns Night
Scotland

Scottish Beef & Potato Pie

Cock-a-Leekie Soup (Chicken & Leek Soup)

Clapshot (Turnip & Potato Puree)

Cranachan (Raspberry Cream)

Petticoat Tail Shortbread Cookies

Scottish Beef & Potato Pie

Makes 4-6 servings

Mrs. Lyn Williamson
Alvie House

For the Beef and Potatoes:

> 1 pound boiling potatoes
>
> 2 teaspoons kosher salt
>
> 2 tablespoons vegetable oil
>
> 1 medium onion, chopped
>
> 3 tablespoons all-purpose flour
>
> 1 pound ground beef sirloin or top round
>
> 1 cup beef broth
>
> 2 teaspoons Worcestershire sauce
>
> 1 tablespoon tomato ketchup
>
> ¼ teaspoon freshly ground black pepper

For the Sauce:

> 2 tablespoons unsalted butter, softened
>
> 2 tablespoons all-purpose flour
>
> 1 cup milk
>
> 1 cup grated sharp white cheddar cheese (about 4 ounces)
>
> 1 large egg yolk
>
> ¼ teaspoon kosher salt
>
> Pinch of grated nutmeg

1 TO MAKE THE BEEF AND POTATOES: Peel and slice the potatoes into ⅜-inch-thick pieces. Put the slices into a pan with cold water to cover, add ½ teaspoon of the salt, bring the water to a boil, and simmer for 2 to 3 minutes or until the potatoes are tender. Drain and set the potatoes aside. Preheat the oven to 375°F.

2 IN A SKILLET over medium-high heat, heat the oil and sauté the onion until lightly golden brown, about 10 to 12 minutes. Stir in the flour with a wooden spoon and cook for 1 minute. Add the ground beef and break it up with the spoon. Sauté the beef for 10 minutes, scraping the bottom of the skillet with the wooden spoon. When the flour and beef are brown, pour in the beef broth, Worcestershire sauce, ketchup, the remaining salt, and the pepper. Bring to a boil, and simmer for 2 to 3 minutes, until thickened. Set aside while you make the sauce.

3   TO MAKE THE SAUCE: Whisk the butter, flour, and milk together in a nonreactive sauce-pan. Heat to a boil, whisking constantly and vigorously, until the sauce is smooth and thickened. Simmer for 2 to 3 minutes, whisking frequently. Remove the sauce from the heat, and whisk in ⅔ cup of the cheese and the egg yolk. Season with the salt and nutmeg.

4   TO ASSEMBLE THE PIE, spread the meat mixture in to a 9-x-9-inch casserole, then cover the meat with the sauce. Top the sauce with the potatoes, overlapping the slices to make a scalloped pattern. Cover with the remaining cheese and bake for 20 to 25 minutes, or until lightly brown. (For an extra-brown top, run the pie under a hot broiler.) Let the pie set at room temperature for 5 to 10 minutes before serving.

ALVIE HOUSE

One place to celebrate Burns Night Dinner is Alvie House, in the town of Kincraig, by Kingussie, in Inverness-shire. It is an Edwardian shooting lodge set above a small loch in the Scottish Highlands. A 13,000-acre estate surrounds the main house and offers all the sports that are dear to a Scotsman's heart: fishing for the wily salmon on the river Spey; pursuing the wild deer in the Kincraig woods; hunting for the nimble grouse on the Highland moor; and, of course, stalking the wee dram wherever you can find it. Alvie House has been home to five generations of the Williamson family. During the 1980s a portion of the estate was turned into a magnificent guesthouse under the direction of Jamie and Lyn Williamson.

Cock-a-Leekie Soup (Chicken & Leek Soup)

Makes 6-8 servings

Mrs. Lyn Williamson
Alvie House

Bouquet garni: 4 sprigs fresh thyme, 4 sprigs flat-leaf parsley, 1 bay leaf, 1 leek green
One (3½ -4 pound) chicken
5 medium leeks, white and light green parts, sliced and washed (about 6 cups)
10-12 cups cold water or chicken broth
1 tablespoon kosher salt, or more to taste
¼ teaspoon freshly ground black pepper, or more to taste
1 cup diced boiled ham (about 4 ounces)
1 cup pitted prunes, quartered

1   TUCK THE HERBS for the bouquet garni into the fold of the leek green and wrap it closed with kitchen string. Remove and discard the gizzards from the chicken.

2   PLACE THE CHICKEN, sliced leeks, and bouquet garni in a soup kettle with cold water or chicken broth to cover. Season with the measured salt and pepper. Bring the soup to a boil, and skim off any foam that rises to the surface. Reduce the heat, so the soup cooks at a very low simmer—bubbles should barely erupt on the surface of the broth. Steep the chicken, covered, for 1½ hours.

3   AFTER THE BROTH HAS SIMMERED, lift the chicken from the pot with tongs or 2 large spoons, and transfer it to a bowl. Continue to simmer the soup, uncovered, for 30 minutes more. When the chicken is cool enough to handle, pull the meat from the carcass and discard the skin and bones. Cut the meat into soup spoon–size pieces.

4   RETURN THE CHICKEN PIECES to the soup, and add the ham and prunes. Simmer gently for 10 to 15 minutes to plump the prunes and combine the flavors. Remove and discard the bouquet garni. Season with salt and pepper to taste. Serve the soup hot.

Clapshot (Turnip & Potato Puree)

Makes 4 servings

4 medium turnips
One (½-pound) baking potato
½ teaspoon kosher salt
3 tablespoons unsalted butter
Freshly ground black pepper
Pinch of fresh grated nutmeg

1 PEEL AND CUT the turnips and potato into 1-inch cubes. Place the vegetables in a saucepan with water to cover, and the salt. Bring to a boil, reduce to a simmer, and cook for about 10 minutes, or until the vegetables are easily pierced with a fork.

2 POUR OFF THE WATER; let the vegetables sit in a strainer or colander for a few minutes to allow all the liquid to drain out. Transfer to the jar of a blender. Puree until smooth. Return the puree to the pan and heat. Stir in the butter and season with salt, pepper, and nutmeg to taste. Serve hot.

Cranachan (Raspberry Cream)

Makes 4 servings

Mrs. Lyn Williamson
Alvie House

2 tablespoons oatmeal, not instant

2 tablespoons chopped peeled almonds

3 tablespoons strawberry jam

3 tablespoons scotch whisky

½ teaspoon minced orange zest

1 cup chilled heavy cream

2-3 tablespoons sugar

1¼ cups frozen raspberries, defrosted

1   HEAT THE OVEN TO 350°F. Spread the oats out on a sheet pan, and toast in the oven for 5 minutes. Add the almonds to the pan and continue to toast for about 5 minutes more, or until the nuts and oats are golden brown. Set aside to cool.

2   WHISK THE JAM, scotch, and orange zest together in a bowl. (If the jam is clumpy, gently heat the mixture on the stove or in a microwave to loosen it up.) Whip the cream in a chilled nonreactive bowl until the cream holds soft peaks. Don't overwhip the cream or it will be grainy when it chills. Fold the jam mixture and half the oats and nuts into the whipped cream.

3   GENTLY STIR THE SUGAR with the raspberries, being careful not to break up the fruit. Spoon about ¼ cup of the raspberries and their juice into the bottom of each of 4 wine glasses. Spoon about ¼ cup of the whipped cream on top of the raspberries. Follow the cream with another layer of raspberries and top that off with the remaining cream. Sprinkle each cranachan with some of the remaining almonds and oats. Refrigerate for at least an hour before serving.

Petticoat Tail Shortbread Cookies

Makes 18 cookies

16 tablespoons (2 sticks) unsalted butter, softened

⅔ cup sugar

1 teaspoon almond extract

2 cups all-purpose flour, sifted

1 large egg yolk

1   IN A MIXING BOWL, cream the butter with the paddle attachment of a standing mixer or with a hand-held beater until light and fluffy, 1 to 2 minutes. Add the sugar and almond extract; continue to beat for 2 to 3 minutes more. Fold the sifted flour into the butter, then add the egg yolk and mix just enough to make a smooth cookie dough. Don't overmix or the shortbread will be tough.

2   LINE A BAKING SHEET with parchment or sprinkle the sheet with flour.

3   TO FORM THE COOKIES: divide the dough into 2 equal pieces. Lightly flour a clean work space and roll one piece into an 8-inch disk. Use a 2- to 3-inch fluted cookie cutter, and cut out the center of the disk. Transfer that single cookie to the baking sheet. Give the remaining circular ring a ruffled edge by crimping the outer edge with your fingertips. Cut the ring into 8 equal-size pieces. Transfer the cookies to a baking sheet. Repeat with the rest of the dough. Refrigerate the cookies for 1 hour before baking.

4   PREHEAT THE OVEN TO 325°F. Bake the cookies for 20 to 25 minutes, until they're lightly browned at the edges. Cool on a rack before serving.

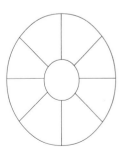

FOOD & ROMANCE

In a city known for a famous pair of star-crossed lovers, romance has never gone out of style. Verona's fountains and festivals still bring people together, just as they did in Shakespeare's "Romeo and Juliet." Once lovers have actually met, sharing food is often the next step of a romance—it is then that they start to learn about each other, and begin the enticing process called courtship.

IN VERONA

Love, Sharing, and Society

Shakespeare's balcony love scene between Romeo, a very young Montague, and Juliet, an even younger Capulet, may be the greatest romantic scene in the history of English literature. It sure has its fans. The story of the two lovers from feuding families has been bringing tourists to Number 23 Via Capello for hundreds of years.

The young lovers, in a desperate attempt to be together, decide that they will drink a potion that will feign death. But the plan gets fouled up, and results in the deaths of both Romeo and Juliet. To me, the confusion and darkness around this hazard-

ous drink is a comment about society. Romeo and Juliet are able to see beyond the feud because of their love. They are wiser than their elders, but the madness of their families destroys them. Their destruction holds a lesson: share the poison of hatred, and you threaten the future of your culture.

As historical figures, Romeo and Juliet may or may not have existed. But their families, and other powerful, and increasingly isolated clans certainly did. Arranged marriages were one of the ways that these families tried to break their self-imposed boundaries. The head of one family decided where an alliance was needed, and made a deal with the head of another family. Marriages that created alliances kept everything functioning and relatively peaceful. Of course, the children that came from such a marriage were the really important focus. The society needed children to bind families together: no children, no future.

If your family did not choose your mate for you, in a kind of preëmptive strike on your emotions, you might actually have a chance to meet someone on your own. Still, if things got serious, you'd ultimately need your family's approval.

One way to meet that "special someone" was to go to a festival.

Festivals were the perfect place to start a romance. Lots of men and women of all different ages were gathered in the same place at the same time. They were eating,

drinking, and dressed in their best clothes. Often, they were masked. If you wore a mask, your identity was a secret. You could easily edge yourself into the crowd at the food tables and meet somebody new.

If your family wasn't in the festival set, the church was the next best place to look over future romantic partners. And as a fallback position, you could always count on the local fountain. Before indoor plumbing made public wells obsolete, young men and women were constantly going off to the fountain to bring home a bucket's worth. That fountain provided the perfect place to meet someone.

Fountains are still thought of as romantic places where lovers meet. They remind us of the places in nature where vastly different species of animals come together to drink. The tavern in the neighborhood where I grew up was usually referred to as "the local watering hole."

The Latin word *companion* literally means "someone with whom we share bread." And sharing is what holds people together, whether they are two lovers, a family, a group of friends, or an entire society. To share food is often an expression of love.

Food and romance got a boost in the 18th century from the "souper intime," an invention of the amorous aristocracy. A very private dinner for two, the "souper intime" required total seclusion. The lavish buffet was set out in advance of the meal. Servants did not appear during the dinner. No one is quite sure just what went on during those romantic little parties (there were no reporters present), but it is my considered opinion that Love Potion #9 played a major part in the festivities. Eventually, "souper intime" could be taken in a restaurant. Small, private rooms were available for the occasion. Waiters entered only by invitation. Such a meal was immortalized in the film version of Henry Fielding's novel *Tom Jones*, in a scene that has permanently altered my view of chicken. A "souper intime" room is still available in Arnaud's Restaurant in New Orleans.

For thousands of years, tradition and ritual have surrounded the foods of lovers. There are many edibles that are believed to arouse sexual desire. Called aphrodisiacs (after Aphrodite, the Greek goddess of love, beauty, and fruitfulness), these foods change depending on where in the world you happen to be. For a long time,

the focus was on any animal that had a reputation for great sexual activity. The hope was that the same abilities would appear in anyone who ate that animal.

Guys would look at a salmon. Finding its way back from the open sea to the river it called home. Swimming against the current for miles. Hurling itself up through waterfalls. And all in the name of love. How about salmon for dinner? (It couldn't hurt.) Clearly, the salmon had a great sexual drive that just might be transferred to the eater. That's one kind of aphrodisiac. But some foods, such as oysters, pomegranates, mushrooms, figs, and passionfruit, *seem* sexual because of their textures. Others get on the list because of their shapes. Bananas, eggplants, carrots, asparagus, cucumbers, and sausages have all, from time to time, been classified as aphrodisiacs.

And then there are foods that come into the culture with a well-established reputation as tasty morsels that will induce thoughts of love. Chocolate is the leading food in this category. The ancient Romans believed that arugula was such a food, and planted it at the foot of statues of Priapus, the Greek god of male sexual power.

Bright colors, especially red, are also thought to be important in meals for lovers. Red is the color of passion. We color hearts red and give red roses. We wear red lipstick and powder on red blusher. And we include red foods in menus: a common double threat is the red strawberry dipped in chocolate.

Couples often combine special foods for eating with special places for meeting. That little restaurant on the corner becomes "our place," and is saturated with meaning and memories. A special meeting place must have certain amenities. It must provide a place to sit, the possibility of light refreshment, and most important, anonymity. The sidewalk cafe is a perfect place to sit and order something to eat and drink in the company of lots of other people without looking expectant. The perfect cover. It's like a little ongoing festival that you can drop into whenever you want.

Restaurants are also excellent places for a romance to blossom. Before you really know each other, the public aspect of the restaurant is very reassuring. Behavior is held in check. This limiting factor actually enhances the couple's intimacy. Since it is under the surveillance of the restaurant's staff and the other patrons, the couple's simple gestures become imbued with much meaning. If one person leans across the table and takes the other's hand, a great cultural taboo against touching at the table has been defied. Violating that unwritten code of behavior brings the couple closer together.

Love and Chocolate: Perugina's Kisses

In the Western world, the food with the most magical, famous, and elaborate history as an aphrodisiac is chocolate. Chocolate had been around in South America for hundreds of years before Europeans tasted it. Legend has it that Cortez was the lucky Spanish explorer who first had the opportunity, when the Aztec ruler Montezuma offered him a cup of hot chocolate. Montezuma recommended chocolate as the appropriate beverage for an amorous evening. For the past five hundred years, that story has been repeated. Whether chocolate really affects your love life is an unanswered question. Every few years, some scientific group announces its research on the subject. Some say that chocolate can have a real effect on your emotions. Others say that there is no physiological effect, except the pleasure that comes from being around the chocolate itself.

One chocolate, however, actually comes with a true story of love, and that is Perugina's "Baci," named for the Italian word for "kisses." Seems that in 1907, the Buitoni family was already a well-known manufacturer of pasta. To add new products to their line, they decided to make the sugared almonds traditionally used in wedding ceremonies. They set up their confectionery in the Italian city of Perugia, named their company "Perugina," and sent Giovanni, the twenty-two-year-old son, to run the factory. As luck would have it, Giovanni fell in love with Luisa Spagnoli, the confectioner that developed many of the company's products. Luisa and Giovanni, working, as they were, in a business environment, did not dare upset the decorum of the place. So they sent secret love messages to each other, hidden in the samples of the candies she was developing. To commemorate that correspondence, Luisa invented Baci. Now Perugina wraps a love note into all the Baci it makes.

Wine and Love

For thousands of years, the land around Verona has been cultivated for wine grapes. Many of those wines have become world famous. But fame brought the ancient problem that plagues both lovers and winemakers. It is good to be popular, to be sought after, to be in demand. But lovers and winemakers that are too responsive to popularity can end up with a compromised reputation. And that's what happened to the region around Verona. The winemakers, flattered by so many ardent fans, finally gave in to the insistent demands of an enamored public, and traded quality for quantity.

Roberto Anselmi, however, decided to come to the aid of his region's reputation. He rejected the idea of mass production, and returned to the small, hillside vineyards. The vineyards are called *capitelli* because of the small chapels built in the fields, and used for centuries by workers stopping for midday prayers.

Anselmi regularly thins his grape bunches, which improves the quality of the grapes that remain. He has reduced the number of grapes grown on each vine and the number of vines in the field. When almost everyone thought that the wines of the area were too fragile to be aged in barrels, Anselmi invented a new approach to barrel-aging that worked quite nicely.

Anselmi is receiving his just desserts in several ways, and one of them is his Anselmi I Capitelli—a sweet dessert wine, known as a Recioto do Soave. It has a flavor with touches of caramelized apricot and peach, honey, and vanilla. A number of leading wine writers have described it as the equal of any of the world's great sweet wines.

Anselmi also makes some elegant dry white wines. San Vincenzo, a classically light and simple Soave Classico, is what Soave was before it started running around. Capitel Foscarino is the name of a five-acre hillside vineyard in Soave. It is also the name of a pale, straw-colored wine made by Anselmi. His Capitel Croce comes from grapes that are grown on a steep hillside vineyard of only six acres. The juice from those grapes is barrel-fermented and aged to produce a wine that is beyond a conventional Soave. In breathing new life into the winemaking region of Verona, Roberto Anselmi reminds us that no reputation is ever truly lost, and that romance and love can blossom where we least expect them.

Recipes for Romance
Verona, Italy

Salmon with Red Pepper Coulis

Herbed Mashed Potatoes

Tortellini with Mushrooms & Tomato

Coeur à la Crème with Lavender & Raspberry Sauce

Juliet's Kisses

Spiced Pumpkin Pecan Muffins

Salmon with Red Pepper Coulis

Makes 2 servings

For the Red Pepper Coulis:

1 red bell pepper, seeded and diced

1 medium shallot, sliced

¼ cup dry white wine or sweet vermouth

2 tablespoons extra virgin olive oil

1 tablespoon minced fresh tarragon, or 1¼ teaspoons dried, crushed

1 teaspoon kosher salt

⅛ teaspoon freshly ground black pepper

3 tablespoons water

¼ teaspoon white wine vinegar

For the Salmon:

Two (6-ounce) salmon steaks

1 teaspoon olive oil

Kosher salt

Freshly ground black pepper

2 sprigs fresh tarragon, for garnish

1   RESERVE 1 TABLESPOON of the red pepper to garnish the finished dish.

2   TO MAKE THE COULIS: Place all the ingredients except the reserved red pepper and the vinegar in a saucepan. Bring to a simmer, cover, and cook for 25 minutes, or until the pepper is soft and tender. Check the sauce as it cooks; if it gets dry, add a bit of water to keep it from browning. Puree the ingredients in a blender or food processor until they become a smooth sauce. Stir the vinegar into the coulis, return it to the pan, and keep warm while you cook the salmon. (The coulis can be made a day ahead and reheated before serving.)

3   PREHEAT THE OVEN to 250°F. Position one oven rack in the lower third of the oven and a second rack in the upper third. Bring 4 cups of water to a boil and pour it into a medium baking pan (the water should be at least 2 inches deep). Carefully place the pan of water on the lower oven shelf.

4   TO COOK THE SALMON: Brush the salmon steaks with oil and place them on a baking or roasting pan on the upper rack. Bake for 10 minutes, turn the salmon over with a spatula, and continue to cook for 5 to 10 minutes longer, depending on the thickness of the salmon. The salmon will keep its translucent color and have a satiny texture. Remove the skin, if desired, and season the fish with salt and pepper to taste. Serve the salmon on warmed plates in a pool of coulis garnished with the reserved diced red pepper and a sprig of tarragon.

Herbed Mashed Potatoes

Makes 2 servings

1 pound baking potatoes, peeled
1 teaspoon kosher salt
⅓ cup half and half
1 tablespoon each minced fresh chives, flat-leaf parsley, and tarragon
2 tablespoons unsalted butter
Freshly ground black pepper

1   PLACE THE POTATOES in a pot with ½ teaspoon of the salt and water to cover. Bring to a boil and simmer until the potatoes are fork tender. Drain and puree the potatoes in a food mill or ricer. Return the potatoes to the pot and keep warm.

2   HEAT THE HALF AND HALF with the herbs and butter. Pour the flavored half and half into the potatoes and stir with a wooden spoon until all the liquid is absorbed. Season with the remaining salt and the pepper to taste. Keep loosely covered and warm until ready to serve.

Tortellini with Mushrooms & Tomato

Makes 2 servings

Executive Chef Agostino Clama
Hotel Due Torri Baglioni

2 quarts water
¼ ounce dried porcini mushrooms
¾ pound ripe tomatoes (1 large tomato or 2-3 plum tomatoes)
2 tablespoons olive oil
2 ounces white mushrooms, sliced
⅛ teaspoon crushed red pepper flakes
8 ounces tortellini (meat or cheese)
1 tablespoon minced fresh flat-leaf parsley
½ teaspoon salt
Freshly ground black pepper

1   BRING THE WATER TO A BOIL. Pour ⅓ cup of the boiling water into a small bowl with the dried porcini and let the mushrooms soak for 10 minutes. Once they are cool and moist, squeeze the mushrooms dry and chop them fine. Save the soaking liquid.

2   TO PEEL THE TOMATOES, remove the blossom end and make a small **x** with the tip of a knife in the other end. Plunge the tomatoes into the boiling water for 30 seconds and then immediately into ice water. Gently peel back their skin. Cut the tomatoes in half and squeeze out the seeds. (If the tomatoes are really juicy, strain the seeds and save the juice to add to the sauce.) Dice the tomatoes.

3   IN A MEDIUM SKILLET set over high heat, heat the oil and sauté the sliced white mushrooms until browned and tender, about 3 to 4 minutes. Add the chopped porcini and 3 tablespoons of the reserved soaking liquid, and cook until the liquid is almost all evaporated, about 4 minutes. Add the tomatoes and red pepper flakes and simmer. While the sauce is simmering, cook the tortellini.

4   SALT THE BOILING WATER, add the tortellini, and cook until tender but not mushy. Drain the tortellini and add them to the sauce. Toss with the minced parsley. Season the sauce with the salt and black pepper to taste. Serve in warmed bowls.

Coeur à la Crème with Lavender & Raspberry Sauce

Makes 2 servings

For the Coeur à la Crème:

> 1 cup mascarpone cheese
>
> ⅓ cup confectioners' sugar, sifted
>
> ½ teaspoon dried crumbled lavender (optional)
>
> ½ cup chilled heavy cream

For the Raspberry Sauce:

> 1 cup raspberries, fresh or frozen defrosted
>
> 2 tablespoons granulated sugar
>
> 1-2 tablespoons orange liqueur (optional)

1   TO MAKE THE COEUR À LA CRÈME: In a standing mixer with the paddle attachment or by hand, cream together the mascarpone, confectioners' sugar, and lavender if used. In a chilled metal or glass bowl, whip the cream until it holds soft peaks. Fold the whipped cream into the mascarpone base.

2   MOISTEN A PIECE OF CHEESECLOTH, about 10 inches square, and line a Coeur à la Crème mold (a perforated heart-shape mold) with the cloth. Spoon the cheese mixture into the mold and smooth it out to fill the mold evenly. Fold the excess cheesecloth over the top, place the mold on a plate, cover with plastic wrap, and refrigerate for at least 2 or up to 24 hours.

3   TO MAKE THE RASPBERRY SAUCE: Combine all the ingredients in a small saucepan. Cover and cook over low heat for 5 minutes, or until the berries liquefy. Using a rubber spatula or spoon, press the softened raspberries through a fine mesh strainer to remove the seeds. Serve warm or chill before serving.

4   TO UNMOLD THE COEUR À LA CRÈME, peel back the cheesecloth, invert the mold onto a large plate, and gently lift. Peel off the cheesecloth. Serve with the warm or chilled raspberry sauce.

Juliet's Kisses

Makes about 3 dozen cookies

Executive Chef Agostino Clama
Hotel Due Torri Baglioni

2 large eggs
8 ounces semi-sweet chocolate, chopped
8 tablespoons (1 stick) unsalted butter
1 cup granulated sugar
1⅓ cups all-purpose flour, sifted
Confectioners' sugar

1   PREHEAT THE OVEN TO 350°F. Grease and flour a large cookie sheet.

2   HARD-BOIL THE EGGS, cool, and peel. Discard the white of one of the eggs. Press the whole egg and the yolks through a fine strainer and set aside.

3   MELT THE CHOCOLATE in a small bowl set over hot but not boiling water or in a microwave oven at half power for 3 minutes.

4   IN A STANDING MIXER or by hand, cream the butter and sugar together until light and fluffy. Add the chocolate and mix until smooth. Stir in the flour and sieved eggs to make a stiff cookie dough.

5   SPOON THE DOUGH in smooth, 1-inch-wide mounds onto the prepared cookie sheet. Bake for 15 to 20 minutes until the cookies are puffed and cracked. Cool and dust with the confectioners' sugar.

Spiced Pumpkin Pecan Muffins

Makes 6 large muffins

Vegetable oil for lining the muffin cups

4 tablespoons unsalted butter

2 large eggs

⅔ cup brown sugar

1 cup pumpkin puree

1½ cups all-purpose flour

2 teaspoons baking powder

1 teaspoon ground cinnamon

½ teaspoon ground allspice

½ teaspoon ground ginger

⅛ teaspoon grated nutmeg

¼ teaspoon salt

⅓ cup finely chopped pecans

1 PREHEAT THE OVEN TO 400°F.

2 LIGHTLY OIL 6 MUFFIN CUPS. In a small pan over medium heat, heat the butter until it begins to brown. Set aside to cool.

3 IN A MEDIUM BOWL, whisk the eggs and sugar together until smooth and airy, about 1 minute. The mixture may lighten in color. Whisk in the pumpkin and browned butter.

4 IN A BOWL, sift together the flour, baking powder, spices, and salt. Gently mix the dry ingredients into the pumpkin mixture. Fold in the pecans, but be careful not to overwork the batter. If there are lumps, they will disappear during the baking. The less you work the batter, the more tender the muffins will be.

5 FILL THE MUFFIN CUPS with batter. Bake for 25 to 30 minutes in the center of the oven. To prevent the muffins from getting soggy after baking, remove the cooked muffins from their cups and cool them on a rack. Serve warm.

CHINESE NEW YEAR IN TAIWAN

T
he most important festival in China is the celebration of the New
Year, which marks the first day of the first lunar month, a date that
falls around the end of the Western month of February. The Chinese
start celebrating the arrival of spring with their New Year, and carry
out a number of rituals at home that signal its beginning.

In the old days, people celebrated the New Year by traveling to the mountains to hunt wild game, then used the meat in offerings to the gods and to their ancestors. These days there's not much hunting in the mountains, but many other ancient rituals are still strictly followed.

First, everything in the home gets cleaned—an undertaking that combines the idea of spring cleaning with the desire to rid the dwelling of any evil spirits that may have taken up residence during the past year. Then old things are replaced. *New* is the operative word in the preparations for the New Year.

The homeowner attaches lucky messages to both sides of the front door. Any visitor from this world or the next would have a hard time missing the greeting! Then the family sets up a table and covers it with offerings for the gods. Generally, the three main meats of the Chinese diet all make an appearance— pork, chicken, and fish dishes are placed on the table. Oranges, which bring good luck, sweet rice cakes, and spirit money are all part of the presentation. Candles are placed in shrines, incense is burned, family prayers are offered, and a little wine is poured, just to keep up the spirits of the spirits.

When the incense has burned down about halfway, the gods are considered to have had their meal, and it's time to go outside and burn the spirit money. The Chinese, like many cultures, believe that what you need and enjoy in this world will be needed and enjoyed in the next. And the way to send things from one world to the other is to reproduce them on special paper, and then to burn them. When the transfer of funds is completed, everyone goes back in the house and helps move the offering table a little to the left of the shrine. This new place is the spot where offerings are made to ancestors, rather than to gods. Gods are slightly to the right—and that's not a political statement. The favorite foods of the ancestors are set out along with a few glasses of rice wine.

It is thought that the ancestors inhale the aroma of the food, which is all they want. The remaining part of the offering is returned to the family and becomes everyone's dinner.

Just before the end of the year, the Kitchen God, who has been hanging on the kitchen wall in the form of a drawing, returns to the other world to report to the Jade Emperor on how the members of the family have behaved during the year. As a general precaution, the Kitchen God's mouth is rubbed with honey in the hope that he will say only sweet things.

The foods of the Chinese New Year are chosen because of their symbolic meaning. Lotus seeds, peanuts, and pomegranates represent a hope for the birth of children during the coming year. The inclusion of a fruit with many seeds often symbolizes a family's desire for many offspring. Grapefruit, oranges, and tangerines bestow their good luck. And candies fill the future year with sweetness. Green foods mark growth and red foods signify good fortune—the same colors and meanings we see in the West as part of the Christmas celebration.

Word-play also has its symbolic role. The Chinese word for *fish* rhymes with the Chinese word for *surplus.* If you eat half a fish on New Year's Eve and the other half on New Year's Day, you might just transfer a surplus of good luck from one year to the next.

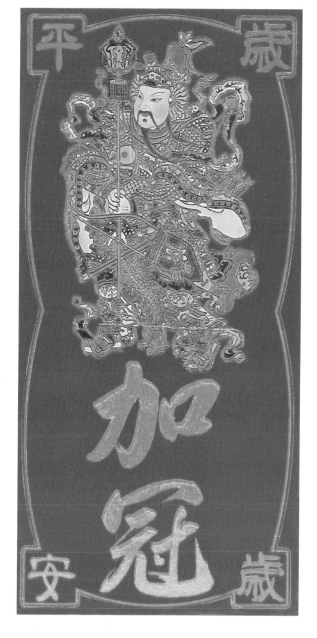

The dumpling is another festival food with great symbolic meaning, and it is particularly important at the New Year. On New Year's Eve, the women of the family gather in the kitchen to make special dumplings—a favorite is stuffed with vegetables. They undertake the task of dumpling-making according to a set of ancient rules. Children are not allowed in the kitchen because they might say something that could interfere with the development of the good luck inside the dumpling.

Custom demands that if there has been any disharmony between the women in the family, now is the time to work things out. It is widely believed that the New Year's dumplings will not cook properly if there is any ill will among the members of a family. If anyone says anything unpleasant, the dumplings will be stolen from the pot by an evil spirit. Never count your dumplings while you're making them. The more you count, the poorer you'll be in the coming year. The dumpling must be wrapped in bamboo leaves so that it doesn't come apart during cooking. If it breaks up in the boiling water, the whole year will be filled with unpleasant experiences that will break up happiness.

For many centuries, it was the custom to place small gold or copper coins inside some of the dumplings, promising a prosperous year to the people who got them. These days, cooks substitute small pieces of candy for the coins, to avoid various dental and swallowing crises. Some New Year's dumplings contain sugar-coated lotus seeds, and if a married woman of child-bearing age receives one of these dumplings, it's considered a sign that she will have a son during the coming year.

People try to go home at the New Year. They renew family ties, find out the current news, and share a reuniting meal. It's also the time that employers give banquets to

thank their employees for working hard during the past year. In earlier times, an employer would place a chicken on the table and point its head toward anyone who was going to be dismissed. Today, the boss points the head toward himself, to avoid any misunderstandings.

During the New Year's celebration, children are given "lucky money" in red envelopes. (In China, red is always the color of happiness and good fortune.) Adults pay off old debts, so they can get started on some fresh ones, and everybody wears new clothing and tries to stay up through the night to welcome in the New Year.

Chinese folklore tells us that, in ancient times, "Year" was a fearsome beast that generally lived very deep in the mountains, minding his own beeswax. But annually, on New Year's Eve, Year would find that his appetite called for human flesh, and came down from his rocky haunts to prey on unsuspecting villagers and townspeople. As a result, a number of monster-avoidance techniques are recommended during the New Year's Eve period. Number One: Stay up all night, so that you can keep a lookout for suspicious-looking characters who might want to eat you. Number Two: Hang strips of red paper on your door—Year just hates red. And Number Three: Set off the noisiest firecrackers you can possibly find, which will give Year a migraine and send him back to the mountains, where he belongs.

When morning comes, everyone congratulates everyone else on not having become Year's midnight snack. Then a ritual offering of respect is made to the family's ancestors—generally a gift of luxurious foods. After this ritual, the gods are venerated. And finally, the younger members of the family show their respect for the older generation. The family visits an incense-filled temple, and goes to see friends and relatives in order to deliver New Year's greetings.

As the New Year gathers speed, the rituals continue. The third day of the New Year is considered a time of bad luck, so many people stay home. For certain animals, however, it is believed to be a good day—especially for field mice, who are thought to hold their weddings on that day. Some people actually scatter rice in the fields just for the affair.

On the fourth day, the gods, who have been on vacation in the other world for the New Year, return to earth. They are welcomed back with firecrackers and offerings of spirit money. The welcoming ceremonies often take place at the end of the day, since no one wants to offend a god who just might be getting back a little late.

On the sixth day, spectacular lion and dragon dances begin. Some are held in front of the presidential offices, and at the Sun Yat-Sen Memorial Halls. The most religious one is held at the Lungshan Temple on Kuangchow Street in Taipei.

The seventh day is the anniversary of the creation of mankind, and is marked by a seven-dish dinner and the lighting of seven candles. Of all the gatherings and festivals involved in the cycle of the lunar year, none is as dramatic or as ancient as the celebration of the Chinese New Year.

The Lantern Festival

It all comes to an end with the ritual of the Lantern Festival, which has been part of the celebration of the New Year for over 2,200 years. The people of ancient China believed that the first full moon of the year sent out a powerful light, making it possible to see the celestial spirits who darted here and there. Torches were added to make the job easier, and eventually, the torches became lanterns.

At some point, the lantern festival became a special event for children. Perhaps it was because the date of the first full moon of the year is also the date on which they go back to school after the New Year holiday. Parents began to construct magnificent lanterns for their children to take to school, and their teachers would light candles inside the lanterns to symbolize everyone's hope that the children would turn out to be bright students. Throughout the centuries, people came together on this day to march about with glorious lanterns. Fireworks were set off, and riddle-guessing contests were introduced.

The traditional food of the Lantern Festival is a sticky rice cake called *yuan hsiao*. It is round, and symbolizes both the new moon and the unity and completeness of the family. Some people believe that these rice cakes contain the central power of aging, and that you will not gain the year of age that comes with the New Year until you eat this cake.

Paper Gods

The Chinese like to keep the images of their gods close at hand. Some images are carved out of wood and stone; some are molded of clay; some cast in metal. But the most common images of Chinese dieties are those that are made of paper. They are an absolutely essential part of Chinese culture. The most popular of these paper images are known as New Year prints.

The tradition of decorating one's home with lucky prints goes all the way back to the tenth century. The most traditional and beautiful examples of the art are printed from wooden blocks carved with an intricate design. The prints vary in size, depending on where they will be in the house, and on how much detail is needed to express the essence of the god's personality. The materials and production are usually quite inexpensive. When it comes to sacrificial offerings, it is really the thought that counts.

Paper gods are available in many shops, but you don't actually purchase them. It would be considered impolite to try to "buy" a god. So you invite the diety to your house, and pay the storekeeper for assisting you with the invitation. You are allowed to buy candles and incense, though.

The dozens of paper gods can be divided into five general kinds. First come the Door Gods, which include Unicorn Bringing Sons, God of a Hundred Sons and a Thousand Grandsons, Protect and Aid the Home (a very popular one), and Bestow Promotions and Bring Prosperity (a big seller in the corporate world).

The second group are the Festival Gods, which include my particular favorite, the Kitchen God. The Kitchen God comes in two forms: homestyle and industrial-strength. For the home, both a god and a goddess are available. Industry just gets the male diety option.

Everyone honors the God of Wealth on the second day of the New Year. In keeping with his commercial affiliations, he is often offered by door-to-door salesmen. This direct marketing ploy puts people in a difficult situation. Even if you have already invited a God of Wealth to your house, it is inadvisable to yell "We don't want any! We've already got one!" That sort of attitude is liable to insult any self-respecting diety, and could easily cut you out of his goodwill for an entire year.

The Congratulatory Gods are a third group of paper dieties. At your first wedding, you'll receive the God of Happiness and the Two Gods of Marital Union. If you are remarrying, you'll need a copy of the God and Goddess of the Bed, a charming couple who have had a hundred children and who have the ability to protect the second wife from any harm at the hand of the first wife's spirit. Useful.

A fourth set of dieties is the Gods of Blessing and Deliverance, who are asked for help according to your specific needs. Health is something people are always hoping for. And finally, there are the Occupational Gods—one for just about any job. The trick is to get the god of your profession lined up with the God of Wealth so that they can work as a team on your behalf in the coming months of the new year.

Recipes for the Chinese New Year
Taiwan

Steamed Seafood Dumplings

Spicy Pickled Cucumbers

Chinese New Year's Omelet

Spicy Chicken Stir-Fry with Peanuts

Braised Whole Fish with Ginger

Cold Noodles with Asparagus & Ginger

Steamed Seafood Dumplings

Makes 35 dumplings

Dim Sum Chef Chou Da-yuan

Grand Formosa Regent

For the Dumplings:

½ pound center-cut cod fillet

1 large egg

¼ pound medium raw shrimp, peeled and deveined

1 tablespoon minced peeled fresh ginger

⅓ cup minced water chestnuts

2 scallions, white and green parts, finely minced

¼ teaspoon ground coriander

1 teaspoon soy sauce

¼ teaspoon freshly ground black pepper

35 won ton wrappers (about 3 inches in diameter)

3-4 large Chinese cabbage or lettuce leaves

For the Sauce:

⅓ cup soy sauce

2 tablespoons rice vinegar

1 tablespoon dry sherry

2 tablespoons minced fresh coriander leaves

⅛ teaspoon ground coriander

¼ teaspoon crushed red pepper flakes (optional)

1   TO MAKE THE DUMPLINGS: Process the cod and egg in a food processor to a smooth puree. Add the shrimp and pulse on and off so the shrimp are coarsely chopped with the fish. Transfer the fish mixture to a medium bowl and mix in the ginger, water chestnuts, and scallions. Season the dumpling filling with the coriander, soy sauce, and pepper.

2   DUST A BAKING SHEET with cornstarch or line it with parchment. Place ⅔ tablespoon of the dumpling filling on the upper half of a won ton wrapper. Fold the skin over the filling and pinch together at the center of the edge. Make 3 small pleats in the side of the skin facing you, to the right side of the center point, and then 3 more on the left side, to seal the dumpling. Press the dumpling skin edges firmly together to seal. Place the dumplings on the prepared sheet pan. Repeat with the remaining filling and won ton wrappers. The dumplings are ready to be steamed, or they can be refrigerated up to 24 hours before steaming.

3   TO MAKE THE SAUCE: Mix all the sauce ingredients together in a small bowl.

4   LINE A STEAMER BASKET with the cabbage leaves. Set the dumplings in the steamer basket, about ½ inch apart. Steam the dumplings in batches if necessary. (If you have a stacking-style steamer, you can steam multiple trays of dumplings at one time.) Place the steamer basket over a pan of boiling water and steam the dumplings for 5 to 7 minutes, or until the filling is completely cooked and the wrapper is tender. Transfer the dumplings to a serving plate with the dipping sauce and serve.

Spicy Pickled Cucumbers

Makes about 2 cups

4 Kirby cucumbers (about 1 pound)

1 tablespoon kosher salt

1 tablespoon vegetable oil

1 medium clove garlic, crushed and peeled

½ teaspoon crushed red pepper flakes

1½ tablespoons dark Chinese or Japanese sesame oil

1 cup rice vinegar

⅔ cup water

6 tablespoons sugar

1 **PEEL THE CUCUMBERS** in alternating strips to make a striped pattern. Slice the cucumbers lengthwise; scoop out the seeds with a spoon and discard them. Cut on the bias into ½-inch-wide slices. Place the slices in a bowl and toss with 1 teaspoon of the kosher salt. Set aside for 30 minutes.

2 **IN A SKILLET,** heat the vegetable oil with the garlic and pepper flakes for 1 minute. Drain the cucumbers of any liquid, add to the oil, and stir-fry for 30 seconds. Add the sesame oil, rice vinegar, water, sugar, and remaining salt. Bring the liquid to a boil to dissolve the sugar, which should take about 30 seconds. Pour the pickles and the liquid into a bowl to cool. When cool, marinate them overnight in the refrigerator. Serve the pickles at room temperature. They will keep, refrigerated, for 1 week.

Chinese New Year's Omelet

Stir-Fry Chef Tsai Kun-zhan
Grand Formosa Regent

> 8 large eggs
> 1 teaspoon kosher salt
> ⅛ teaspoon freshly ground black pepper
> ⅛ cup chopped water chestnuts
> 4 scallions, white and green parts, thinly sliced
> 1 teaspoon dark Chinese or Japanese sesame oil
> 3 tablespoons vegetable oil

1 WHISK THE EGGS in a medium bowl with the salt and pepper. Mix the water chestnuts, scallions, and sesame oil into the eggs.

2 HEAT THE VEGETABLE OIL in an 8-to-10-inch non-stick skillet over medium-high heat. Pour the egg mixture into the pan. Let the eggs begin to set, then gently stir the middle of the omelet a couple of times with a fork and cook for 1 to 2 minutes. Cover the omelet and cook over medium-low heat for 2 minutes more, or until the eggs are almost set. When the omelet is almost set, carefully flip it over onto a flat plate larger than the pan, then slip the omelet back into the pan to cook the other side for another minute.

3 INVERT THE OMELET from the pan to a plate, slice it into wedges, and serve immediately.

Spicy Chicken Stir-Fry with Peanuts

Makes 4 servings

Stir-Fry Chef Tsai Kun-zhan
Grand Formosa Regent

For the Marinade:

    1 large egg white
    1 tablespoon sugar
    1 tablespoon soy sauce
    ½ teaspoon kosher salt
    ⅛ teaspoon freshly ground black pepper
    ½ teaspoon cornstarch
    1 pound skinless and boneless chicken breast meat, cut into ½-inch dice

    2 cups vegetable oil

For the Stir-Fry:

    ¾ teaspoon crushed red pepper flakes
    2 teaspoons balsamic or black Chinese vinegar
    1 tablespoon soy sauce
    ⅛ teaspoon sugar
    1 teaspoon cornstarch dissolved in 2 tablespoons water
    ⅓ cup unsalted roasted peanuts
    1 tablespoon minced fresh coriander
    Cooked white rice for serving

1   TO MAKE THE MARINADE: Mix the egg white, sugar, soy sauce, salt, pepper, and cornstarch together in a medium bowl. Add the chicken pieces and set aside to marinate for 15 minutes.

2 WHEN READY TO SERVE, in a medium heavy-bottomed saucepan or wok, heat the oil to 350°F. Remove the chicken pieces from the marinade. Deep-fry the chicken pieces for about 1 minute. Carefully pour the chicken and oil into a strainer or colander set over a bowl to drain the oil completely from the chicken. Reserve the oil.

3 TO STIR-FRY: Heat 2 tablespoons of the strained oil in a medium-size skillet or wok. Add the red pepper flakes to flavor the oil and cook for 30 seconds to 1 minute, then add the chicken, vinegar, soy sauce, and sugar, and heat for 1 minute. Add the cornstarch mixture, bring to a boil, and stir in the peanuts. Transfer the stir-fried chicken to a warmed platter, sprinkle with the coriander, and serve immediately with rice.

Braised Whole Fish with Ginger

Makes 4 servings as part of a banquet

Stir-Fry Chef Tsai Kun-zhan
Grand Formosa Regent

One (2-inch) piece fresh ginger, peeled
One (2-pound) snapper, scaled, trimmed, gutted, and gills removed
2 tablespoons vegetable oil
4 scallions, white and green parts, sliced into 1-inch strips
¼ teaspoon crushed red pepper flakes
2 tablespoons soy sauce
1½ cups chicken broth
1 teaspoon cornstarch dissolved in 1 tablespoon water

1   SLICE THE GINGER into paper-thin rounds. Slice the rounds into narrow strips. Rinse and dry the fish. Make 3 slices, 3 inches long on each side, in the skin of the fish.

2   IN A LARGE HEAVY-BOTTOMED SKILLET or wok, heat the oil. Add the ginger, scallions, and red pepper flakes and stir-fry for 1 minute.

3   PLACE THE FISH in the pan along with the soy sauce and chicken broth. Bring the broth to a simmer, baste the fish, and cover. After 8 minutes, slip a large spatula under the fish and turn, baste, and braise it for 5 to 7 minutes more, or until fish is cooked but still moist.

4   CAREFULLY TRANSFER the fish with a large spatula to a lipped platter, cover and keep in a warm place. Combine the dissolved cornstarch with the braising liquid and cook over high heat for 1 minute, just until the sauce starts to thicken. Pour the sauce over the fish and serve.

Cold Noodles with Asparagus & Ginger

Makes 4 servings

For the Dressing:

1½ teaspoons kosher salt

¼ teaspoon freshly ground black pepper

2 tablespoons rice vinegar

1 tablespoon Chinese black or balsamic vinegar

2 teaspoons soy sauce

4 teaspoons finely minced peeled fresh ginger

½ teaspoon finely minced orange zest

⅓ cup vegetable oil

1 tablespoon dark Chinese or Japanese sesame oil

For the Noodles:

½ pound Chinese egg noodles

¾ pound asparagus

4 radishes, thinly sliced

1 scallion, white and green parts, thinly sliced

2 tablespoons minced fresh coriander, plus sprigs for garnish

1 TO MAKE THE DRESSING: In a large bowl, whisk together the salt, pepper, vinegars, soy sauce, ginger, and orange zest. Slowly whisk in the vegetable and sesame oils. Set aside.

2 TO MAKE THE NOODLES: Bring a medium pot of water to a boil, salt the water, and cook the noodles until al dente, according to the package directions. Drain the noodles into a colander and rinse them under cool water. Shake the noodles free of excess water. Add the noodles to the dressing, toss to coat, and set aside.

3 PEEL THE BOTTOM PART of the asparagus stalks with a vegetable peeler and trim the tough ends. Cut the asparagus on the bias into ¼-inch-thick slices about 1½ inches long. Steam the asparagus and radishes in a steamer basket or bamboo steamer over boiling water for 2 minutes. Remove the steamer tray and rinse the vegetables under cold water to stop the cooking.

4 TOSS THE NOODLES with the cooked asparagus, radishes, scallions, and minced coriander. Place in a serving bowl and garnish with sprigs of coriander.

I n the middle of the fifteenth century, a Parisian theologian compared the people of a country to wine fermenting in a barrel. Sometimes, he wrote, barrels of aging wine need to be opened just to keep them from exploding. The wine of human madness, he believed, needed to be released at least once a year, in order to transform itself into the good wine of pious devotion.

CARNIVAL IN

NEW ORLEANS

Carnival, that all-out, city-wide bash for which New Orleans is justly famous, has its roots in an ancient Roman holiday called the Feast of Saturn. This festival, encouraged by the government, was calculated to release tensions between the "rich-and-famous" and the "*never*-to-be-rich-and-famous." In Rome, there were many more slaves than there were slave-owners. During the festival, all sorts of wild partying went on between all classes of society. The Feast of Saturn helped distract the slaves from doing the math and realizing that they might be able to overthrow the whole arrangement.

When Christianity became the official religion of the Roman Empire, the Feast of Saturn was converted into Carnival, the last opportunity to live it up before the forty days of Lent, a time of fasting and abstinence. Carnival was imported to the New World by its original French and Spanish settlers. Even today, many of the rituals of a New Orleans Mardi Gras are the same as those followed in France and Spain. The ethnic origins of the festivities are still alive and well, and are still presented as dramatically as ever.

The Idea of Carnival

Carnival is chaotic: it turns life upside-down. It removes the recognizable structure of day-to-day life. During the festivities, people are allowed to cross over barriers, break rules, and violate customs. A carnival is almost always somewhat indecent, openly obsessed with the erotic, and demanding

of all kinds of excess. There's overeating, overdrinking, and noise. Expense is not spared, and costumes and floats come in all shapes and sizes. Famous people, cultural symbols, and social events are ridiculed. People at all levels of society get a part of the action. Yet the festivities only last for a little while, and they show people that rebellion, disorder, and general chaos are not what they want to live with all the time. Order and organization are essential for the survival of a community, and these are always reestablished at the end of any carnival.

Carnival in New Orleans

A fascination with other times and places is an important ingredient of Carnival, and in New Orleans the past is constantly being dragged out and put on view. Most of the krewes—Carnival societies whose members celebrate and parade—have names taken from Greek, Roman, and Egyptian mythology. The Mystic Krewe of Comus, the Krewes of Rex, Proteus, Hermes—each makes reference to an ancient mythological character.

In New Orleans, the first documented Carnival street procession with masks took place in 1837. It developed from a mix of French, Spanish, and Portuguese traditions; African rituals; and the masked balls that were held by the aristocratic families of the Confederacy. For the most part, the pageants of the 1800s used fairly acid humor, and ridiculed much of life in New Orleans.

Carnival has always been a time that ordinary people who have little opportunity to show their creativity in their everyday lives suddenly have the opportunity to display their imagination. The Mardi Gras Indians are a perfect example. Groups from New Orleans' black community call themselves "tribes," and wear costumes inspired by Native American dress. Every year, these costumes are different and are often refashioned from the previous year. This tradition is one of the most original and authentic surviving parts of the New Orleans Carnival.

Parading

O ver the years, Carnival in New Orleans has, in many ways, become a parade. Americans love parades because they give individuals a chance to belong to a group and to demonstrate that affiliation to a large audience. The word *parade* comes from the old Spanish word *parada*, which meant "the stopping." It was an army word that was used to describe the period of time that a foreign army stayed in an occupied town. The soldiers marched through the streets, which gave them the chance to show their strength and awe the locals. It may seem odd that something as regimented as an army would have its part in the history of Carnival, but soldiers are from the realm of war, which is the ultimate chaos.

Women began to parade openly only in 1941, with the foundation of the Krewe of Venus. Men and women did not parade together until the 1960s. Yet even as early as 1912, there were bands of "Baby Dolls"—tough women—who walked along the street instead of riding on a float. These days there are so many krewes that the New Orleans newspaper, the *Times-Picayune*, has a home page on the World Wide Web that tells you how you can quickly become a member and join a parade.

In ancient carnivals, nuts and sweets were tossed to spectators. And this ritual survives today: an essential part of Mardi Gras is its crowds grasping for necklaces and the plastic coins called doubloons. The distribution of "wealth" to the populace is a way of letting everyone be a part of Mardi Gras action. The symbolism? The people on the floats have everything they want, and are moving through life at a clip. The spectators are not moving forward, and are watching life go by. The distribution of trinkets keeps the watchers amused and in place. Maybe it's a comment on consumerism. The tradition celebrates the American myth of equal opportunity, but also makes fun of it.

The word *carnival* derives from the archaic Italian word *carnelevare,* which means to "lift," or give up, meat. Most people mistakenly think that the word comes from the Latin *carne vale,* which would mean "farewell to meat."

The Foods of Carnival

The Christmas season officially ends on January 6th, which is variously known as Twelfth Night, Epiphany, or Kings' Day. It may be the end of Christmas, but it's the beginning of Shrovetide, a period that continues until Mardi Gras. The last Monday of Shrovetide is known as Collop Monday, because people once ate collops—eggs fried on top of bacon—on that day. Bacon and eggs were two of the most common foods that were given up for Lent, and this day was a last opportunity to eat them. Nowadays, *collop* has come to mean a small piece of meat, usually bacon.

Collop Monday is followed by Shrove Tuesday. The word *shrove* comes from *shrive,* which means to hear confession and to receive absolution. Before the Protestant Reformation in England, this was the day to confess your sins and cleanse your soul in preparation for Lent. A bell tolled to remind people to get "shriven." It was also the day for eating pancakes, which were made with lots of milk, butter, and eggs, and therefore were not on the Lenten menu. After the Reformation, confession and the Pope were out, but pancakes stayed in. Shrove Tuesday became Pancake Tuesday, and the bells became a reminder to make the pancakes.

Mardi Gras wouldn't be Mardi Gras in New Orleans without King Cake. For hundreds of years, King Cake was traditionally served at a ball that was held on

Twelfth Night. It marked the beginning of the Carnival season. Made of a rich, yeasty dough, the crownlike ring is topped with colored sugars—green for faith, gold for power, and purple for justice. At the stroke of midnight, everyone at a New Orleans Mardi Gras party sits around the table and is served a piece of cake and a cup of champagne punch. Hidden in the cake is a bean, a pecan, a coin, or a tiny baby doll. Whoever finds the token becomes the king or queen of the group. If the winner is male, he chooses his queen; if a woman, she chooses her king, and they reign until the following week, when the next party takes place, and the ritual is repeated. In many Creole homes, you will find a small jewelry box containing a bean or a baby doll—a remembrance of the time the owner was king or queen of a Carnival party.

To say that the King Cake tradition is still alive and well is more than an understatement. Each year, well over one million of these cakes are sold during Carnival. They have become so popular that bakers now produce them throughout the year, shipping them all over the world. And if you are ever at a Carnival party and your slice of cake doesn't contain the little prize that makes you king or queen, don't feel too bad. Along with the prize and the royal moment comes the responsibility for organizing and paying for the next week's party!

The Restaurant Tradition in New Orleans

The people of New Orleans are devoted to their restaurants. Some maintain traditions, rituals, and recipes that go back more than two hundred years. This deep appreciation of good food and good restaurants can be traced to two big events.

The first was the French Revolution in the late 1700s, when the people of France did away with Louis XVI, Marie Antoinette, and about five thousand of their closest friends and relatives. Most of these victims were quite well-off, and had household staffs that included chefs, saucemakers, bakers, and pastry masters. This unexpected rise in the employer mortality rate left many chefs out of work. Word spread that there was a place in America that was like a little Paris, where the people spoke French and loved French cooking. Many chefs packed up their knives and came to New Orleans.

The slave revolt on the island of Saint Dominigue, which began in 1791 and ended in 1804 with the defeat of the French, was the other major historical event that affected New Orleans and its future restaurants. During the period of the revolt, so many refugees came to New Orleans that the population tripled. The Saint Dominigue refugees began the theater, the opera, and the sugar industry, and made major contributions to the cultural and business life of the city.

Creole and Cajun Food

The first French and Spanish colonists in New Orleans did not have the ingredients they were used to using in Europe. So they took the foods they found in their new environment and combined them with their traditional French and Spanish cooking techniques. The result was the earliest rendition of Creole cooking.

Many Creoles were wealthy plantation owners, and their kitchens were staffed with skilled and sophisticated chefs who knew how to take an old recipe and make it work in a new place. You can see how these chefs adjusted their recipes when you look at the history of a single dish. When the French arrived in New Orleans, they brought with them their love of a classic French fish stew called bouillabaisse.

Unfortunately, New Orleans did not have the classic ingredients, so they used local fish from the lakes, rivers, and the Gulf of Mexico. Crabs and shrimp were added. The Spanish settlers tossed in some red peppers. The Africans brought in the okra, and the Native Americans tossed in the file powder, which was also called sassafras. Bouillabaisse had become gumbo. And pretty much the same thing happened when the Spanish recipe for paella changed into jambalaya.

Traditional Cajun food is the strong "down-home" country cooking of rural New Orleans communities. Peppery, pungent, hot, and spicy, very often all the ingredients will cook in one pot. Rice is served on the side to quell the heat. Until the mid-'70s, Creole food could have been described as the food of the city and Cajun the food of the country. Since then, however, there has been so much exchange between the two styles that we now have a third cuisine, which is often described as "Louisiana."

Carnival
New Orleans

Chicken & Sausage Gumbo

Blue Cheese & Ham Custard

King Cake

Chocolate Bread Pudding

Chicken & Sausage Gumbo

Makes 4 servings

6 chicken legs and 6 thighs, skinned

¾ teaspoon kosher salt, plus extra to taste

½ teaspoon freshly ground black pepper, plus extra to taste

¼ cup vegetable oil

½ pound andouille or Kielbasa sausage, cut into ¾-inch pieces

1 medium onion, diced

3 medium cloves garlic, minced

1 green bell pepper

1 red bell pepper

⅛ teaspoon cayenne pepper (optional)

6 cups chicken broth

1½ cups coarsely chopped canned tomatoes with their juice

1 teaspoon ground coriander

1 teaspoon dried thyme, crushed

2 bay leaves

¼-½ teaspoon crushed red pepper flakes

¼ cup all-purpose flour

½ pound fresh okra, cleaned, tops trimmed and pods sliced into rings,
  or frozen defrosted

Cooked white rice for serving

1   SEASON THE CHICKEN with the salt and ¼ teaspoon of the black pepper. Heat the oil in a large stewpot and brown the chicken over high heat, 7 to 10 minutes. Add the sausage and cook for 2 to 3 minutes longer, turning often. Remove the sausage and chicken and set aside.

2   DRAIN ALL BUT 3 TABLESPOONS of the oil from the pot and reserve the pan drippings for making a roux. Add the onion and garlic to the pot and fry over medium heat for 3 to 4 minutes, scraping up any browned bits on the bottom of the pot with a wooden spoon. Add the bell peppers, the cayenne (if used), ¼ teaspoon of the black pepper, and cook for 5 minutes more or until the vegetables are softened. Return the meat to the pot, along with the chicken broth, tomatoes, coriander, thyme, bay leaves, and red pepper flakes. Simmer the stew uncovered for 45 minutes. Skim any excess fat and scum that may come to the surface of the stew.

3   WHILE THE MEAT IS STEWING, make the roux. Heat 3 tablespoons of the reserved pan drippings in a small cast-iron skillet, and stir in the flour with a wooden spoon. Cook over medium heat, stirring constantly, until the roux is chocolate brown, about 7 to 8 minutes. Carefully scrape the roux into a heatproof bowl—it is very hot and will continue to cook in the bowl. Set aside.

4   ADD THE OKRA TO THE STEWPOT. Continue to simmer over medium heat for 10 minutes, or until the okra softens. Whisk the roux into the stew and bring to a boil. Continue to simmer the stew for 15 minutes. Adjust the seasoning to taste with salt and pepper. Remove the bay leaves. Serve over the rice.

Blue Cheese & Ham Custard

Makes 4 servings

Executive Chef Jeff Tunks
Windsor Court Hotel

> 3 large eggs
> 1½ cups heavy cream
> ½ teaspoon kosher salt
> ¼ teaspoon freshly ground black pepper
> ½ cup diced proscuitto (about 2 ounces)
> ⅓ cup crumbled blue cheese, such as English Stilton, Roquefort,
>   or Maytag Blue (about 2 ounces)
> 4 large sprigs watercress

1 PREHEAT THE OVEN TO 350°F. Line a roasting pan with paper toweling. The paper will help prevent the ramekins from shifting.

2 MIX THE EGGS AND HEAVY CREAM together in a bowl with the salt and pepper until just combined. If the custard mix gets over-aerated the custards will cook unevenly. Set the custard mix aside.

3 DIVIDE THE PROSCUITTO AND CHEESE into four 1-cup ramekins. Pour the custard into the ramekins, and gently spoon any air bubbles off the surface of the custard. Transfer the custards to the roasting pan.

4 POUR ENOUGH BOILING WATER into the roasting pan so that it reaches halfway up the ramekins to create a water bath. Cover the pan tightly with foil. Carefully transfer the pan to the center shelf of the preheated oven and bake for 30 minutes. When making custards, it is important to remember that cooking times vary, and fresher eggs cook faster than older eggs. To check the custards, fold the foil back and gently jiggle a ramekin. If the custards are set, they shake as a firm unit; if underdone, waves of custard will shiver in the center. If the custards need more time, bake them longer, checking every 5 minutes until done. Remove the custards from the oven and the water bath.

5 COOL THE RAMEKINS AT ROOM TEMPERATURE for 15 to 20 minutes before serving. Serve the custards in the ramekins, set on small plates and garnished with the watercress sprigs. These custards are best served slightly warm or at room temperature.

Chocolate Bread Pudding

Makes 4-6 servings

2 cups milk

2 cups half and half

6 ounces semi-sweet chocolate, chopped

1 teaspoon vanilla extract

½ teaspoon ground cinnamon

4 large eggs

1 cup light brown sugar

2 tablespoons unsalted butter, melted for the baking dish

6 cups (1-inch pieces) quality French bread, left out overnight

½ cup chopped pecans

½ cup heavy cream

2 tablespoons confectioners' sugar

1 tablespoon dark rum

1   IN A MEDIUM SAUCEPAN, bring the milk and half and half just to a boil. Remove the pan from the heat and add the chocolate, vanilla, and cinnamon. Whisk briskly until the chocolate is melted.

2   IN A MEDIUM BOWL, whisk together the eggs and brown sugar. Slowly whisk the chocolate-flavored milk into the eggs.

3   BUTTER A ROUND BAKING DISH that is 8 inches in diameter and 4 inches deep, or an equivalent size casserole. Put the bread into the dish and cover with the custard; stir in the remaining butter. Let the pudding sit for 30 minutes, occasionally pressing the bread cubes into the liquid to saturate them, until the bread absorbs most of the custard. Preheat the oven to 325°F.

4   SPRINKLE THE TOP OF THE BREAD pudding with the pecans. Cover the bread pudding with foil and bake for 40 minutes. Remove the foil and continue to bake for another 20 minutes, or until the pudding is set. Remove from the oven and cool slightly.

5   WHIP THE CREAM in a chilled bowl until the cream holds soft peaks; don't overwhip the cream or it will be grainy. Fold in confectioners' sugar and the rum. Serve the bread pudding warm, with a dollop of the whipped cream.

King Cake

Makes 8 servings

For the Dough:

> ½ cup milk
>
> 1 envelope active dry yeast (2 ¼ teaspoons)
>
> ⅓ cup granulated sugar
>
> 3 cups all-purpose flour, plus up to ½ cup more if necessary
>
> 12 tablespoons (1½ sticks) unsalted butter, softened
>
> 4 large eggs
>
> Zest of 1 lemon, minced
>
> ½ teaspoon salt

For the Filling and Decoration:

> 2 tablespoons butter, melted
>
> ⅓ cup light brown sugar
>
> 1 tablespoon ground cinnamon
>
> 1 large dried bean or whole almond

For the Decorative Icing:

> 2 cups confectioners' sugar
>
> 2-3 tablespoons water
>
> Green, yellow, red, and blue food coloring

1 TO MAKE THE DOUGH: Gently heat the milk in a small saucepan to slightly warmer than body temperature (105˚ to 110˚F). Pour the milk into a bowl, sprinkle the yeast over the surface, and add a teaspoon of the sugar and a tablespoon of the flour. Stir to combine, and let the yeast plump with the milk before whisking. Set aside to proof for about 10 minutes.

2 IN A MIXING BOWL, with the paddle attachment on a heavy-duty mixer, cream together 11 tablespoons of the butter and the remaining sugar until light and fluffy, 1 to 2 minutes. Add the yeast mixture and mix for 1 minute. Add an egg and mix thoroughly; follow with a third of the flour. Repeat with the remaining eggs and flour. Add the lemon zest and salt, and continue to mix on low speed for 8 to 9 minutes, until the dough is smooth, shiny, and elastic, and pulls away from the side of the bowl. If very soft, add up to ½ cup of flour. Scrape the dough from the mixing bowl and knead lightly to form a ball. Butter a medium-size bowl with the remaining tablespoon of softened butter. Transfer the dough to the bowl and turn it in the bowl to coat with the butter. Cover with plastic and set in a warm spot to proof for 1 hour, or until doubled in bulk.

3 AFTER AN HOUR, turn the dough out of the bowl, punch it down, and knead lightly to form into a ball. Put the dough back in the bowl, covered, and refrigerate for at least 2 hours or for up to 24 hours.

4 TO FORM THE CAKE: Flour a clean work space and roll the dough into a 20-x-10-inch rectangle, keeping the thickness consistent throughout. If the edges get thin, trim them to keep consistent. Cut the dough lengthwise into 3 strips. Paint each strip of dough with the melted butter, leaving a ½-inch border clean along the length of each of the strips. (Reserve any leftover butter for brushing on the cake before baking.) Sprinkle the butter with the brown sugar and cinnamon.

5 LINE A BAKING SHEET WITH PARCHMENT. Fold each strip over, lengthwise and toward the clean edges, to enclose the cinnamon and sugar, and pinch the seam to seal the dough closed. Braid the 3 ropelike pieces together. Transfer the braid to the baking sheet, and form the braid into a wreath by pressing the ends together. Cover with a towel, and set aside to proof for 40 minutes. Preheat the oven to 350°F.

6 BRUSH THE CAKE with the reserved melted butter, and bake for 20 minutes, until golden brown. Tent the cake with foil and continue baking for 25 minutes. Keeping the cake on the baking sheet, cool on a rack. After the cake has cooled, carefully tuck the bean or almond into the underside of the cake.

7 TO MAKE THE ICING: Whisk the confectioners' sugar with the water in a medium saucepan and heat very gently to dissolve the sugar. Divide the icing into 3 small bowls and add the food coloring to make a mild green, a golden yellow, and a purple (½ drop red and ½ drop blue). Brush the ridges of the dough while it is still warm with alternating Mardi Gras colors. Cool and serve.

NOTE

Be very careful not to swallow the bean or the almond. Be especially careful with children.

A FAMILY'S SUNDAY

DINNER IN FRIULI

T he tradition of uniting the family at table on the weekly day of rest crosses many national boundaries. The meal is always held for the same reasons that larger, more elaborate feasts are celebrated. It preserves the family's understanding of itself as a group. It is an opportunity for talk, reminiscence, and the social training of children. But this meal isn't just an opportunity to preserve memories. It also nourishes new ones.

Friuli-Venezia Giulia, the district that covers the northeastern corner of Italy, is a place known for seafood, asparagus, corn, fruit, and wine, but its real claim to fame is its intense cultivation of family life. A farming area, Friuli has never been an easy place to live. The ancient Romans had an outpost here, and Attila the Hun passed through on his way back from bringing down the Roman Empire. After that the Venetians showed up, followed by the Austrians. Constant foreign rule caused the Friulians to look for comfort within the family unit, and they found much that brought happiness there.

Marking the Sabbath

In most Western countries, Sunday is marked as the Sabbath, the "day of rest" stipulated by the Old Testament. God rested on the seventh day after his creation of the earth and heavens, and his people were exhorted to do likewise. Although many religions still interpret the Sabbath strictly, making sure that their members do nothing that could be construed as working on that day, many people in our society have lost touch with the meaning of the word *rest*.

A body "at rest" is a body that is not in motion, not moving, and not exerting itself. But in our contemporary world, an activity is considered "restful" as long as it is outside the area of one's official job. "Rest" is often considered anything that is something you *want* to do, and can include extraordinary levels of physical effort and strain.

In most Westernized nations, Sunday is a feast day. It's not that you eat a lot, but that most people get that day off from work. For Christians, Sunday is a recollection of Easter, and functions as a small feast day every week. It is never a day of fasting. Even during Lent, Sundays are exempt from dietary stricture.

We have become so devoted to our day of relaxation that we have added Saturday to Sunday, inventing the weekend. The weekend is a creation of the twentieth century. In most Western nations, Saturday was a day that businesses were open and children went to school for part of the day. Saturday only became a second day of relaxation in the 1950s. The weekend actually promotes the idea of Sunday as a feast day, because feasts need preparation. Saturday gives everyone time to get ready for Sunday.

Feasts are different from everyday meals, and the Sunday family dinner is no exception. It must be a proper meal, with as many traditional aspects as possible, and with as many family members as can be brought together. When Friulian winemaker Livio Felluga invited me to join his family for a Sunday dinner in the middle of the day, I was aware of the honor of being allowed to join in this very intimate family gathering.

Sunday Dinner with the Family of Livio Felluga

On Saturday the Felluga household begins to make preparations for the Sunday gathering. The kitchen team consists of Leda, who has been the family cook for at least two generations of Fellugas; Livio's daughter Elda; Elda's daughter Letizia; and a ringer brought in from out of town: me.

It takes many hands to prepare a festive family dinner, and everyone in the Felluga household will make something and take part in the meal's creation. Coming together to make the food is as important as coming together to eat it. Gathering in the kitchen allows time for being together and for each person to contribute something unique and creative to the occasion. Unlike the passive entertainments of contemporary life, a family dinner is a participatory activity—everyone gets to join in.

Meals, particularly special meals served at home, always contain symbols of togetherness and separation. How the table is set can be very significant. The family table is a wonderful study of territorial marking. A table can seat only a certain number of people. If you are seated at the table, you are part of a chosen group. If you are not, you are an outsider. The dining table reinforces the idea of being together and separate at the same time— of being an individual within a family. Although single placemats may be the norm for weekday meals, the Sunday family dinner table gets one big tablecloth. But on that tablecloth, which holds everything and everyone together on one field, there are individual place settings, individual dishes, individual glasses, knives, forks, and spoons. Individual, but clearly part of a group.

The Sunday meal is also made special by the use of objects that are the host's "Sunday best." Almost all the implements used at the meal are different from the ones that are used during the week—special table linens, china, silver, and glasses. And the entire meal is presented in the dining room, not on the kitchen table, where meals are often served during the week.

Sunday midday dinner is held at the home of Livio and Bruna Felluga, the ranking members of this part of the family. Getting together for the meal keeps Livio and Bruna in touch with all their various relatives, but it also provides an opportunity

for the other members of the family to stay in touch with each other. There are sixteen people at lunch: Grandfather Livio, Grandmother Bruna, their three sons, their daughter, two daughters-in-law, seven grandchildren, and me.

For millions of years, when we sat down to eat, we sat around a fire. We remember the importance of fire to survival when we light our tables with candles. A meal with candlelight is always special because candles provide a flattering glow, are a luxury in this era of electric lighting, and only burn for a short time. At a family meal on Sunday, they may remind us of the short time we have together. They remind us to enjoy the warmth of the occasion while we can.

Children in many cultures actually learn to speak at mealtime. Sociologists believe that a family meal puts young children in a situation that makes it easier and more rewarding to understand the use of language. The children pay attention and see cause and effect. They see people ask for things and get them. The children begin to comprehend the raw power of a phrase like, "May I please have some more cookies, Grandma?" Adults also pay more attention to the language and behavior of their children during these family meals. After all, often their own parents are watching to see how they are doing at rearing their families. The children learn to say "please" and "thank you," and to wait their turn to speak properly in public.

The menu for a Sunday family meal must be different from what people consider "everyday" food. Often the dinner revolves around special recipes that are thought of as family heirlooms. Whether a food is, or is not, proper for this meal is often a decision based on the family's history of likes and dislikes.

The sharing of wine is an important symbolic act at the family table. Since the Fellugas are a winemaking family, the selection and presentation of the wine is an even more important ritual, concerning, as it does, the family's business as well as the family's pleasure. Since ancient times, wine has been thought to be nourishing and nurturing. When it is presented at the dinner table, it is kept separate from other food and drink. Even when almost everything else comes to table as a single serving, the wine is served in a bottle or decanter, and is divided in front of the family, reminding everyone of their common starting point. Poured into a distinct and tall glass, the wine sits just outside the boundary of the place setting, in deference to its mythical power.

Bread, like wine, is a product of fermentation, and, like wine, it is presented at table in an area that is just outside of the place setting. The fermented nutrient of wine stands to the right of the plate; the fermented nutrient of bread lies to the left.

After dinner is over, the adult members of the family retire to the *fogher*, a special room at the end of the house that has a bench running around the walls and an open hearth at its center. The name comes from the Latin word for "hearth" or "center of the house." The branches that burn in the Felluga hearth have been pruned from the family vines. For centuries the hearth was the architectural heart of the Friulian home.

The Wines of Friuli

Livio Felluga is considered one of the fathers of Italian winemaking. When the Italian government was choosing the wines for the heads of state attending the Economic Summit in Venice, they served Livio Felluga's whites. The Felluga vineyards in Friuli cover almost four hundred acres of the rolling countryside, and the family has been producing wine for four generations. Yet it is still a family business that involves every family member.

Friulians were exporting wine to Greece and Rome over two thousand years ago. They quickly learned to terrace their hillsides, because the soft and crumbly soil that was ideal for grapes was also especially well suited to sliding off hillsides in winter rains. Terraces cost a lot to maintain and keep yields low, but they keep the quality of grapes very high. Friuli's mild, breezy climate maintains its "natural air conditioning" because air currents come down from the Alps on one side and up from the Adriatic Sea on the other. This lower temperature gives the grapes extra time to ripen, and slow maturing lets them develop more flavor. Yet the real key to Friulian wine is the relationship between its soil and its vines.

In order to make a great wine, you need a vine that is highly stressed. You do that by planting it in poor soil. The more the vine struggles, the better the final wines. Rich soil is great for potatoes or corn, but for the vine, poor soil is best. In fact, there is a saying in Friuli, spoken from the point of view of the vine: "The poorer the place you put me, the richer I will make you." Although the soil in their vineyards may be poor, the Friulian people are rich in their heritage of family tradition.

Recipes for a Family's Sunday Dinner
Friuli, Italy

Barley Soup

Gnocchi with Asparagus & Ham Sauce

Chicken Felluga

Spring Green Salad

Apple Strudel

Barley Soup

Makes 4-6 servings

Mrs. Leda Della Rougre

Livio Felluga Winery

1 pound asparagus stalks (not tips)

2 tablespoons olive oil

2 leeks, white parts plus an inch of green, well rinsed and cut into thin half-moon slices

1 cup diced carrots

8 cups chicken broth

1 cup barley

1 medium zucchini, diced

1½ cups chopped Swiss chard or any dark leafy green of your choice

¼ cup roughly chopped fresh flat-leaf parsley leaves

⅓ cup freshly grated Parmesan cheese

1   PEEL THE ASPARAGUS STALKS with a vegetable peeler to remove their tough fibrous skin. Cut the cleaned stalks into ½-inch pieces.

2   HEAT THE OLIVE OIL in a medium soup pot. Over medium-low heat, cook the asparagus, leeks, and carrots, without browning, for about 7 to 10 minutes.

3   POUR IN 6 CUPS of the chicken broth and bring to a boil. Add the barley and simmer for about 25 to 30 minutes, or until the grain is tender. When ready to serve, add the remaining chicken broth, bring to a simmer, and add the zucchini, Swiss chard, and parsley, and simmer for 4 or 5 minutes, until the zucchini is cooked through. Serve in warm bowls with the cheese sprinkled on top.

Asparagus & Ham Sauce

Makes 4 servings

Mrs. Leda Della Rougre

Livio Felluga Winery

1 tablespoon olive oil

½ pound asparagus, cut into 2-inch-long pieces

1 cup diced boiled ham (¼ pound)

¾ cup white wine

2 cups chicken broth

6 tablespoons unsalted butter, cut into pieces and chilled

½ teaspoon salt, or to taste

¼ teaspoon freshly ground black pepper

1 IN A LARGE SKILLET, heat the oil and sauté the asparagus until lightly browned, 3 to 4 minutes. Remove the asparagus from the pan and set them aside while you make the sauce.

2 ADD THE HAM to the skillet and cook 2 to 3 minutes, until lightly browned. Add the wine and boil over high heat until it is reduced to about ¼ cup. Add the chicken broth, and reduce by a third. Lower the heat and whisk the butter into the sauce to thicken it. Season with the salt and pepper.

Gnocchi

Makes 4 servings

Mrs. Leda Della Rougre
Livio Felluga Winery

2½ pounds baking potatoes (about 4)
1 large egg
3 teaspoons salt
1¼ cups all-purpose flour, plus ½ cup more as needed
4 quarts water
1 recipe Asparagus and Ham Sauce (recipe precedes)
½ cup freshly grated Parmesan cheese

1   PREHEAT THE OVEN TO 350° F. Bake the potatoes for 45 minutes or until a fork inserted in the center comes out clean. To make the peeling of the hot potatoes a little easier, hold the potato with an oven mitt or kitchen towel and scrape out the flesh with a spoon. Puree the potato flesh through a ricer or food mill. As you are ricing the potatoes, let them fall evenly in one layer onto a large pan; this helps the potatoes cool and reduces excess moisture. Refrigerate until cool, about 15 minutes.

2   TRANSFER THE POTATOES to a clean work space and pull them together, making a well in the center. Crack the egg into the center and add 1 teaspoon of the salt. With your fingertips, work the potato and egg together to make a rough dough. Sprinkle 1 cup of flour over the potato mix and gently combine. If the dough feels wet, add a bit more flour (up to 1½ cups). Knead the dough until it is smooth and uniform, 3 to 4 minutes. If you are uncertain about the dough, pinch off an inch piece and boil it. If it is mushy you will need to add a bit more flour.

3   FORM THE DOUGH into a rectangle and cut it into 8 equal pieces. On a flat work space, roll each piece into a ropelike cylinder, about 18 inches long and the width of your finger. This can be awkward at first, but glide your fingers out over the dough, working it back and forth while gently pulling outward. Lightly dust each piece with flour.

4   PLACE 2 LENGTHS of dough horizontally in front of you. With a knife, cut across the dough to make ¾-inch pieces. Repeat with the remaining lengths.

5   SPREAD THE GNOCCHI in a single layer on a tray so they don't stick together, and refrigerate for 2 to 3 hours, until ready to serve. To cook the gnocchi, bring the water to a boil with the remaining 2 teaspoons of salt. Gently add the gnocchi to the boiling water and cook until the gnocchi float back up to the surface, 2 to 3 minutes. Drain the gnocchi and toss with Parmesan cheese.

NOTE

If you are going to freeze the gnocchi, add the full amount of flour to the recipe; otherwise they will be mushy when boiled.

Chicken Felluga

Makes 4 servings

Mrs. Leda Della Rougre
Livio Felluga Winery

4 sprigs fresh rosemary, or 1 tablespoon dried
One (2-3 pound) chicken, cut into 8 pieces
2½ cups white wine
2 teaspoons kosher salt
¼ teaspoon freshly ground black pepper
2 tablespoons olive oil
4 medium onions, quartered

1   PULL THE LEAVES from the rosemary stalks. In a nonreactive bowl, combine the chicken, 1½ cups of the white wine, and half of the rosemary leaves. Marinate in the refrigerator for at least 2 hours or overnight.

2   HEAT THE OVEN TO 350°F. After the chicken has marinated, discard the marinating liquid. Dry the chicken well with paper towels and season it with the salt and pepper. Heat the olive oil in a large skillet and brown the chicken over medium-high heat. Transfer the chicken to a roasting pan. Discard the excess fat from the skillet, add the remaining wine and rosemary, and bring to a boil. Scrape up any browned bits on the bottom of the skillet and pour the wine over the chicken. Tuck the onions around the chicken and cook in the oven for 40 minutes, or until firm to the touch.

3   PLACE THE COOKED CHICKEN pieces on a serving platter. Put the roasting pan directly on a flame to cook the wine and onions over high heat. Boil the cooking liquid to reduce by half and glaze the onions. Spoon the onions over the chicken and serve.

Spring Green Salad

Makes 4 servings

Mrs. Leda Della Rougre
Livio Felluga Winery

For the Vinaigrette:

1½ tablespoons red wine vinegar, preferably Italian

4-5 tablespoons extra virgin olive oil

1 clove garlic, crushed

½ teaspoon fresh thyme leaves, or ⅛ teaspoon dried (optional)

½ teaspoon kosher salt

¼ teaspoon freshly ground black pepper

For the Greens:

2 heads bibb lettuce, washed, dried, and gently torn into 2-inch pieces (about 3 cups)

1 cup washed and dried watercress leaves

1 cup washed and dried arugula leaves

1 cup torn, washed, and dried escarole leaves

¼ cup roughly chopped fresh flat-leaf parsley leaves

1   TO MAKE THE VINAIGRETTE: Place all the ingredients in a jar or plastic container with a tight-fitting lid. Close the top and shake vigorously until the dressing looks creamy. Set aside until ready to use. If the dressing separates, just shake vigorously before using.

2   FOR THE SALAD: Place all the cleaned greens in a bowl. Remove the garlic clove from the dressing. Pour the dressing over the salad and toss gently.

Apple Strudel

Makes 4-6 servings

Mrs. Leda Della Rougre
Livio Felluga Winery

½ cup unseasoned bread crumbs

8 tablespoons (1 stick) unsalted butter

3 Golden Delicious or Granny Smith apples, peeled, cored,
  and sliced into ¼-inch pieces

Zest of 1 lemon, minced

⅓ cup raisins

¼ cup pine nuts

1 teaspoon ground cinnamon

⅓ cup granulated sugar

5-6 sheets phyllo dough

1 tablespoon unsalted butter, melted

Confectioners' sugar

1   PLACE 3 TABLESPOONS of the bread crumbs in a bowl and set aside. Melt the butter and skim off the foam that forms on the surface. Let the melted butter sit for 5 minutes until it settles with a milky liquid on the bottom. Carefully spoon 4 tablespoons of the golden-colored butter off the top to a small bowl and set aside.

2   TOAST THE REMAINING BREAD crumbs in the remaining butter until golden brown, 3 or 4 minutes. In a medium bowl, mix together the toasted bread crumbs, the apples, lemon zest, raisins, and pine nuts.

3   PREHEAT THE OVEN TO 350°F. Lightly flour a cookie sheet.

4 IN A SMALL BOWL, mix together the cinnamon and the sugar. Lay the phyllo sheets out on a clean work space and cover them with a damp towel. Gently spread 1 sheet of phyllo out on a work space with the longer side facing you. Working quickly so the phyllo doesn't dry out, lightly brush it with the reserved melted butter, and sprinkle it with about 1 teaspoon of the cinnamon sugar and about a teaspoon of the reserved bread crumbs. Lay a second sheet of phyllo on top of the first sheet and brush with more butter. Sprinkle on more cinnamon sugar and bread crumbs. Repeat this process with 3 more sheets of phyllo, for a total of 5 layers.

5 COMBINE THE APPLE MIXTURE with the remaining cinnamon sugar. Lay the apple mix across the middle of the phyllo in a strip about 4 inches wide. Pick the far edge of the dough up over the apples and roll the phyllo around the apples to make a tight cylinder. Tuck the ends in to seal the strudel. If the layers around the strudel tear, use the extra sheet to wrap around the cylinder and make a smooth surface.

6 CAREFULLY LIFT THE STRUDEL to the cookie sheet. With a paring knife, make 4 small slits in the top of the strudel to let steam escape during baking. Brush with the melted butter. Bake the strudel for 45 minutes, or until golden brown. Cool for 5 to 10 minutes, then dust with the confectioners' sugar and serve warm.

*L*ike most holidays, Easter marks a series of passages—darkness into light, winter into spring, death into life. Because food is so essential to existence, it is a powerful symbol for any celebration that deals with rebirth or the return of the growing season. No matter what culture or religion, the message is always the same: life, in one form or another, will always have the power to renew itself.

EASTER IN FLORENCE

The History of Easter

Easter is a celebration of cosmic events as well as a religious festival. It is a celebration of the arrival of the sun, of warmth after winter, of spring. The word *Easter* is derived from *Eostre,* the name of the Teutonic goddess of spring. Most early cultures that went through a barren winter and a rebirth of vegetation in the spring also had some sort of celebration to mark the return of the growing season. According to myth, Demeter, the ancient Greek goddess of agriculture, had a daughter who was held in captivity in the underworld during part of each year. Only when she was released did the growing season return. The idea of the resurrection of a beloved child as a mark of spring goes back to the stories of the very earliest religions. The celebration of Easter is part of that tradition.

Easter is also part of the tradition of the Jewish holiday of Passover. Passover begins on the night of the spring equinox. (An equinox is a twenty-four-hour period when the length of the day's sunlight is equal to the length of the day's darkness. This occurs twice a year—once in the fall and once in the spring.)

This feast reminds the current generation of the Jews' escape from slavery, and their passage out of Egypt. It tells the story of the last of the plagues, when the angel of death struck down the firstborn of the Egyptians but "passed over" the children of the Israelites, whose homes were marked with the blood of a lamb. Like the Greek story of Demeter and her daughter, the Jewish springtime festival celebrates the "sparing" of a favorite child from death—in this case, a firstborn.

The Last Supper was originally a Passover meal, attended by Jesus and his twelve disciples. It foreshadows the sparing of Jesus from death on the cross—this favorite, firstborn son rises again, foiling death, just like Demeter's daughter.

The central Christian feast of Easter celebrates the resurrection of Christ on the third day after his crucifixion. Easter is celebrated on the Sunday following the first full moon after the spring equinox. The moon returns from oblivion, just as Christ returns from the dead. The celebration of the Eucharist, in which the worshipers at a church are invited to partake of the body and blood of Christ in their symbolic forms of bread and wine, reminds Christians of their participation in the Resurrection. Christians are invited to think of every Sunday as a small celebration of Easter.

Easter at the Cathedral

Florence has a special historical relationship to Easter. The city celebrates the Easter feast over five days, starting on Holy Thursday and continuing through the weekend to Easter Monday. The ritual begins at about five o'clock on the evening of Holy Thursday with the washing of the feet, Mass, a procession removing the Eucharist—the consecrated elements of bread and wine—to a separate place, and private prayer throughout the night.

In some churches there is a pre-Mass Seder, often held with Jewish groups. Priests from small local churches visit the cathedral for the blessing of oil that will be used during the ceremonies in their own villages.

On Good Friday, the day of Jesus' death, the altars are stripped and all flames are extinguished in every church. No candle will be lit again until the dark night between Saturday and Sunday.

The Easter vigil begins at ten o'clock on Saturday night. The congregation gathers in the dark church, each person holding an unlit candle. In Florence, this ritual takes place in the vast cathedral under an enormous fourteenth-century vaulted ceiling. A fire is set—a kind of bonfire—far from the altar. The bishop and all of the clergy proceed from the altar to this fire, which provides the only source of light in the entire church. At the fire, the bishop blesses a monumental candle—often about six feet high. The candle symbolizes not only Christ, but the column of fire that led the people of Israel through the Red Sea and across the desert to safety. The bishop uses a wick to take fire from the bonfire and lights the new Easter candle, which will burn beside the altar during every Mass for the rest of the year. Five pieces of incense are pressed into the candle, representing the five wounds of Christ.

The deacon then holds up the candle—*Lumen Christi,* the light of Christ, signifying his resurrection from the dead. Acolytes—young church assistants—take flame from the candle and begin to light the candles of the faithful, communicating the spiritual light and life of Christ to those who believe in him. By the time the deacon brings the great paschal candle to the altar, the entire church is filled with points of light drawn from the single light that is Christ. The deacon then sings the ancient Easter hymn proclaiming that the sin of Adam and Eve was a "happy fault" because in the end it caused God to send a savior. In this ritual, all of the history of human salvation is recalled. It represents the resurrection of Christ from the dead as the fulfillment of all forms of salvation, from the ancient people of Israel back to Adam and Eve.

A series of readings from the Old Testament tells the story of the creation and the sacred history of the world, beginning with Genesis. The Mass begins. The *Gloria* is sung for the first time since the fasting and penitence of Lent began, six weeks earlier. A version of the *Alleluia*—meaning "praise God"—is sung because, again, all *alleluias* have been silenced throughout Lent. (The beginning of Lent, after a festival of merrymaking and revelry called Carnival, was once marked by the Burial of the Sausage. A large sausage was interred as a sign that meat-eating was barred for six weeks.)

On Sunday morning, a grand procession of people dressed in period costumes fills the streets of Florence, taking part in a ritual called the Explosion of the Cart. Pairs of white oxen adorned with flowers and ribbons, their horns and hooves

gilded, drag a cart through the city until they reach the front of the cathedral. The cart carries an elaborately decorated pyramid set on top of a box. The cart used today was originally built in 1764 and is nicknamed the "Big Old Bum" because of the way it teeters into the piazza.

At about ten o'clock, the fire arrives at the cathedral. The fire is struck from three flints in a nearby church. The flints are said to have come from the Holy Sepulcher, the tomb of Christ. They are reputed to have been given as a reward to Pazzo de' Pazzi for having been the first knight to scale the walls of Jerusalem during a Crusade in the eleventh century. (The Pazzi were a powerful Florentine family at the time. They instituted the ceremony of the exploding cart, which has taken place in front of the cathedral for six hundred years.)

A wire is stretched along the central nave of the church to the cart, which is standing, freed from its oxen, in the piazza beside the baptistery. A rocket in the shape of a dove is attached to the wire. A wick in the dove is ignited from the fire lit by the three flints and the dove shoots down the wire, out of the cathedral doors,

and into the wagon which is draped in fireworks. If the dove succeeds in lighting the fireworks on the first try, it means the harvest will be especially good this year.

The explosion of the cart is technically the explosion of the fireworks on top of the cart. The cart itself remains intact. As the noise of the fireworks resounds throughout the piazza, numerous bells start to ring—the great bells of Giotto's Campanile, church bells, altar bells, even cowbells lend their clanging to the celebration. The explosion, the colorful shafts of light, the smoke billowing into the cathedral, and the joyous cacophony in the cathedral itself are a spectacular expression of jubilation at the event of Christ's resurrection.

What is the meaning of this ritual? The dove came out of the darkness and brought light, in the form of fireworks. The thunder of the explosion recalls Christ breaking out of his tomb. The thunder implies rain, the symbol of baptism. Fire and water, darkness into light, silence to noise—death into life.

In Florence, Easter Monday is the last day of the holiday. People go off into the country to picnic and to enjoy the spring weather. It is a day for family walks, perhaps reminding believers of the time when the risen Christ walked with two of his disciples on their way to Emmaus, a town near Jerusalem, on the day after Easter.

Easter Lunch at the Villa di Capezzana

Count Ugo Contini Bonacossi, his wife, the Countess, and their family come together every year for an Easter lunch at their villa. The main course of the meal—roast lamb—is served from a single dish, instead of in individual portions brought to each place. This dish symbolizes the central unity of the family, from which all its individuals get their strength.

All the wines served by Count Ugo are made at his family's winery, Tenuta di Capezzana, which dates from the year 804. The actual estate goes back to Roman times. "Family winery," in this case, could not be a more accurate description. Count Ugo's son Filippo is an agronomist who looks after the vineyards, and his son Vittorio is a consultant on winemaking. His daughter Benedetta handles the public relations, and her husband designs the labels for the wine. The Countess oversees the property, and their daughter Beatrice is in charge of sales.

The vineyards are high in the hills, about fifteen miles west of Florence. Count Ugo's estate is actually surrounded by the Chianti region, but the wines of Capezzana are produced under a different set of regulations. In 1716, the Grand Duke of Tuscany, Cosimo de Medici III, marked off this district as special; its wines are similar to those of Chianti, but wine authorities describe the wines of Capezzana as more refined. Today Capezzana produces several outstanding red wines, but it is renowned for its Villa De Capezzana Carmignano and Carmignano Riserva. Wine authorities believe that their elegant smoothness comes from an addition of Cabernet Sauvignon grapes to the Sangiovese harvest.

The Wine of Easter

Of all the gatherings and celebrations in the Christian tradition, none is more clearly associated with wine than Easter. At the Last Supper, Jesus told his disciples that the wine they drank was his blood, and the bread they ate, his body. In so doing, he made wine an essential element in the future rituals of the Church.

Early Romans developed vineyards throughout western Europe, so it was not difficult for early Christians to find wine for their services. With the fall of Rome, however, the cultivation of the vineyards became, in many places, the responsibility of the Church, and it kept the skills of winemaking alive through the Dark Ages. Many monasteries acquired large properties and developed new winemaking skills and methods. In a stunning display of real estate savvy, these monasteries allowed local aristocrats to donate valuable vineyards to the church, in exchange for continual remembrance in the prayers of the monks.

During the Middle Ages, the Church played an important part in the feudal system and used its extensive land holdings to consolidate its power. Like other feudal landlords, the Church collected rent from the people who lived on its land, and often that rent was paid in the form of wine. Unlike most agricultural products, wine lasts a long time and, in some cases, even improves with aging. These special attributes made wine a favorite form of rental payment. The monks, interested in stockpiling this drinkable currency, taught the people who lived on the land how to grow grapes and how to make wine, exacting a portion of the vintage at the end of the process. In another wine-in-payment policy, wealthy landowners often gave wine to the church in the hope of someday receiving "celestial privileges."

When Spanish explorers headed for the New World, members of the clergy were part of the expedition, and they established vineyards in the earliest Spanish colonies. The original vineyards of California and South America were the work of Catholic missionaries.

Conte Contini Bonacossi

VILLA DI CAPEZZANA

Carmignano

1988

Recipes for Easter
Florence, Italy

Chicken Liver Toasts (Crostini)

Spring Peas with Pancetta

Roasted Leg of Lamb with Garlic & Rosemary

Dipping Cookies (Cantucci)

Zabaglione

Chicken Liver Toasts (Crostini)

Makes 6 servings

1 pound chicken livers

2 tablespoons olive oil

½ teaspoon kosher salt

¼ teaspoon freshly ground black pepper

1 cup sliced red onions

2 teaspoons minced garlic

½ teaspoon dried sage, crushed

8 juniper berries, crushed (optional)

⅔ cup sweet vermouth

12 slices Italian-style bread cut into ½-inch slices

1 TO CLEAN THE LIVERS: Remove any dark or green spots and separate the 2 lobes of the livers. Dry the livers with a paper towel.

2 HEAT THE OLIVE OIL in a large skillet and season the livers with the salt and pepper. When the oil is hot, add the livers to the pan one at a time, taking care not to overcrowd the pan. If necessary, cook the livers in 2 batches. Cook the livers over high heat until browned, 2 to 3 minutes, then turn and cook until springy to the touch, another 1 to 2 minutes. The livers should be rosy pink inside. Remove them from the pan using a slotted spatula. Set aside.

3 REDUCE THE HEAT to medium and add the onions, garlic, sage, and juniper berries to the pan. Cook until the onions are translucent, about 5 minutes. Add the vermouth and, with a wooden spoon, scrape up any browned bits that may have collected in the pan. Reduce the liquid until syrupy, 1 to 2 minutes.

4 IN A FOOD PROCESSOR OR BLENDER, puree the livers with the onions until smooth. Place the puree in a bowl and refrigerate for 2 to 3 hours. This dish may be prepared a day ahead.

5 WHEN READY TO SERVE, toast or grill the sliced bread, spread 1 to 2 tablespoons of the chicken livers on the warm bread, and serve.

Spring Peas with Pancetta

Makes 6 servings

Countess Lisa Contini Bonacossi
Capezzana Winery

1 tablespoon olive oil

¼ pound pancetta, diced

1 cup chicken broth

1¼ pounds fresh peas (about 4 cups shelled) or two 10-ounce packages frozen

1 medium clove garlic, crushed

¼ teaspoon freshly ground black pepper

Salt

1   IN A MEDIUM SKILLET, heat the olive oil and cook the pancetta over medium heat until crispy, about 10 minutes. Drain excess fat.

2   ADD THE CHICKEN BROTH, peas, garlic, and pepper. Simmer uncovered for 8 to 10 minutes until all the liquid is absorbed and the peas look glazed. Season with salt to taste and serve.

Roasted Leg of Lamb with Garlic & Rosemary

Makes 6-8 servings

Countess Lisa Contini Bonacossi
Capezzana Winery

One (7-8 pound) leg of lamb, hip/aitch bone removed, shank in
4 medium cloves garlic
1½ teaspoons kosher salt
½ teaspoon freshly ground black pepper
1½ tablespoons minced fresh rosemary, or 2 teaspoons dried, crushed
3 tablespoons balsamic vinegar
2 tablespoons extra virgin olive oil
2-3 fresh rosemary sprigs, or 4-5 flat-leaf parsley sprigs for garnish

1 TO PREPARE THE LAMB: Trim the excess fat and membrane from the leg, particularly at the broad end. The trimmed leg should have a thin film of fat, which will cook up to a crispy skin.

2 PREHEAT THE OVEN TO 450°F.

3 MAKE A PASTE BY CRUSHING TOGETHER the garlic and ¾ teaspoon of the salt with the flat side of a large knife. In a small bowl, mix together the paste with half the pepper, the rosemary, 1 tablespoon of the balsamic vinegar, and 1 tablespoon of the olive oil. With a paring knife, make 7 or 8 slits in the meat about an inch wide and 2 to 3 inches deep. With your fingers, poke the paste into the slits. Rub any excess over the surface of the lamb. Brush the leg with the remaining oil and season with the remaining salt and pepper. The leg can be prepared to this point and refrigerated up to a day ahead. (Before roasting, bring the lamb to room temperature, so that it cooks evenly.)

4   PLACE THE LAMB on a rack thickest part up, bone down, in a roasting pan and roast for 20 minutes. Reduce the temperature to 350°F and baste the leg with the pan drippings and the remaining balsamic vinegar every 15 to 20 minutes. Cook the lamb for 1¼ to 1½ hours, or until an instant-read thermometer poked into the thickest part of the leg reaches a temperature of 125°F to 130°F for rare to medium-rare. If you like your lamb cooked medium to medium-well, cook to 140°F to 150°F. Remove the leg from the oven to a warm spot and let it "rest" for 15 to 20 minutes before carving. This keeps the meat juicy.

5   TO CARVE, hold onto the shank bone with a napkin and, with a sharp knife, slice parallel to the bone. Lay the slices out on a heated platter and garnish with the fresh herbs.

THE EASTER BUNNY

Not actually a part of the meal, but essential to the celebration, the Easter bunny was originally an Easter hare, an animal sacred to the goddess of the moon.

People have often imagined that they saw a hare in the moon, rather than our current "man in the moon." The hare's reputation for productivity makes it an ancient symbol of fertility. It symbolizes the power of the life-force, always returning, like spring from winter, like the moon. During the last few hundred years that hare has turned into the Easter bunny, usually made of chocolate and carrying an egg.

The egg is a traditional symbol of birth, and its yolk is a symbol of the sun. The bunny holding, or surrounded by eggs unites the sun and the moon. The symbols of the season bring together sun and moon, day and night, life and death, the rebirth of spring from winter and the rising of Christ from the dead.

Dipping Cookies (Cantucci)

Makes 40 cookies

3 cups all-purpose flour

1 cup sugar, plus 1 tablespoon

⅛ teaspoon salt

1 teaspoon baking powder

4 large eggs

1½ teaspoons vanilla extract

¾ cup whole unblanched almonds

¾ cup whole hazelnuts

1   PREHEAT THE OVEN TO 325°F. Line a cookie sheet with parchment paper.

2   SIFT THE FLOUR, 1 cup of the sugar, the salt, and the baking powder into a large mixing bowl. In a small bowl, lightly whisk the eggs and vanilla together. Make a well in the flour, pour in the eggs and, with a fork or your finger, pull the dry ingredients into the wet to make a soft dough.

3   TURN THE DOUGH OUT onto a clean work surface and gently knead the nuts into the dough. Let the dough rest for 5 minutes.

4   DIVIDE THE DOUGH into 4 pieces and form each piece into a log 10 inches long by 2 inches wide. Place the logs on the prepared cookie sheet 2 inches apart, brush them with water, sprinkle on the remaining tablespoon of the sugar, and bake for 25 minutes. The logs should be firm but still pliable. Cool for 10 minutes.

5   WHEN THE LOGS ARE COOL, use a serrated knife to cut them on an angle into 1-inch slices. Lay the cookies out on the cookie sheet. Lower the oven temperature to 300°F. and bake for 35 minutes. To check that the cookies are dry enough, remove one from the oven and let it cool. The cookies should be dry and crisp. Cool completely and store well covered.

Zabaglione

Makes 6-8 servings

Countess Lisa Contini Bonacossi
Capezzana Winery

5 large egg yolks
5 tablespoons granulated sugar
¼ cup sweet marsala wine
¼ cup Grand Marnier or other orange-flavored liqueur
½ cup heavy cream
1½ tablespoons confectioners' sugar

1   TO COOK THE ZABAGLIONE: Set up a double boiler or set a medium-size stainless-steel bowl over a pot of simmering water. Check to make sure the bottom of the bowl is not touching the water, or the eggs may scramble and overcook. Whisk the egg yolks, sugar, marsala, and Grand Marnier together and place them in the pot or bowl over the simmering water. Continue to whisk vigorously until the eggs increase in volume and thicken; this should take 2 to 3 minutes. It's important to move the whisk around the bowl so the eggs cook evenly. If the edges of the eggs start to scramble, remove the bowl from over the water and continue to whisk. The final zabaglione should be like an airy pudding.

2   WHISK THE ZABAGLIONE over a bowl of ice to cool, then set aside. Whip the cream over the ice until it stands in soft peaks, then sift in the confectioners' sugar. Fold the whipped cream into the cool zabaglione and refrigerate for 1 to 2 hours. The zabaglione can be prepared a day ahead. Serve it with panettone or pound cake.

THE SPRING FIESTAS OF SEVILLE

H oly Week and the Seville Fair are the two events that come together to become the spring festivals of Seville. The Seville Fair follows on the heels of Holy Week, and the two fiestas balance and complete each other. Taken together, they signify an important rite of passage, a passage from winter to spring—a passage from sad, dark hours to times of light and joy. And all the foods that are part of these fiestas are symbols of that passage.

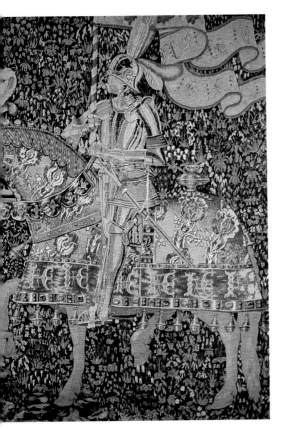

Seville is the capital of the region of Andalusia, in southern Spain. This area has been inhabited for at least five thousand years. During the Bronze Age, the ancient Phoenicians began to trade with the local people for tin and tuna, and by 1100 B.C. the Phoenicians had settled comfortably in the area. In the third century B.C., the Romans took the place over and built aqueducts to bring water in from the hills. Visigoths, a loose association of Germanic tribes, pushed the Romans out and remained in Andalusia until A.D. 711. Later, in the ninth century, the Moors arrived from North Africa, and conquered virtually all of the territory that is now called Spain.

The city of Seville is a magnificent layer cake. Each slice has a first layer that was created during the Bronze Age. Additional layers were added by the Phoenicians, Carthaginians, Greeks, Romans, Jews, Moors, and Christians. When you take a bite out of Seville, all the flavors blend together.

Holy Week in Seville

The weeks of the spring fiestas are one of the best times to see all the layers of the cultural cake. There are actually two weeks, one very different from the other. The first, Holy Week—the week during which Christ was arrested, condemned, and crucified—is a week of symbolic conflict between good and evil. The stories told are of great terror and ultimate heroism. After a desperate struggle, the forces of goodness and light triumph over evil and darkness. As the Passion of Christ is played out along the streets of the city, Seville is transformed into the town where the original events occurred.

During the 1300s the people of Seville began to group themselves into brotherhoods—or, in Spanish, *cofradias*. Each brotherhood agreed to produce an image from the Passion of Christ or a sorrowing Virgin, and to venerate that image throughout the year in a brotherhood chapel. Today, there are fifty-five brotherhoods, each with up to three thousand members, including both men and women. People may be born into a brotherhood—children automatically belong to their mother's—but anyone can join one if two of its members can be cajoled into making recommendations.

The most important acts of veneration each year are the fifty-five processions, one for each brotherhood, which take place during Holy Week. Each brotherhood owns from one to three floats—or *pasos*—with scenes showing Christ's Passion, and one canopied statue of the weeping Virgin. Many of the statues are famous works of art created by great baroque and twentieth-century sculptors. All the statues are very realistic and must be approved by the general public. If the people don't like a new image, it is removed, no matter how expensive it was to create.

Floats are elaborately decorated, and the statues in the processions wear real clothing. The clothing, the embroideries and lace, the candles, and the flower decorations (red carnations for Passion scenes; lilies, roses, jasmine, and wax flowers for the Virgins) are all made and maintained by women—as are the remarkable clothes of the walkers in the processions.

Each float weighs between two and three tons and is carried through the streets of Seville by a group of young men. For years, the floats were carried by professional stevedores. Eventually, however, their fees became too expensive for the brotherhoods. People thought that carrying the floats through Seville would come to an end, but the young men of each brotherhood came together to do the job, and the general opinion is that the young men do an even better job than the stevedores did. There is an art to carrying the floats: the trick is to make them swing and sway so the figures seem alive and moving.

Only a few of the members of a brotherhood actually walk in the procession. These members wear long robes in the colors of the brotherhood, and pointed headgear called *capirotes* that cover their faces. The pointed headgear, which looks rather terrifying, was originally designed to hide the identity of the person inside, giving him a chance to withdraw into himself. The disguise gave men the opportunity to act piously, which was not an easy thing for them to do in a culture that often viewed religious behavior in public as unmanly. Under the hood, emotions remain private. The pointed hats also make the official walkers clearly visible above the crowd. Nowadays, more and more women walkers are included in the processions. Women have always belonged to the brotherhoods, but have not officially walked until recently. In the past, women secretly joined the processions wearing their fathers' or brothers' outfits, with gloves to hide their hands.

Some people who wear the robes of their society take the cardboard cones out of their hoods. The hanging hood increases their humble appearance and is a sign of penance. The visual symbol is likened to that of a rooster that has become crestfallen and is therefore no longer "cocky."

The floats carried through the streets of Seville express all human suffering through the symbols of Christ and the Virgin Mary. Christ's suffering represents persecution and pain in action. The images of the weeping Madonnas show the pain of looking on, of knowing that you are helpless to prevent the suffering of someone you love.

The Holy Week processions are often a very emotional experience for those who participate. Moments of sympathy, sorrow, gratitude, and intense feelings of love for Christ occur often throughout the week. One of the most dramatic moments during the processions is the singing of a saeta. *Saeta* is the Spanish word for "arrow," in this case an arrow of emotion, passion, and sentiment. The arrow passes symbolically between one of the statues being carried through the streets and one of the people watching the procession. A viewer becomes overwhelmed with feeling, and expresses this flood of emotions by singing an intimate story of love and sadness. Writing and singing saetas is an art form; a saeta may be rehearsed, or it may be improvised on the spur of the moment. When a saeta is sung during the procession, the float is put down and the crowd becomes silent. It is a truly climactic moment in the celebration, but it is also a very personal moment, and usually only the singer knows when and where a saeta will take place. Sometimes the singer only finds out because she is suddenly singing!

The brotherhood processions wind through Seville, turning the city into a labyrinth with the cathedral at its heart. They continue all day and all night for seven days—each one takes from eight to twelve hours to follow its path through the city because each float must pass through a specific pattern of streets and must stop at the cathedral. Holy Week ends with a final procession that concludes at the very moment of midnight, when the bells of the cathedral start to toll, announcing that Easter has begun. Life and light have triumphed over death and darkness.

The Holy Week processions remind everyone that there are journeys in life that we must make if we are going to find our way in the outside world and places we must visit if we are eventually to find our way into our inner heart.

The Seville Fair

Shortly after Holy Week ends, Seville turns to Fair Week. This is a celebration of life, of the sensuous aspects of existence. The fair started hundreds of years ago as a cattle market, and some of its rituals are designed to show the superiority of humans over animals. Horses are celebrated for their ability to increase human power by raising us up and lending us their strength. Bullfights take place to illustrate man's skill and daring in the face of extraordinary animals.

The fair has always been a sort of balance to Holy Week. The fair stands as the secular complement to Holy Week's religious fervor. Whereas Holy Week takes over the streets of the city and uses them as the stage for its festival, the fair moves outside the city and sets up a make-believe Seville.

Each year an enormous, newly designed entrance gate is built for the fair. The people of Seville are highly interested in the actual design of the doorway, its presentation, and opening. One of the hallmarks of almost any festival is the production of elaborate architecture that is destroyed as soon as the event is over. Taking away the physical elements that contained the celebration is a way of keeping each

occasion unique and memorable—and it's in the tradition of sheer extravagant waste that has often been considered a must for a good festival.

On each of the six days of the fair there is a parade along the main street. Men in leather pants, boots, and stiff-brimmed hats ride along on horses. It is considered extremely chic to have an elaborately dressed, highly adorned woman sitting side-saddle behind the man. Her attire is dictated by tradition: her dress has an extravagant flounced skirt and a long, tight bodice with frilled sleeves. She wears a long, fringed shawl, a carnation in her smooth hair (which is pulled back into a bun), and enormous earrings. It is also considered appropriate to ride a horse and buggy in the parade. These are driven by men in somber, dark clothing and black hats. The horses, however, are decked with bells and pom-poms, plumes and bobbles. The women who ride in carriages also wear the traditional brightly colored, flounced dresses of old Spain.

Inside the fair, the basic structure is a little red or green striped canvas house called a *caseta* or "little house." Inside, the casetas are furnished with all the elements you would expect to find in one of Seville's private houses: curtains, carpets, mirrors, tables, chairs, pictures, and places to cook. The family or business that set up the caseta invites people to stop in and have something to eat and

drink. The canvas city has strings of lights overhead, and the roads are covered with a special yellow sand brought in from a nearby town. Acrobats, shooting booths, and conjurers add a carnival atmosphere while fireworks displays, flower shows, and exhibitions of painting attract the stares of passers-by. Concerts, a poetry festival, theatrical events, flamenco dancers, and mechanical rides also add to the excitement of the fair.

The people of Seville consider themselves great presenters of dramatic displays. They need an audience to share the experience, and so in many ways they are very open and hospitable. But Seville has had a long history of invasion by foreign powers, and so the individual family of Seville has become very private. Everyone is ready to go out eating and drinking and dancing, but the operative words here are *go out* rather than *go home*. It is a very special occasion when an old and prominent Seville family entertains at home. But at the fair, everyone enjoys a week of make-believe visits in others' houses. Every night for six nights there is music and flamenco. The music often features guitar playing, clapping, and rhythms that originated in Moorish times. Just before dawn everyone finds a soft spot and goes to sleep for a few hours until the next morning, when the fair begins again.

About Sherry

Over two thousand years ago, the Greeks shipped wine out of southern Spain. Today, the region still produces a lot of wine. But the truly unique drink to come out of this part of the world is not just wine—it's wine that has been fortified to become sherry. The world's largest producer of sherry is a company called Gonzalez Byass. It produces Tio Pepe, which is made in the town of Jerez de la Frontera, not far from Seville. The soil of Andalusia is filled with the fossilized shells of the marine life that lived in the sea that once covered the Andalusian hills. These shells keep the soil rich in limestone, which winemakers like because it helps hold moisture in this hot, sunny climate.

On a day of the winemakers' choosing, the grapes are picked and crushed. The crushed grapes start to ferment. Yeast, which has been growing naturally on the outside of the grapes, suddenly comes in contact with the juice of the crushed grapes. The yeast acts on the sugar in the grape juice, turning some of it into carbon dioxide gas and alcohol.

The cellarmaster selects the best of the winemakers' work and determines which sherry shall be made from which wine. Bottled sherries are usually not wines made from the harvest of a single year. They are a blending together of sherries from different years.

During the fermentation of a wine that is destined to become a *fino* or an *amontillado*, a flower-like yeast forms spontaneously on the top surface of the wine. It is called the *flor* and has a yeasty breadlike aroma that it gives to the wine. This flor is known to form only in the area around Jerez.

A *fino* is a very light, dry, delicate sherry. The differences in taste between a *fino*, an *amontillado*, and an *oloroso* are similar to the differences between an almond (the fino), a hazelnut (the amontillado), and a walnut (the oloroso).

The aging of the wine takes place according to a method called the solera system, which is used in the making of sherry and *brandy de Jerez*. The wine barrels are held in rows, one on top of the other. The newest wine, from this year's vintage, goes into the cask on the top. The most mature wine is at the bottom. When the producer is ready to bottle the sherry, a portion is drawn off from the bottom. The portion that was drawn off is then replaced with wine from the barrel just above. The process is repeated until all the barrels have been refilled from the row above except for the row on top—which is refilled with new wine. Each one of the oak casks can be used to make sherry for three or four years, after which it retires to Scotland where it is used to age scotch whisky.

After the wine is drawn off, it is fortified with distilled grape alcohol made from the same type of grape as the wine. The addition of the alcohol to the wine is one of the essential elements in the production of sherry.

The ancient Egyptians used stills to make alcohol, but it was not for drinking. Their alcohol was used as a solvent into which charcoal dust was mixed to produce the eye makeup worn by women. When the Moors took over Spain in the 700s, they introduced the distillation process to the local winemakers, who used it to develop sherry. It is said that during the week of the Festival of Seville, more sherry is poured in that city than during an entire year in North America.

Recipes for the Spring Fiestas
Seville, Spain

Spring Vegetable Stew

Stuffed Squid

Fish Baked in a Salt Crust

Cheesecake with Orange Honey Sauce

Spring Vegetable Stew

Makes 6-8 servings

Executive Chef Fernando Cordoba

El Faro Restaurant, Jerez

8 cups water

1 tablespoon kosher salt, or to taste

10 ounces green beans, trimmed and split into ½-inch pieces

3 small carrots, peeled, cut into 1-inch diagonal pieces

8 asparagus tips

2 pounds peas in the pod, or 2 cups shelled peas

2 pounds baby artichokes, or 18 ounces frozen artichoke hearts

1 lemon

⅓ cup extra virgin olive oil

1 large bread roll (about 3 ounces), cut into ½-inch cubes

1½ cups chopped onions

6 cloves garlic, sliced

2 bay leaves

1 teaspoon dried thyme, crushed

1 red bell pepper, seeded and diced

1 ancho pepper, crushed

8 small red potatoes, skins on, quartered

2 tablespoons minced fresh flat-leaf parsley

Freshly ground black pepper

1   BRING THE WATER to a boil with a teaspoon of kosher salt. Boil the beans for 1 minute, remove the beans with a slotted spoon, and rinse under cold water. In the same water, repeat this procedure with the carrots, cooking for 4 minutes. Repeat this procedure with the asparagus, cooking for 2 minutes. Save the water that the vegetables were cooked in to use as the broth for the stew.

2   IF YOU ARE USING fresh peas, shuck the peas. To enhance the broth for the stew, save about half the pea pods. Add the pods to the water the vegetables cooked in. Simmer for 15 to 20 minutes and strain and reserve.

130

3   IF USING FRESH BABY ARTICHOKES, prepare them for cooking by cutting off the upper quarter-inch of the pointed tops and trimming the stems; snap off 2 or 3 layers of the tough outer leaves until you reach tender yellow leaves. Cut the artichokes in half vertically with a paring knife, and cut out the spiky choke. Rub the artichokes with a cut lemon as you clean them, and place them in water with lemon juice until ready to cook.

4   HEAT THE OIL in a soup pot and then sauté the bread until golden brown on all sides. Set the bread aside to cool. Add the onions, garlic, bay leaves, and thyme to the pot and cook over medium-high heat until softened and fragrant, 3 to 4 minutes. Add the red bell pepper and continue to cook for 2 minutes. Add the artichokes and reserved vegetable broth. Add the ancho pepper and potatoes to the pot. Bring to a simmer and cook uncovered for 20 minutes.

5   CRUSH THE BREAD with the remaining salt and add this to the soup to thicken it. Add the carrots. Simmer the stew for 10 to 15 minutes, or until the artichokes are tender and the stew is thick. The stew can be prepared to this point a day ahead.

6   WHEN READY TO SERVE, add the peas and cook for 5 minutes over medium heat. Add the asparagus, green beans, parsley, and fresh black pepper to taste and heat through. Serve immediately.

EL FARO

Just south of Seville is the town of Jerez, and just outside Jerez is the restaurant El Faro. It's one of the most picturesque restaurants in Spain. The restaurant's specialty is fish, which makes a lot of sense, since the area has been famous for its seaports and fishermen for thousands of years. In a back room, El Faro has an extensive collection of the wines, sherries, and brandies of Spain. The room also has a row of tables at which guests can stand and eat small plates of traditional *tapas,* or appetizers. The restaurant itself is decorated with locally produced arts and crafts. Fernando Cordoba, the owner and chef, comes from a family of restaurateurs. He likes to take the classic home recipes of his native region and adapt them to more modern tastes.

Stuffed Squid

Makes 4-6 servings

For the Squid and Stuffing:

> 1 pound cleaned squid (about 8 medium squid)
>
> 2 tablespoons olive oil
>
> 1 teaspoon dried thyme, crushed
>
> 1 tablespoon minced garlic
>
> 1 cup minced onions
>
> ¼ cup finely diced serrano ham or prosciutto
>
> 2 tablespoons finely chopped toasted almonds
>
> 2 tablespoons plain bread crumbs
>
> 2 tablespoons minced fresh flat-leaf parsley
>
> ½ teaspoon salt
>
> Freshly ground black pepper

For the Sauce:

> 2 tablespoons olive oil
>
> 2 tablespoons dry sherry
>
> ⅔ cup clam juice or fish broth
>
> 1⅓ cups canned tomatoes, roughly chopped
>
> 1 medium onion, sliced
>
> 3 cloves garlic, sliced
>
> 1 carrot, sliced
>
> 1 bay leaf
>
> Pinch of crushed red pepper flakes (optional)
>
> ½ teaspoon salt
>
> Freshly ground black pepper

1   TO MAKE THE SQUID AND STUFFING: Separate the squid bodies and tentacles. Pat the tentacles dry with a paper towel and chop them into small pieces. Flush the bodies clean with water; dry and set them aside. Make sure the plastic-like stiff membranes are removed and discarded.

2 IN A MEDIUM SKILLET, heat the oil and thyme and sauté the garlic and onion for 5 minutes, or until the onions are translucent. Stir in the ham and the chopped squid tentacles and cook over high heat until the squid firms, 2 to 3 minutes. If the squid throws off a lot of liquid, remove it from the pan with a slotted spoon and reduce the liquid down to a couple of tablespoons. Add the liquid to the reserved squid mixture.

3 MIX IN THE ALMONDS, bread crumbs, and parsley. Season with the salt and freshly ground black pepper to taste.

4 LOOSELY STUFF THE SQUID bodies with the mixture. Don't overstuff the bodies; the squid shrinks when it cooks and if they are too full, they will burst. Thread the squid closed with toothpicks.

5 TO COOK THE SQUID AND MAKE THE SAUCE: Heat the olive oil in a large skillet and sauté the stuffed squid about 2 minutes on each side. Add the sherry and reduce by half. Add the remaining sauce ingredients except the salt and pepper. Scrape any pan drippings into the liquid. Season with the salt and freshly ground black pepper to taste. Braise, covered, for 1 hour, or until tender.

6 WHEN THE SQUID IS TENDER, remove it from the braising liquid to a serving platter. Remove the bay leaf. Remove the toothpicks and spoon the tomato sauce over the squid. Serve warm or at room temperature, with warm bread to sop up the sauce.

Fish Baked in a Salt Crust

Makes 2-3 servings

Executive Chef Fernando Cordoba
El Faro Restaurant, Jerez

6-7 cups kosher or coarse sea salt
One (2-pound) sea bass or red snapper, gutted, gills removed, but scales intact
3 tablespoons extra virgin olive oil
1 lemon, quartered

1   HEAT THE OVEN TO 425°F. Pour a ½-inch-deep bed of salt into a roasting pan or casserole. Lay the fish on top and bury the fish in the remaining salt. Cook in the oven for 20 to 25 minutes, or until an instant-read thermometer, poked into the thickest part of the fish, reaches 130° to 135°.

2   REMOVE THE FISH FROM THE OVEN, crack the outer shell of salt, and remove the excess salt. Peel back the skin and gently lift off the top fillet to a serving dish. Carefully pull off the bones, head, and tail. Transfer the second fillet to the serving dish and serve with a light sprinkling of olive oil and lemon juice.

THE STORY OF TIO PEPE

Tio means "uncle" in Spanish. The founder of the Gonzalez Byass company had been making a particular style of sweet sherry, which was fine, except that his old uncle, Tio Pepe, wanted some sherry like the kind he used to drink when he was younger—dry and light. So Gonzalez produced some especially for him. He kept it in casks that were stored separately in a back room. Tio Pepe would come in with his friends to have a little party. He put his name on the barrels so no one would get into his private reserve. Eventually, however, Tio Pepe's sherry became the world's most popular brand.

Cheesecake with Orange Honey Sauce

Makes 6-8 servings

Executive Chef Fernando Cordoba
El Faro Restaurant, Jerez

1 pound cottage cheese
1 cup cream
5 large eggs
1¼ cups sugar

For the Sauce:

½ cup orange juice
3 tablespoons honey

1   POUR THE COTTAGE CHEESE into a sieve set over a pot and let it drain overnight in the refrigerator, covered with plastic wrap, to remove any excess moisture.

2   PREHEAT THE OVEN TO 325°F. In a blender, mix the drained cottage cheese with the cream until smooth. In a medium bowl, whisk together the eggs and sugar until slightly thickened. Stir the cheese mixture into the egg mixture.

3   POUR THE CHEESECAKE mixture into a glass loaf pan, about 8 x 4 x 2 inches. Place the loaf pan in a larger pan and pour hot water into the outside pan until the water comes halfway up the outside of the inside pan. Bake for 1¾ to 2 hours, or until the cheesecake is lightly browned on top and set. Turn the oven off and cool the cheesecake in the oven for 15 to 20 minutes. Refrigerate for 2 to 3 hours before serving.

4   TO MAKE THE SAUCE: Pour the orange juice and honey into a small saucepan. Bring to a simmer and boil until thickened, about 10 minutes. Set aside.

5   WHEN READY TO SERVE, turn the cake out onto a plate or cutting board. Cut the cake into slices and serve with a drizzle of the orange honey sauce on top.

A birthday party celebrates two important themes: it is a rite of initiation and a ceremony of measurement. How old are you now? How far have you come? Celebrating the date of someone's birth sets the stage for moving into another cycle of life. We traditionally place candles on top of a birthday cake—one for each year of a person's life. The candles are lit, representing the life-force within us. But they, like life itself, last only for a short time. The "birthdayer" is required to blow the candles out with one breath, as if to say, "The past years of my life are over and gone, but I still have the breath of life within me! I am in control. I can blow these candles out and start anew." With one blow, we celebrate our luck in still being alive, and start our new year with a hopeful wish for the future.

THE BIRTHDAY PARTY

The Idea of the Birthday

The ancient Romans were the first people to celebrate birthdays. Every god had a temple, and everybody had a favorite god. People celebrated the anniversary of the opening of their favorite god's temple. Soon, they began to celebrate the birthday of the favorite god of important people. And before long, they were also celebrating the birthdays of those important people, like the emperor. And we still do the same thing today. The British, for example, celebrate their queen's birthday. And in the United States, there are celebrations for the birthdays of Presidents Washington and Lincoln and civil rights leader Martin Luther King.

Early Christians did not accept the idea of celebrating the emperor's birthday as if he were a god. Their refusal to do so caused the first persecutions, giving Christianity some of its earliest martyrs. In fact, the early Christians deliberately celebrated deaths rather than births (they did not celebrate Christ's birth until the fifth century) since death was the beginning of eternity, and the day of liberation. An infant was named after a favorite saint, who was then perceived as a model and spiritual guide throughout the person's life. Orthodoxy and Catholicism still celebrate saints' days as well as birthdays.

Today, in the West, we celebrate birthdays every year, and some birthdays are more important than others. A baby's first birthday is very special—the child has made it through the perils of infancy. The sixteenth birthday symbolizes the change from childhood to adulthood, and marks sexual maturity. For centuries, the twenty-first birthday signified a legal "coming of age." At thirty, people were considered responsible. In the ancient world, a man became a citizen at thirty and did not marry until that age. (In Denmark, people play pranks on 30-year-olds who are still unmarried.) Forty was thought to be the halfway point in life, and fifty was supposed to be the beginning of the peak decade in one's career. Sixty-five was the official time to retire, and seventy was thought of as the threshold of old age. After ninety, every year was marked by a celebration of sheer survival.

As the number of older people in our society increases, however, there have been changes in the meaning attached to some of these birthdays. Forty is now considered too young to be called middle-aged. Fewer and fewer people are retiring at sixty-five. And at seventy many people are quite active. One hundred is, of course, a very big deal. Every morning, national television shows congratulate people who have reached their hundredth year.

In Eastern societies, it is customary to note the number of years someone has lived, but not bother too much about the actual date of birth. When the first moon of the new year arrives, *everybody* is considered to be one year older. In China, Korea, and Japan, the sixtieth year traditionally marks a major transition into old age, a transition from an active life to one of contemplation.

In most parts of the world, people never really kept records of birth dates. The church kept a record of baptisms, but quite often people were just not that interested in knowing exactly when they were born. Many cultures also felt that counting the years of life that had already been lived was an unlucky practice.

Modern American society, however, is definitely a measuring culture. Governments and institutions love to categorize people by their age, and these institutions tell you when you can drive, when you can vote, and when you can take a bus at a discounted rate. They even tell you when you're too old to order from the children's menu. I know. I've tried.

A Brief History
of Orlando and Disney World

Birthday celebrations are often more important to children than they are to adults, and the location of the party can be crucial. One of the world's favorite places for a family gathering or celebration is Walt Disney World in Orlando, Florida.

Ponce de Leon, the Spanish explorer, was the first European to record his trip to Florida. He wandered through in 1513 looking for the "fountain of youth," but never found it. He also missed the real idea behind the fountain. It's not something that makes your body young again. It's a state of mind; a way of thinking about life. And today it really does exist in Florida—at Disney World.

The Walt Disney World Resort is one of the world's great entertainment destinations. It actually includes three major theme parks: the Magic Kingdom, EPCOT, and the Disney-MGM Studios. The Magic Kingdom features Cinder–ella Castle, Adventureland, Frontierland, Fan–tasyland, and Tomorrowland. One part of EPCOT takes a look at future technology with such interactive exhibitions as Spaceship Earth, Communicore, and Computer Central, and gives us information about the planet in the One Land Pavilion and The Living Sea. The other part is called the World Showcase, and it has areas devoted to the history and culture of eleven nations. The most recent addition, the Disney-MGM Studios, gives us a look at the realities and illusions involved in making movies. Michael Eisner, the chairman of the Walt Disney Company, gave the definitive description of the park when he opened the studios in 1989. He welcomed everyone to "a Hollywood that never was—and will always be."

The Birthday Party

It's important to have people around to witness the celebration of your initiation into a new stage of life. Other people need to see that you are moving on. They reinforce your image of yourself as a changed person. Whom you choose to be at such a celebration is a sign of your power. Who could forget Marilyn Monroe singing "Happy Birthday" to John F. Kennedy? Now *that's* a guest list.

The birthday party host usually puts a great deal of effort into the planning of the celebration. Food, toys, and games are all offered, in partial payment to the all-important guests. Everyone that comes to an official birthday party must bring a present; it is an essential part of honoring the birthday person. At a child's birthday, games generally express group togetherness, and often involve numbers. In some cultures, the child is playfully whacked for the number of years lived. Whackings are a common part of initiation rites.

Everybody joins in the appreciation of the birthday person. A traditional song is sung. The music of "Happy Birthday to You" was written in 1893 by two sisters, Mildred and Patty Hill, who lived in Louisville, Kentucky. In 1924, words were added to their music, but no one knows who wrote them. The tune is the most-frequently sung music in the Anglo-Saxon world.

Birthday parties are the most common occasion for dining out, and during the dinner the birthday person is often singled out and sung to. Tradition has it that the "birthdayer" should at least pretend to be embarrassed! Surprise parties let the birthday person know that a conspiracy of happiness has taken place, and that effort has been taken on their behalf by caring friends.

The birthday cake is the centerpiece of a birthday party, but it is not made according to a particular formula. Unlike a wedding cake or Christmas fruitcake, a birthday cake can be quite unique and generally "says" something about the person being celebrated. Often the honoree chooses the kind of cake. The sharing of the cake symbolizes the unity of the people at the event.

Recipes for a Birthday Party
Walt Disney World

Mini Crab Cakes with Rémoulade Sauce

Florida Tomato Salad with Parmesan Crisps

Sautéed Florida Grouper with Tomatoes, Artichokes, & Olives

Devil's Food Birthday Cake

Orange Cream Angel Food Birthday Cake

Mini Crab Cakes with Rémoulade Sauce

Makes about 30 small cakes

2 tablespoons unsalted butter

2 scallions, white and green parts minced

1 rib celery, minced

1 medium clove garlic, minced

1 pound lump crab meat, cleaned and picked over to remove any bits of shell

2 large eggs, lightly beaten

2 teaspoons fresh lemon juice

2 tablespoons whole grain mustard

2 tablespoons minced fresh flat-leaf parsley

1 teaspoon kosher salt

¼ teaspoon freshly ground black pepper

Pinch of freshly grated nutmeg

⅓ cup cracker meal, plus more for dredging

⅔ cup vegetable oil, for frying

Rémoulade Sauce (recipe follows)

1   IN A MEDIUM SKILLET, heat the butter; add the scallions, celery, and garlic, and cook over medium heat until the vegetables are translucent, about 3 to 4 minutes.

2   IN A MEDIUM BOWL, combine the cooked vegetables with the crab, eggs, lemon juice, mustard, and parsley. Season with the salt, pepper, and nutmeg. Add the cracker meal and stir well to combine thoroughly. Form heaping tablespoons of the crab mixture into 1½-inch- round cakes. Roll the cakes in additional cracker meal and place them on a baking pan. Refrigerate for at least 30 minutes before cooking.

3   WHEN READY TO SERVE, heat a large skillet. Pour the oil into the skillet to a depth of ½-inch. Heat the oil over medium heat, keeping the oil at a low simmer; cook and brown the cakes for 1 to 2 minutes on the first side and about 1 minute on the second side, or until they are cooked through and golden brown. Transfer the cakes to paper towels to drain. Serve the cakes warm, with the Rémoulade sauce.

Rémoulade Sauce

Makes about 1 cup

⅔ cup mayonnaise

2 scallions, white and green parts chopped

2 tablespoons finely minced fresh flat-leaf parsley

2 tablespoons minced fresh dill

1 teaspoon fresh lemon juice

2 tablespoons drained white horseradish

4 tablespoons whole-grain mustard

1 tablespoon ketchup

1 teaspoon Worcestershire sauce

1 tablespoon sweet paprika

½ teaspoon kosher salt

⅛ teaspoon freshly ground black pepper

Tabasco to taste

IN A SMALL BOWL, whisk all of the ingredients together and refrigerate until ready to serve.

Florida Tomato Salad with Parmesan Crisps

Makes 4 servings

Executive Chef Brian Tossell
Walt Disney World Dolphin Hotel

For the Parmesan Crisps:

Vegetable oil
6 ounces fresh Parmesan cheese, shredded

For the Dressing:

2 tablespoons fresh lemon juice
4 teaspoons Dijon-style mustard
½ teaspoon sugar
1½ teaspoons dark Asian-style sesame oil
1 tablespoon minced fresh chives

For the Salad:

6 medium ripe tomatoes
4 medium shiitake mushrooms, stems trimmed
1 tablespoon minced fresh tarragon
½ teaspoon kosher salt, or to taste
⅛ teaspoon freshly ground black pepper
5 cups oak leaf or other baby lettuce, washed and dried

1   TO MAKE THE CRISPS: Heat the oven to 425°F. Have an overturned medium-size bowl ready to use as a mold for the cheese crisps. Lightly oil a cookie sheet or non-stick baking sheet. Sprinkle a quarter of the cheese into a rough 9-inch circle on the sheet. Bake the cheese in the oven for 5 to 6 minutes or until it just turns golden brown. Remove the pan from the oven. Working quickly and carefully, scrape the cheese off the pan in one piece. Use a plastic or metal spatula or pastry scraper, and complete the procedure before the cheese has a chance to harden. Carefully transfer the cheese crisp to the overturned bowl and gently press it over the outside of the bowl to make a free-form basket shape. Cool the crisp on the bowl, remove it, and repeat with the rest of the cheese to make a total of 4 crisps. These can be done a couple of hours ahead and stored at room temperature.

146

2 TO MAKE THE DRESSING: In a medium bowl, whisk the ingredients together and set aside.

3 TO MAKE THE SALAD: Bring a large pot of water to a boil. Make a small **x** with the tip of a knife on the bottom of each tomato. Plunge the tomatoes into the boiling water for 30 seconds and then immediately into ice water. Gently peel off their skins and remove the stem ends. Blanch the shiitake mushrooms in the boiling water for 1 minute. Drain.

4 CUT A ⅓ WEDGE OUT from each of 4 tomatoes. Scoop out the center of these tomatoes and set the shells aside for filling with the salad. Save the tomato centers for the salad itself.

5 SEED AND DICE the 2 remaining tomatoes and the reserved tomato centers. Slice the shiitake mushrooms into thin strips. Add the cut tomatoes, mushrooms, and tarragon to the prepared dressing and toss to combine thoroughly. Season with salt and pepper.

6 WHEN READY TO SERVE, divide the greens among 4 plates. Place a Parmesan crisp on each plate. Carefully place a hollowed-out tomato shell in each crisp. Spoon the salad into the tomatoes so it appears to cascade from each tomato. Serve immediately.

Sautéed Florida Grouper with Tomatoes, Artichokes, & Olives

Makes 4 servings

Executive Chef Waldo Brun
Walt Disney World Swan Hotel

For the Vegetables:

4 ripe plum tomatoes

3 tablespoons olive oil

1 medium shallot, minced

2 tablespoons minced garlic

¼ pound white mushrooms, quartered

3 tablespoons pitted sliced black olives, Gaeta or Kalamata

1 tablespoon minced fresh thyme, plus sprigs for garnish

1 (9-ounce) package of frozen artichoke hearts, thawed

1 teaspoon kosher salt

¼ teaspoon freshly ground black pepper

⅓ cup white wine

2 tablespoons unsalted butter

For the Fish:

⅓ cup flour

1 teaspoon kosher salt

½ teaspoon freshly ground black pepper

4 (6-ounce) skinless grouper or red snapper fillets

3 tablespoons olive oil

1   TO PREPARE THE VEGETABLES: Bring a medium pot of water to a boil. Make a small **x** with the tip of a knife on the bottom of each tomato. Plunge the tomatoes into the boiling water for 30 seconds, and then immediately into ice water. Peel off their skins and remove the blossom ends. Cut the tomatoes in half, squeeze out the seeds, and dice. Set aside.

2   IN A LARGE SKILLET, heat the olive oil and sauté the shallot and garlic over high heat for 1 minute. Add the mushrooms, olives, and minced thyme, and continue to cook, stirring occasionally, for 3 to 4 minutes. Add the tomatoes and artichokes, and season with the salt and pepper. Cook for 1 to 2 minutes, or until juicy. Add the white wine and cook over high heat to reduce the liquid by about a quarter, 2 to 3 minutes. Keep the vegetables warm while you cook the fish.

3   TO PREPARE THE FISH: Combine the flour, salt, and pepper, and spread the mixture out on a large plate or piece of wax paper. Pat the fish dry and roll it in the flour to coat evenly. Shake off any excess.

4   HEAT A LARGE SKILLET, big enough so the grouper can lie flat while cooking. Use 2 pans if necessary. Heat the oil and then lay the fish in the hot oil. Sauté the fish over medium-high heat for 4 to 5 minutes on the first side, or until lightly browned. Flip the fish and continue to cook on the other side for 1 to 2 minutes, or until cooked through but still moist. The fish should be light brown and crisp, and slightly firm to the touch.

5   REHEAT THE VEGETABLES if necessary, and whisk in the butter. Transfer the fish to 4 warmed plates or a platter and spoon the artichoke mixture on top. Garnish with fresh thyme sprigs and serve immediately.

Devil's Food Birthday Cake

Makes 8 servings

Pastry Chef Jean-Paul Fagot
Walt Disney World Dolphin Hotel

For the Cake:

2¼ cups cake flour

2 cups sugar

¾ cup unsweetened cocoa powder

2 teaspoons baking powder

½ teaspoon baking soda

½ teaspoon salt

12 tablespoons (1½ sticks) unsalted butter, softened

4 large eggs

1¾ cups buttermilk

1 teaspoon vanilla extract

For the Chocolate Ganache:

1 pound semi-sweet chocolate, chopped into small pieces, or semi-sweet chocolate chips

2 cups heavy cream

For the Decoration:

2 ounces white chocolate

½ teaspoon corn or canola oil

1   TO MAKE THE CAKE: Preheat the oven to 350° F. Lightly butter two 10-inch cake pans and line the bottoms with parchment paper. Sift together the flour, sugar, cocoa, baking powder, baking soda, and salt. In a medium-size bowl, mix the sifted ingredients with an electric hand-held mixer for 30 seconds. With the mixer still running, alternately add half the butter and 2 of the eggs, and then the remaining butter and the remaining eggs. Mix until the ingredients are evenly combined, about 1 minute. Scrape down the sides of the bowl to combine the ingredients. Continue to mix on low speed and add the buttermilk and vanilla. Increase the speed and beat the batter for 3 to 5 minutes, until fluffy.

2　DIVIDE THE BATTER between the prepared cake pans, and bake for 30 to 40 minutes, or until a cake tester or toothpick comes out clean when inserted in the center. Cool the cakes for 10 minutes, then carefully unmold them onto a cake circle or plate and cool on a rack.

3　TO MAKE THE CHOCOLATE GANACHE:　Place the chocolate in a medium bowl. In a saucepan, bring the heavy cream to a boil. Pour the cream over the chocolate and whisk until completely smooth. Let the ganache come to room temperature and then refrigerate for 2 hours. For icing the cake, the ganache should be set but still spreadable.

4　SLICE EACH CAKE HORIZONTALLY into 2 layers. Set one layer on a cake circle and spread the top with about a ¼-inch of chocolate ganache. Repeat with the other layers and ganache to build the cake. Spread the top and the sides of the cake with a thin smooth layer of ganache. Chill the cake for 20 minutes.

5　GENTLY HEAT THE REMAINING chocolate ganache in the top of a double boiler over simmering water until it is pourable but not warm. To glaze the cake, set it on a rack over a pan and pour the ganache over the cake. Let the glaze drip down the sides of the cake. Chill the cake for 20 minutes. If there is extra ganache, melt it again, cool, then pour it over the cake as before.

6　TO DECORATE THE CAKE:　Melt the white chocolate with the oil. Place the white chocolate in a pastry bag with a $1/16$-inch open tip. Press the white chocolate to the tip of the bag. With gentle pressure, practice writing a couple of letters on a piece of wax paper. Then write your birthday message over the top of the cake. Chill the cake until ready to serve, but set it at room temperature for 20 minutes before serving.

Orange Cream Angel Food Birthday Cake

Makes 8 servings

Pastry Chef Richard Carpenter
Walt Disney World Swan Hotel

For the Cake:

> 1 cup cake flour
>
> ½ cup confectioners' sugar
>
> ½ cup finely ground almonds
>
> 1⅓ cups egg whites (about 10 large whites)
>
> ¼ teaspoon fresh lemon juice
>
> Pinch of salt
>
> 1 cup granulated sugar
>
> 1 teaspoon vanilla extract
>
> ¼ teaspoon almond extract

For the Orange Cream:

> ½ cup orange juice
>
> 1 envelope unflavored gelatin (1 scant tablespoon)
>
> 1½ teaspoons grated orange zest
>
> 1 cup heavy cream
>
> 3 tablespoons confectioners' sugar

For the Glaze:

> ¼ cup ground almonds
>
> 1 cup confectioners' sugar
>
> 3 to 4 tablespoons strained orange juice

1   PREHEAT THE OVEN to 350°F. Sift the flour and confectioners' sugar together 3 times into a medium bowl. Whisk in the almonds and set aside.

2 IN A STANDING MIXER or in clean bowl with a hand-held electric mixer, whip the egg whites together with the lemon juice and salt on low speed until foamy. Increase the speed and continue to whip the whites while slowly pouring in the granulated sugar. Beat the whites until they reach a moist, firm peak. Add the extracts. Do not over-whip the whites.

3 GENTLY FOLD THE FLOUR MIXTURE into the egg whites in 3 separate additions. Transfer the batter to a unlined 10-inch tube pan and bake for 30 to 40 minutes. The cake is done when it springs back when pressed with a finger. Cool, inverted, for 1 to 1½ hours.

4 TO MAKE THE ORANGE CREAM: When the cake is cool, put the orange juice in a small bowl. Sprinkle the gelatin over the surface of the juice and set aside for 5 minutes to soften the gelatin. Place the bowl over a pot of simmering water and whisk to dissolve the gelatin thoroughly. Remove from the heat and add the orange zest. Cool to room temperature.

5 WHIP THE CREAM to the soft peak stage and add the confectioners' sugar. Fold a third of the whipped cream into the orange juice and then fold it back into the rest of the cream. Refrigerate the cream for 5 to 10 minutes while you slice the cake.

6 TO ASSEMBLE THE CAKE: Cut the cake horizontally with a serrated knife into 3 equal layers. Whip the cream lightly. Place the bottom layer on a cake circle or plate and spread the cake with a third of the cream. Lay the second layer on top and spread with an equal amount of cream. Place the top layer back on the cake and smooth the remaining cream over the sides of the cake. Refrigerate for ½ to 1 hour.

7 TO MAKE THE GLAZE: Holding the almonds in the palm of your hand, gently press them halfway up the sides of the cake. Rotate the cake by supporting it with your opposite hand as you coat all the sides of the cake. Whisk the confectioners' sugar with the orange juice to make a smooth glaze. Pour the glaze over the top of the cake and let it drip down the sides. Keep in the refrigerator until ready to serve.

ods, ghosts, and ancestors play major roles in the celebrations of China—and in the most positive ways! When you pay respect to your ancestors you express your gratitude for the life they gave you, but you also help them with their lives in the hereafter. These rituals connect you to the past, and, since you teach your children the same rituals, they connect you to the future. That sense of connection is the most valuable aspect of celebrating each of the Chinese festivals.

THE MOON FESTIVALS OF CHINA

The Festivals of the Lunar Calendar

Western countries use the Gregorian calendar to break time into pieces. This system is based on the number of days it takes the Earth to orbit the sun—three hundred sixty-five and ¼ days. China, however, uses an entirely different calendar to measure out the year. It's called the lunar calendar, and it is based on the amount of time it takes for the moon to orbit the Earth. Time is measured from new moon to new moon—twenty-nine and ½ days. For thousands of years, the Chinese have used a lunar calendar to organize their lives.

Since China was predominantly agricultural for most of its history, daily life was centered around the farming activities of rural communities. The moon calendar showed people when to plant and when to harvest. Celebrations developed naturally from the cycles of the farming year. The New Year and the Lantern Festival come along when the winter weather makes field work difficult. The Tomb-Sweeping Festival gets the family out to enjoy spring's first good weather. The Dragon Boat Festival comes after the first harvest, and the Mid-Autumn ceremony follows the last harvest.

When the Republic of China was founded in 1912, the Western Gregorian system was adopted as the official calendar. The idea made perfectly good sense from a commercial point of view. But the new calendar was only incorporated into the business life of the community. Personal life, religious life, and family life are all still centered around the moon and its phases. All of the major gatherings and celebrations of China have their origins in celestial events.

The Tomb-Sweeping Festival

In the Republic of China, as in Chinese communities throughout the world, one of the year's major occasions is the Tomb-Sweeping Festival, which takes place in the beginning of April. It is a day when all the members of a family, both young and old, pay their respects to their ancestors by visiting the family tombs, cleaning up the gravesites, and making ritual offerings.

The ceremonies are usually performed at dawn or in the early morning hours. The spirits of the departed are thought to sleep during the night and the idea is to catch them "at home" with the offerings before they leave for the day. The family burns incense and sacrificial paper money—a specially-printed money that is believed to turn into real money in the afterlife as its smoke passes up into the heavens—then sweeps and manicures the gravesite. People bring fresh flowers, and sometimes a new bush is planted. Often a complete meal will be placed on a tray and presented to the ancestor. Traditionally, the tray contains foods that were favorites of the dear departed. One of the many nice things about spirit ancestors and gods is that they don't actually *eat* the food. They only take in the aroma. When they have done that, they like *you* to take the food home and eat the rest yourself. The spirits consider your eating of their leftovers an additional tribute to their memory.

The festival is an enjoyable family outing centered on remembering those who have gone ahead to the afterlife. The Chinese take pleasure in the continuance of their family relationships with their ancestors, and use this festival to stop and think about the interrelatedness of life and death. Far from being a somber or morbid occasion, the festival connects the present generation with the past in a warm and tender way. Because the whole family is involved in the tasks of the festival, everyone comes away with a renewed sense of relationship to the past. By caring for the tombs of your relatives in the spirit world, you express your hope that they will care for you in your world, and you teach your children to continue to honor what you have honored.

The Dragon Boat Festival

The fifth day of the fifth lunar month is the date for the Dragon Boat Festival, one of the most colorful celebrations in the Chinese year, and it has a great story behind it. It seems that, during the Warring States Period (about 300 B.C.) there lived a poet named Ch'u Yuan, who was much beloved by the people. He was also an advisor to the emperor, by whom he was not so much beloved. The poet became deeply depressed over the state of the country, and finally clasped a stone to his chest and threw himself into the Mi-lo River, which winds through the province of Hunan. The people of the area immediately launched their boats to save him, or at the very least, to retrieve his body and give him a proper burial. When they were unable to find him, they threw rice into the river, hoping the sea-creatures would eat the rice and not eat their beloved poet. The throwing of the rice became an annual event. About two hundred years later, a ghost appeared and identified himself as the spirit of the great poet. He expressed his appreciation for the annual offering of rice, but pointed out that very often the rice was stolen by the monster who caused floods. The ghost asked that the rice be wrapped in leaves and tied with five-colored string, neither of which was on the monster's diet. The custom of eating *tsung tzu*, dumplings made with glutinous rice and wrapped in bamboo leaves, is a reminder of the rice that was thrown into the river to save the poet.

158

The dragon boat races that take place during the festival commemorate the search to save Ch'u Yuan, and they also demonstrate the Chinese devotion to cooperation and teamwork. Each boat has a crew that includes a helmsman, a drummer, twenty-two oarsmen, and a flag catcher. Two boats compete against each other in each race, with the process of elimination eventually producing a winner. Teams come from all over the world to take part in the races.

The dragon of Chinese mythology controls the rainfall and all the waters of the earth. This makes him essential to the survival of life. Dragon heads and tails are secured to the boats, and a Taoist priest brings them to life by burning incense, setting off firecrackers, dotting the dragon's eyes with paint, and burning sacrificial paper money.

Like many important festivals throughout the world, the particular date of the event coincides with happenings in the heavens. The great poet's death occurs at the summer solstice—the longest day of the year. Summer is the time of China's hottest weather, and it is considered a dangerous period when life is deemed to be out of balance. Evil spirits abound, and the festival's noise and confusion scare off any that may be lurking in the waters. At night, lighted paper lanterns float down the rivers, symbolically releasing wandering spirits from the Buddhist purgatory.

The Mid-Autumn Festival

Ancient Chinese legend holds that the Mid-Autumn Festival falls on the birthday of the earth god known as *T'u-ti Kung*. The festival marks the end of the growing season and the beginning of harvest time. People take this opportunity to thank the god of the earth and the god of the moon for the good things that have happened during the year. The moon god is the great patron of family and good fortune, and the Mid-Autumn Festival is a time that the family gazes at the moon together. It is also a time that lovers are joined in prayer for their continued togetherness. Of all the celebrations of the year, the Mid-Autumn Festival is the most poetic and most nostalgic.

There are many folk stories about happenings concerning the moon, but the most important is said to have taken place about four thousand years ago. It concerns Hou Yih, a skilled archer and master architect. One day, ten suns appeared in the sky. The emperor called upon Hou Yih to shoot down the nine additional suns, which he promptly did. Because of this marvelous feat, he came to the attention of the Goddess of the Western Heaven, who commissioned him to build a jade palace for her. He did such a magnificent job that the goddess rewarded him with a pill that would give him everlasting life. But she warned him not to take the pill until he had prepared himself by completing a year of prayer and fasting. Hou Yih returned home, hid the pill, and began his prayers. In the meantime, his wife, a woman whose incredible beauty was only matched by her awesome curiosity, discovered the pill, swallowed it, and was immediately drawn up to the moon. The legend claims that her beauty is greatest on the night of the Mid-Autumn Festival.

In another version of the story, however, Hou Yih's wife acts with selfless heroism. In this rendition of the legend, Hou Yih is an arrogant ruler who gets his hands on the magical herb of longevity. His wife saves the kingdom from an eternity of tyrannical rule by taking all of the drug herself. The overdose sends her to the moon, but the people are saved.

The food most often associated with the Mid-Autumn Festival is the moon cake, a round pastry stuffed with a sweet filling that symbolizes family unity. It is common practice to give moon cakes to friends and relatives during this time. In ancient China, the giving of moon cakes was once used as a cover for revolution. During

the thirteenth century, the Mongols conquered most of China and set up the Yuan Dynasty. A warrior named Chu Yuan-chang decided to revolt against the Mongol's rule, and sent the signal for the uprising by hiding messages inside moon cakes. It worked. The invaders were overthrown, and moon cakes became more popular than ever.

The Chinese word for grapefruit is *yu*, which sounds like the word for "protection." Much grapefruit and pomelo are eaten during the Mid-Autumn Festival with the hope that the moon god will protect the family from peril during the coming year.

Recipes for the Moon Festivals of China
Taiwan

Bok Choy, Mushroom, & Bean Curd Soup

Chicken Fried Rice

Scallops & Shrimp in Lettuce Leaves

Stir-Fried Lettuce

Beef with Ginger & Bell Peppers

Sherry-Braised Duck with Aromatic Spices

Bok Choy, Mushroom, & Bean Curd Soup

Makes 4 servings

> 1 cup water
>
> 8 dried shiitake mushrooms
>
> 6 cups chicken broth
>
> One (1-inch) piece of fresh ginger, peeled, sliced into thin rounds,
>   then sliced into thin strips
>
> 2 scallions, white and green parts thinly sliced
>
> 2 tablespoons vegetable oil
>
> 1 pound bok choy (about ½ head), sliced into ½-inch pieces
>
> ½ teaspoon kosher salt
>
> ⅛ teaspoon freshly ground black pepper
>
> 4 ounces firm bean curd, diced

1 BRING THE WATER TO A BOIL. Pour the hot water into a bowl with the dried shiitake mushrooms. Set aside to let the mushrooms hydrate for about 20 minutes. Save the soaking liquid. Trim and discard the mushroom's tough stems. Slice the mushrooms into ⅛ inch strips.

2 IN A MEDIUM SOUP POT, simmer the chicken broth with the mushroom soaking liquid (be careful not to add any grit or sand that may be at the bottom of the mushroom broth). Add half the ginger slices and all the scallions to the broth and simmer for 10 minutes.

3 HEAT THE OIL in a large skillet or wok. Stir-fry the bok choy over high heat for 3 minutes, or until crisp-tender. Season the bok choy with the salt and pepper. Add the bok choy, mushrooms, and bean curd to the broth, and continue to simmer for 5 minutes.

4 SERVE THE SOUP in bowls with the remaining ginger sprinkled on top.

Chicken Fried Rice

Makes 4 servings

Executive Chef Ip Chi-chiu
Grand Formosa Regent

2 cups vegetable oil

1 pound boneless, skinless chicken breast meat, cut into ½-inch dice

3 large eggs, lightly beaten

½ teaspoon salt

3 cups cold cooked white rice (1 cup raw rice)

½ cup frozen peas, defrosted, or fresh peas, cooked

¼ teaspoon freshly ground black pepper

2 teaspoons soy sauce

1 cup thinly sliced iceberg lettuce

1   SET A STRAINER or colander over a bowl. Heat the oil in a medium saucepan or wok to 350°F. Add the chicken and stir-fry, stirring once or twice, for 1 to 2 minutes, or until the meat is almost cooked. Carefully pour the chicken and oil into the strainer to drain the oil and reserve it.

2   HEAT ¼ CUP of the strained oil in a large skillet or wok over high heat. Season the eggs with ¼ teaspoon of the salt. Scramble the eggs in the skillet for 30 seconds to 1 minute, then add the rice and peas. Stir-fry for 2 to 3 minutes to evenly combine the rice, eggs, and peas and to heat through.

3   ADD THE CHICKEN, the remaining salt, and the pepper, and stir-fry for 30 seconds. Add the soy sauce and lettuce and stir-fry for another minute, or until all the ingredients are hot. Transfer the rice to a platter and serve.

Scallops & Shrimp in Lettuce Leaves

Makes 4 servings

Executive Chef Ip Chi-chiu
Grand Formosa Regent

4 large leaves of iceberg lettuce

¼ pound ground pork

1 cup vegetable oil, plus 2 tablespoons

½ pound medium raw shrimp, peeled and deveined, diced

½ pound raw sea scallops, cleaned and diced

½ cup minced mushrooms

1 rib celery, minced

⅓ cup minced water chestnuts

2 tablespoons minced peeled fresh ginger

1 cup diced bamboo shoots (one 8-ounce can)

½ teaspoon kosher salt

2 teaspoons soy sauce

2 tablespoons oyster sauce

2 tablespoons rice wine vinegar

2 scallions, white and green parts thinly sliced

⅓ cup cilantro leaves, minced

1 tablespoon cornstarch mixed with 1 tablespoon water

¼ cup chopped macadamia nuts

1 TRIM THE LETTUCE LEAVES with kitchen shears or a knife into neat bowl-like shapes, 4 to 5 inches across. Set the lettuce leaves on a serving platter.

2 HEAT A LARGE SKILLET or wok. Add the ground pork, break up the meat, and cook for 2 to 3 minutes, or until the meat is completely cooked through. Remove the pork from the pan and set it aside. Wipe the pan clean.

3 SET A STRAINER or colander over a bowl. Heat 1 cup of the oil in the skillet or wok to 340°F. Add the shrimp and scallops and fry for 1 minute, or until the shrimp and scallops are translucent. Carefully pour the seafood and oil into the strainer to drain the oil.

4   HEAT THE 2 TABLESPOONS of oil in the skillet or wok. Add the mushrooms, celery, water chestnuts, and ginger, and stir-fry over high heat for 1 minute. Add the bamboo shoots and cooked pork, and continue to stir-fry for 1 minute more. Season with ¼ teaspoon salt.

5   RETURN THE SEAFOOD to the pan and season the mixture with the rest of the salt, and the soy and oyster sauces. Add the rice wine vinegar and stir well, deglazing the pan, scraping the bottom of the pan with a wooden spoon, until the vinegar is reduced by one-third. Add the scallions and cilantro, and combine well. Add the dissolved cornstarch and continue to stir-fry for 1 minute more.

6   LADLE THE SEAFOOD into the lettuce cups, sprinkle with the nuts, and serve.

Stir-Fried Lettuce

Makes 4 servings

Executive Chef Ip Chi-chiu
Grand Formosa Regent

½ cup chicken broth

2 teaspoons Chinese hot chili oil

2 teaspoons peanut or vegetable oil

1 tablespoon minced peeled fresh ginger

1 head iceberg lettuce, cut into 2-inch squares, washed and dried

½ teaspoon kosher salt

2 teaspoons cornstarch dissolved in 2 teaspoons water

1 tablespoon soy sauce

1   HEAT THE CHICKEN BROTH, oils, and ginger in a large skillet or wok. Add the lettuce and cook over high heat, stirring constantly, for 3 to 4 minutes, until the lettuce is cooked but still firm to the bite.

2   ADD THE SALT, cornstarch mixture, and soy sauce, and cook for 30 seconds to 1 minute more. Transfer the lettuce to a platter and serve hot or at room temperature.

Beef with Ginger & Bell Peppers

Makes 4 servings

Executive Chef Ip Chi-chiu
Grand Formosa Regent

For the Marinade:

    2 tablespoons soy sauce

    1 tablespoon dry sherry

    4 teaspoons sesame oil

    ½ teaspoon sugar

    1 teaspoon rice wine vinegar

    1 pound flank steak, sliced against the grain, on an angle, cut into 4-x-½-inch strips

For the Stir-Fry:

    3 tablespoons vegetable oil

    2 medium cloves garlic, sliced

    4 teaspoons peeled minced fresh ginger

    3 bell peppers, 1 red, 1 yellow, and 1 green, seeded and cut into 1-inch pieces

    ¼ teaspoon kosher salt

    ⅛ teaspoon freshly ground black pepper

    1 tablespoon soy sauce

    1 teaspoon Chinese black vinegar or balsamic vinegar

    1 teaspoon cornstarch dissolved in 1 tablespoon water

1   TO MAKE THE MARINADE: In a medium bowl, whisk the ingredients together, add the flank steak, stir to coat the meat, and marinate at room temperature for 45 to 60 minutes.

2   TO STIR-FRY: When ready to serve, heat a large skillet or wok. Heat 2 tablespoons of the oil and stir-fry the garlic and ginger over high heat for 30 seconds. Add the peppers, stir-fry for 3 minutes, and season with the salt and pepper. Transfer the peppers to a bowl and keep warm.

3   HEAT THE REMAINING OIL in the pan, add the beef, and stir-fry over very high heat for 2 to 3 minutes. Return the peppers to the pan, add the soy sauce and vinegar, and combine with the beef. Add the dissolved cornstarch and continue cooking for 1 minute, until the sauce begins to thicken. Transfer to a platter and serve immediately.

Sherry-Braised Duck with Aromatic Spices

Makes 4 servings

One (3-4 pound) Long Island duck, fresh or frozen and defrosted

6 scallions

1½ cups dry sherry

⅓ cup soy sauce

6 quarter-size slices peeled ginger

3 whole star anise

2½ cups water

2 tablespoons sugar

8 dried shiitake mushrooms

1 medium turnip, peeled and cut into ½ moons

1   REMOVE THE GIZZARDS and neck from the cavity of the duck. Trim the excess fat and skin from the duck's neck and tail. Cut off and discard the wing tips and tail. Pierce the duck skin all over with the tines of a fork to help render the fat.

2   HEAT A LARGE SKILLET OR WOK. Carefully lower the duck, breast side down, into the pan and sear the duck over medium heat until it is golden brown, about 10 minutes. Poke a wooden spoon into the duck and rotate the bird onto its side. Brown the bird for 5 to 7 minutes. Rotate and brown the bird on the other side and then the back, until all sides have been well browned and most of the duck fat has been rendered. Transfer the duck to a plate and discard the rendered fat.

3   LAY THE SCALLIONS in the center of a casserole that will fit the duck snugly. Place the duck breast side down on the bed of scallions. (The scallions provide a buffer so the duck skin doesn't scorch.) Add the sherry, soy sauce, ginger, and star anise, bring to a boil, and then add 1-1/2 cups of the water. Reduce the heat so the liquid simmers gently. Baste the bird with the sauce, cover, and simmer the duck for 1½ hours. Check the duck periodically to make sure the sauce is not simmering too quickly, and to baste the bird.

4   AFTER THE DUCK has simmered for 1½ hours, poke a wooden spoon into the cavity and turn the bird onto its back. Add the sugar to the braising liquid. Baste the duck and continue to braise, covered, for another hour. Check periodically to make sure the sauce is simmering gently and to baste the duck.

5   BRING THE REMAINING 1 cup of water to a boil and pour it into a bowl with the dried shiitake mushrooms. Set aside for 20 minutes to hydrate. Once the mushrooms are soft, trim and discard their tough stems.

6   WHEN THE DUCK IS FULLY TENDER, carefully remove it to a plate with a pair of tongs and cover it with foil to keep warm. Strain the sauce and skim the fat from the surface, or pour the liquid through a degreasing cup.

7   RETURN THE SAUCE to the pan and simmer it with the mushrooms and turnip for 10 minutes.

8   TO SERVE, slice the duck into serving pieces and arrange it on a large platter. Spoon the sauce and vegetables over the duck and serve warm or at room temperature.

JUNE'S FEAST DAYS

IN PORTUGAL

Portugal spends June commemorating the great apostolic saints of Catholicism. The festivities include sports events, religious rituals, street parades, and block parties. There are dinners in little town squares all over the country.

Portugal runs along the southwestern edge of Europe, where the land ends and the sea begins. Its capital city, Lisbon, stands just below the midpoint of the coastline. For hundreds of years, Lisbon was home to the ruling families of Portugal and the center of one of the world's most powerful nations. In the middle of the fifteenth century, the king of Portugal described himself as "the lord of navigation, conqueror of Ethiopia, Arabia, Persia, and India." And that was his most *modest* title.

Celebrating the Saints

Among Catholics, every saint is accorded a feast day, and the feast days for many saints who played an active role in spreading Christianity happen to fall in the month of June. June's the perfect time of year for a party, and the feast days bring everyone outdoors to parade, dance, and have a great time.

St. Elmo, St. Boniface, St. Ephrem the Syriac, St. Antony of Padua, St. Vitus, St. John the Baptist, St. Irenaeus, and the saints Peter and Paul all have feast days in June. Many other saints are also remembered during the month. Although sainted now, these early Christians were once just people going about life like you or me. But their ethical choices changed their lives completely. The Portuguese feel that these

saints can understand the problems of real life, and they rely on their guidance through difficult times. The celebration of their lives is a month-long festival that celebrates the triumph of the human spirit over confusion, desolation, and despair.

The Foods of the Festival

The Portuguese celebrate with traditional dishes—roasted lamb, pork, or goat; grilled sardines; seafood stews; and a special sweet rice that reminds everyone of the sweetness of beatitude. You'll find *pataniscas de bacalhau*, pieces of codfish that have been fried in a seasoned batter; *salada de feijao frade*, a salad of black-eyed peas, hard-boiled eggs, and onions; *sardinhadas*, grilled sardines, for which the Portuguese have an endless appetite; *carapauzinhos*, a tiny fish called whitebait that is floured and deep-fried; and *peixinhos da horta*, green beans sautéed in butter.

St. Antony of Padua

Although all the June saints are honored during the month-long celebration, St. Antony of Padua is especially dear to the hearts of the Portuguese. Many people think of St. Antony, or St. Anthony, as an Italian, but he was actually born in Portugal and lived most of his life in Lisbon. He was originally christened Fernando in 1195, and joined the Augustinian order at St. Vincente de Fora, which still exists. He then worked and studied in Coimbra, the center of intellectual life in the Portugal of the time. In 1220 he heard of the martyrdom of a small group of Franciscan missionaries who had been killed while trying to convert the Moslems in Morocco. Fernando, aged 25, decided that his intellectual life was too comfortable and worldly, and he joined a group of Franciscans at a small and very poor hermitage outside Coimbra called St. Antony's. Taking the name of the hermitage as his own, he set off to convert the Moslems. As fate or Providence would have it, his ship sank, and Antony found himself in Sicily. In Italy, he met Francis of Assisi, and so impressed him that the Franciscans

became an order of preachers. A great linguist, Antony was instrumental in founding the Franciscan preaching style—it was simple, direct, and based on natural imagery. When St. Antony died, at 36, he was taken back to Padua, a city that has remained faithful to its *Santo* ever since.

The Portuguese carry out, as assiduously as the Italians do, the custom of St. Antony's Bread. When you pray to the saint, you offer him bread to give to the poor. The modern custom is to sell bread rolls, *paezinhos de Santo Antonio*, in June, and to give the money to the poor.

A specifically Portuguese custom is the building of "thrones" for St. Antony on his feast day. These used to be made out of matches, matchboxes, and other found materials by street urchins. Today the thrones are made by rival neighborhoods, who compete for the tallest or most elaborate models.

A Short History of Port

The city of Oporto, with a population of about one million people, is the industrial center of northern Portugal. Like Lisbon, it sits atop a group of hills looking down on a river. The Douro River, which opens out into the Atlantic Ocean, has made the city an important port for over two thousand years. The shipbuilders of Oporto redesigned the local rivercraft, and ended up with the famous caravels that sent Portugal into its great age of exploration.

Directly across the river is an area known as Vila Nova de Gaia. Originally a separate settlement, it has become almost a part of Oporto, especially since a graceful bridge was designed to connect the two communities by Alexandre-Gustave Eiffel, of Eiffel Tower fame. Vila Nova de Gaia is the heart of the world's port wine business.

There are many legends about how port came to be, but they all have certain elements in common. About two thousand years ago, the ancient Romans began to grow grapes in the region around Oporto. During the fourteenth century, English traders exchanged wool and cotton for Portuguese wine and olive oil. At some point, the winemakers of the region started to use brandy to stop the fermentation process when it reached a balanced sweetness. The English loved

this new product because it tasted great and traveled well. A number of English families moved to Oporto and set up businesses for the production and exportation of port, and in the seventeenth century, John Croft began to ship great quantities of port back to England. Interestingly, the Portuguese themselves never drank port until very recently. Today the French consume more port than anyone else in the world. They drink port as an aperitif. The English run a close second, drinking port after dinner.

Drinking Port: Ruby, Tawny, or Vintage?

All ports start out as ruby ports. When aged in wood they become tawny ports. Tawny port is a blend of ports from a number of different years. Each has spent from eight to sixteen years maturing in an oak cask. During that time, the port becomes mellow, and its color lightens to a burnt orange. Vintage ports are made from the wine of one outstanding year. Only two or three years from every ten will be good enough to bottle as a vintage. These ports are rare and fine, aging in the bottle for fifteen or twenty years before being offered to the public. Their deep, balanced flavor is the reason that port has been famous for hundreds of years.

Good port can age sixty years or more. In England, a father often laid down a few bottles when a child was born, in order to be able to drink it a few decades later at an important occasion. Most people knew they would not live to drink their best bottles. "Unless you are a babe in arms it will see you out" was the traditional wisdom.

Late-bottled vintage port was developed because British restaurateurs wanted a port that had much of the taste of a great vintage port but did not need twenty years in the bottle or decanting at the table. This port is made from the wine of one year and aged in wood for about five years.

Today, port is often brought to the table as a dessert by itself, or with walnuts, a blue cheese, apple tarts, or something with chocolate in it. Of all alcohol-based drinks, port probably makes the most comfortable marriage with chocolate.

The British Factory House

Built in 1790, the British Factory House in Oporto houses a club of the directors of port-shipping companies. For over two hundred years, the members of the British Factory House have been known for the quality of their food and wine, but especially for the quality of their port. And during their two hundred years, they have been practicing a number of rituals in connection with their favorite drink.

Dinner is served in the dining room, which has a magni–
ficent mahogany table that seats forty-six people. After
dinner, members pick up their napkins and move to an
adjoining room with another magnificent mahogany table
that seats forty-six people. The members sit in the same
seating arrangement as in the first room. The second room
has no electric lights, just candles. There is no tablecloth.
Bowls of fruits and nuts and decanters of port decorate
the table. This room, free from the aromas of cooked food,
suits the sensibilities of the serious port drinker.

Port-drinking Traditions

They all know the traditional rules practiced in any port-drinking group.
The decanter sits in front of the host. He will usually start the decanter on
its rounds by pouring a glass for the person on his right, then for himself.
He then passes the decanter to his left. From that point on, the port must be kept
moving, though it is rude to ask for it to be passed. Failing to keep the port in
motion is very bad form, and if you do, you may become known as a "bottle–
stopper," a sad fate. For this reason, round-bottomed decanters were invented,
so that the decanter could only rest when it was safely back in its holder in front
of the host.

The Story of Lancers

In 1944, the farms and vineyards of Germany, Italy, France, and Spain were in
total disarray. World War II was still being fought, and the last thing on anyone's
mind was wine. Except for one mind. Andre Behar, a wine importer from New
York, believed that the American troops stationed in Europe during the war had
developed a taste for wine, and that they weren't going to stop drinking it when
they got home. He knew that Germany, Italy, France, and Spain were not going
to be in any shape to be making wine in the near future. But Portugal, a neutral
country in the war, was untouched. Its winemaking tradition and facilities were
in perfect shape.

In Azeitao, just outside of Lisbon, Mr. Behar found a local rosé that he felt would appeal to American tastes. He chose a bottle for it that reminded him of the clay amphoras used by the ancient Romans when they took wine from the area back to Rome. He named the wine Lancers, after a painting by the seventeenth century Spanish artist Diego Velazquez, and put a picture of a caravel on the label. The ship reminded him of the past glories of Portugal, when explorers like Vasco da Gama and Magellan traveled around the world.

Eventually, Lancers became the most popular Portuguese wine imported into the United States. It is still made in the same small part of Portugal where Mr. Behar found it.

The winery buys fermented grape juice made to its specifications by local farmers. The juice is held in tanks that get their shape from ancient Moorish structures. Both the form and the color of the tanks reduce the effects of the sun's rays and help to keep down the vat's internal temperature. The juices are then blended to create white, red, rosé or blush wines. After the blending, the wine is filtered and chilled.

The first time a wine is chilled, it may develop a few ice crystals that settle to the bottom of its bottle. Lancers doesn't want that to happen in your refrigerator, so the first chilling takes place at the winery, where the wine can be filtered of any sediment.

The technique that is used to give the wine its slight effervescence was invented by a group of Russian scientists. The tanks are filled with swirling strips of wood, and the wine is poured in. At the same time, a little yeast is added, along with some grape juice. The living yeast settles onto the surface of the wood, spreads out, and keeps in contact with the wine. The yeast interacts with the natural sugar in the grape juice and produces the tiny little bubbles that are found in Lancers. The wines move through the vats in a continuous process that lasts for twenty-eight days. One more filtration, and the bottles are filled.

Recipes for June's Feast Days
Portugal

Salt Cod & Potato Puree

Portuguese Seafood Stew

Roast Pork with Black Pepper, Garlic, & Paprika

Sweet Rice Pudding

Salt Cod & Potato Puree

Makes 4-6 servings

Executive Chef Bernard Guillot
Hotel da Lapa

For the Puree:

  1 pound dried salt cod fillets
  3 cups milk
  5 medium cloves garlic
  2 medium boiling potatoes (about 1 pound)
  ¼ cup extra virgin olive oil
  1 teaspoon kosher salt, or to taste
  ½ teaspoon freshly ground black pepper

For the Seasoned Oil:

  ⅓ cup extra virgin olive oil
  ¼ cup minced fresh coriander leaves
  Freshly ground black pepper
  15-20 slices sourdough bread or Italian loaf, toasted

1 TO MAKE THE PUREE: Purge the fish of salt and hydrate the flesh by putting the salt cod in a bowl and covering it with cold water. Refrigerate and soak the fish for 24 hours, changing the water 2 or 3 times during the soaking. After the fish has soaked, discard the water and trim any dark skin or spots. Put the fish in a skillet with the milk. Smash 3 of the garlic cloves, peel them, and add them to the fish. Peel and cut the potatoes into ¼-inch slices; add them to the pan. Heat the milk to a simmer. Place a lid slightly ajar on the pan, and simmer for 12 to 15 minutes, or until the potatoes are tender and the fish flakes easily.

2   TRANSFER THE FISH, garlic, potatoes, and ½ to ¾ cup of the cooking liquid to the bowl of a food processor. Process into a smooth puree and slowly pour in the olive oil while the machine is running. (If the puree is too stiff, adjust the consistency with a bit more of the hot milk.) Mince the remaining garlic and add it to the puree. Season with the salt and pepper. Return the puree to the pan, and cook over medium heat, stirring constantly, for 2 to 3 minutes. Keep warm while you make the seasoned oil.

3   TO MAKE THE SEASONED OIL: Heat the olive oil in a small saucepan with the minced coriander. Cook until the oil bubbles, and then swirl the pan over the heat for about 30 seconds. Set aside and keep warm.

4   TO SERVE: Use a spatula to form the cod puree into a 6-inch-round "cake" on a large platter, or make 4 individual "cakes" on separate plates. Drizzle some of the seasoned oil over the cake. Pass the rest of the oil on the side. Garnish with freshly ground black pepper, surround the cake with toasted bread, and serve warm.

Portuguese Seafood Stew

Makes 4 servings

Executive Chef Bernard Guillot
Hotel da Lapa

¼ cup extra virgin olive oil

2 medium leeks, white and light green, sliced and washed

1 yellow or red bell pepper, diced

4 large cloves garlic, minced

½ pound small white mushrooms, wiped clean and quartered

2 medium carrots, peeled and diced

2½ teaspoons kosher salt

½ teaspoon freshly ground black pepper

1 cup white wine

2 bay leaves

3 cups tomato puree

2 cups fish broth or clam juice

2 boiling potatoes, peeled and diced

2 tablespoons finely minced fresh ginger

1 medium zucchini, diced

12 littleneck clams in their shells, scrubbed clean

16 medium mussels in their shells, scrubbed clean

¾ pound large shrimp, peeled and deveined

¼ cup minced fresh coriander leaves

Salt and freshly ground black pepper

¾ pound snapper fillet (skin on), cut into 1½-inch-wide slices

1 HEAT THE OIL IN A LARGE STEWPOT. Add the leeks, pepper, and garlic, and sauté over medium heat until the vegetables are soft, about 5 minutes. Add the mushrooms and carrots and season with 1½ teaspoons of the salt and the pepper. Sauté for 1 minute. Add the white wine and simmer until the liquid is reduced by half, about 7 minutes. Add the bay leaves, tomato puree, and fish broth, and continue to simmer over medium-low heat, covered, for 15 to 20 minutes.

2   WHILE THE STEW BASE is simmering, put the potatoes in a small saucepan with water to cover, add the remaining 1 teaspoon salt, bring to a boil, and simmer for 3 to 4 minutes, or until the potatoes are tender. Drain the potatoes and add to the stew. (The base can be prepared up to this point a day ahead, cooled, and refrigerated.)

3   WHEN READY TO SERVE, bring the stew to a boil, add the ginger and zucchini, and simmer, covered, for 1 to 2 minutes. Stir in the clams, cover the pan, and cook the clams for 5 to 6 minutes, or until the shells just begin to open. Stir in the mussels, shrimp, and coriander. Season the broth to taste with salt and pepper. Tuck the snapper pieces into the stew and continue to cook, covered, for 3 to 4 minutes. The stew is ready when the clam and mussel shells open fully and the shrimp turn a light pink and begin to curl. Swirl the pan to mix the stew without breaking up the snapper. Serve immediately in large warmed bowls.

SINGING THE FADO

Fado, the singing of epic songs filled with memories both sad and glorious, is a Portuguese musical tradition. The word *fado* comes from the word *fate*. These songs were originally sung by sailors longing for their homeland and loved ones, and often express the hope that the singer will be reunited with the people and places he loves. These songs were also sung by those on shore who hoped to see their loved ones again. Although tourist establishments abound, get someone to lead you to a place where the authentic *fado* is sung. For, when it is authentic, *fado* is an intensely personal expression—the words are not as important as the emotions are. In the presence of a real *fado* singer, the room of listeners often falls silent, coming under the spell of these songs of human destiny and longing.

Roast Pork with Black Pepper, Garlic, & Paprika

Makes 4 servings

4 medium cloves garlic

¼ cup chopped fresh flat-leaf parsley, plus several sprigs for garnish

2 teaspoons freshly ground black pepper

1 teaspoon hot paprika

1 tablespoon kosher salt

3 tablespoons extra virgin olive oil

One (3½-pound) center-cut pork rib roast

1   PREHEAT THE OVEN TO 350°F. Puree the garlic, parsley, black pepper, paprika, salt, and olive oil in a blender to a smooth paste. Paint the entire surface of the pork loin including the bones with the paste.

2   SET THE ROAST, ribs down, in a roasting pan, and cook for 1 hour. After an hour, tip the roast so the bones point straight up, baste with any pan juices, and raise the heat to 450°. Continue to cook the roast for another 20 to 25 minutes, until the internal temperature of the pork reaches 155° to 160° on a thermometer. The roast should be golden brown and firm to the touch.

3   REMOVE THE PORK ROAST from the oven and let it rest at room temperature, loosely covered with foil, for 10 to 15 minutes before slicing. Cut the roast between the bones, lay the chops on a warm platter, garnish with parsley sprigs, and serve.

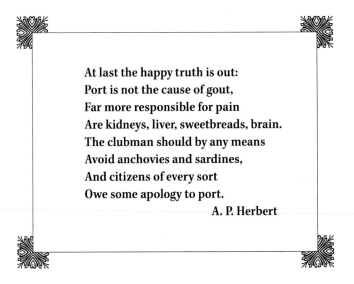

At last the happy truth is out:
Port is not the cause of gout,
Far more responsible for pain
Are kidneys, liver, sweetbreads, brain.
The clubman should by any means
Avoid anchovies and sardines,
And citizens of every sort
Owe some apology to port.

A. P. Herbert

Sweet Rice Pudding

Makes 4 servings

Executive Chef Bernard Guillot
Hotel da Lapa

1½ cups water
1 cup raw medium- or short-grain white rice
2 pieces lemon zest, about 1 inch wide x 3 inches long
2 cinnamon sticks
5 cups milk
1 cup sugar
2 large eggs, plus 1 large egg yolk
Ground cinnamon, for garnish

1   BRING THE WATER and rice to a boil in a medium saucepan. Stir the rice with a wooden spoon to loosen it from the bottom of the pan, and add the lemon zest and cinnamon sticks. Simmer, uncovered, over medium heat for 5 to 7 minutes, until the water is absorbed and tight bubbles form on the surface of the rice. Stir the milk into the rice, and continue to cook for 17 to 20 minutes, until the rice is tender.

2   WHEN THE RICE IS TENDER, add the sugar, and stir constantly until the sugar dissolves and the kernels are shiny. Remove the pan from the heat and whisk in the eggs and yolk. Return the pan to medium heat and stir with a wooden spoon for 2 to 3 minutes to thicken the mixture. Remove and discard the cinnamon sticks and lemon. Pour the rice pudding into a round shallow serving dish.

3   COOL THE PUDDING to room temperature and then refrigerate it for at least 1 hour before serving. Lightly dust the surface of the rice pudding with ground cinnamon to make a lattice or other decorative pattern.

SAINT JUHANNUS DAY

Midsummer Day, the longest day of the year, also tells us that winter is on its way—that after this festival of light, shorter days will follow. We are reminded to begin new things as the old are coming to an end; to rejoice in sunlight, though darkness will soon come. As a celebration, Midsummer Day balances Christmas Day. It reminds us that the darkest days of December are actually days of rebirth—a rebirth that will eventually bring us the brightest days of summer.

the property of a man she fancied would surely secure him as a husband. Rituals like these show the Finns' blending of Christian symbolism with older pagan beliefs.

Many Midsummer superstitions and customs involve the prediction of the future, especially of marriage. Sun and water show up again and again as themes of fertility on Midsummer Eve. One old Finnish practice is to pour an egg white into a glass that is half full of water, then set it on a window ledge or in a place where it will be "in the eye of the sun" during Midsummer Day. The next morning, you read your future in the swirly shapes. Sun, eggs, and water come together, three fertility symbols acting in one ritual.

Along with these three symbols, plants, especially flowers, play their role in the prediction of connubial bliss. At Midsummer, a young woman picks seven or nine different kinds of flowers and makes them into a wreath, which she tucks under her pillow. That night, she dreams about the man she will marry.

In another tradition, women take a look into the future by baking a "silent cake." In this custom, a group of women bake a cake without talking to each other, then each takes a small bit of the edge of the cake and sleeps with it under her pillow, dreaming about the future and about her future husband. It's a holiday that's tough on pillowcases.

Trees played an important part in the beliefs of paganism, and the birch tree has its place in the traditions and customs of Finland. In all of Scandinavia, the leafing of the birch marks the beginning of the agricultural year. (In England, the traditional financial year began on the first of April because that was the day the birch was said to start leafing, probably a leftover from Scandinavian policy.) The birch also plays a significant role in the Midsummer celebrations of Finland—as the pine is to Christmas, so is the birch to Midsummer.

It represents beginnings, and during the three-day festival its branches decorate city buses, office buildings, railway engines, cars and cows.

Not surprisingly, more people get married in Finland during the Midsummer celebrations than on any other weekend of the year. It seems that all the seeing-into-the-future customs put you in a good position to make a wise decision. The theme of marriage resonates throughout Finland on Midsummer weekend. The joining together of man and woman, and their traditional symbols of fire and water, is celebrated in an important ritual that begins late on Midsummer's Day.

The festivals of the longest days of the year are always marked by fires, both large and small. The ancient ritual of lighting fires to encourage the sun at the summer solstice is one of the oldest in Europe. In Helsinki, thousands of people gather to watch a solemn ceremony in which a newly married couple is rowed across the water to a small island. The couple is chosen to represent all the men and women married that day in Finland, and their collective hope for a bright future. On the island, a huge tower has been constructed of fir trees and the hulls of boats. Together, the bride and groom set the tower ablaze. The ancient ritual is an appeal to the sun, a request for its eternal warmth and light.

Midsummer Day in the Country

Finland celebrates St. Juhannus' Day over a long weekend. The Finns rush from the cities to a lake shore—the country is dotted with thousands of lakes—and stay at family cottages or visit with friends. It is a time for renewing friendships and for reacquainting oneself with nature. People light bonfires that burn throughout the night. "Night" is not actually a descriptive term, for it never actually gets dark at Midsummer in Finland. The sun merely dips below the horizon for a few hours, creating a sense of late afternoon, then comes right back up.

There is music. People dance and sing late into the evening. Water, swimming, and sauna are all important elements of the festivities. In Finland, the sauna is a very distinct form of social gathering. It is possible for a Finnish family to have a sauna and no house, but it is virtually impossible to have a house and no sauna. An old Finnish saying goes, "First you build the sauna and then you build the house."

The Food of Midsummer

After they have taken their Midsummer sauna, the Finns sit down to a lavish meal. Supper tables are often decorated with birch branches and flower garlands, and with the traditional summer delicacies: preserved meats and liver pâté with pickled apples; mixed forest mushrooms; simple salads; cold grilled salmon; glassblower's herring; marinated Baltic herring; gravlax and boiled new potatoes; Finn Crisp with pâté; caviar and fresh brie; Finnish blue cheese and Emmental. And then, of course, there's grilled herring, cold smoked salmon and prawns, warm sweet pancakes, cloudberries, raspberries, marinated melon, grilled Lapland cheese, and Midsummer strawberries.

A variety of breads—most made with rye flour—have been part of the Finnish diet for hundreds of years. Rye has a reputation for being a healthy food. If a man is strong, the Finns say, "He has rye in his wrist." During the summer, new potatoes are everywhere. And the smaller, the better. Cooked in water with salt and dill, they're served with just a touch of butter. The Finns believe that potatoes cooked *before* Christmas should go into boiling water.

After Christmas, however, they should start in cold water, and be brought to a boil. The newer the potato, the less water it needs.

Traditional Finnish food includes sauna-smoked ham. In the old days, they would actually hang a ham in the sauna and use the smoke from the fire to preserve the meat. Cozy in here. Just you, me, and the ham. Reindeer meat, which is low in fat and free of antibiotics, is another specialty. Licorice is a big favorite in Finland, and comes in both salted and sweet varieties. *Piirakka*, a traditional pastry made of dough filled with mashed potatoes or rice, is a Finnish classic, originally created in Karelia, in the northeast part of the country.

Finland's "Little Water"

A land of glaciers, lakes, and rivers, Finland is also a land of vodka. The word *vodka* means "little water," a term of endearment. It's appropriate, for vodka is certainly dear to the Finns, and pure water is important to vodka's production. The spot where the government produces its Finlandia vodka was chosen because it was the site of a well with extraordinarily pure water. The well and its water are still there, pure as ever.

Vodka, first produced in Russia, eventually became the national drink of all the countries surrounding the Baltic Sea. The drink was originally made by farmers using a fairly straightforward process. A food high in complex carbohydrates, like potatoes or beets, was crushed into a mash. Then yeast and water were added. The yeast caused fermentation, which meant that the sugar in the potato (or beet) was turned to alcohol and carbon dioxide. The gas floated away, and the potato and alcohol were put into a still. As the still heated, the alcohol turned into a gas and rose. The mash and its impurities were left behind. Forced down a tube that passed through a bucket of snow, the gas recondensed into liquid, which dripped out into a bucket. The result was pure alcohol, to which the farmer added water to make vodka.

Eventually, the Finnish kings decided that this was much too valuable a process to be left to amateurs, and the crown became the exclusive producer of vodka. Today, Finland is a democracy, but the government is still in charge of all vodka production. Instead of potatoes or beets, the government makes its mash from barley, and its sophisticated stills and quality-control system make one of the purest vodkas in the world.

Vodka, Cocktails, and Finnish History

Vodka distilling played an important role in Finnish history. In 1939, the Soviet army invaded Finland, and the Finns defended themselves in one of the most hostile environments in the world. They fought back with everything they had, which wasn't much. Finnish ski troops learned to cover themselves in

white overalls, which made them impossible to see during the winter war. They built dams and flooded areas in the way of the Soviet advance. They conducted troop movements in the forest, so that they would be hard to see. On the other side, the Soviets had hundreds of tanks, and they used their tank commands as the primary units of their advance.

The Finns had few anti-tank guns and few anti-aircraft guns, but they did have vodka plants. The women working in those plants put a little alcohol, some tar, and a few other ingredients in a bottle, and taped two giant matches to the outside. A Finnish soldier would light the matches, run up to a Soviet tank, and drop the bottle down the tank's exhaust pipe. The glass broke, the liquid exploded, and the tank was immobilized. The Finns named this little cocktail after the Soviet Foreign Minister of the time—a Comrade Molotov.

Partly because of this difficult past relationship with Russia, the Finns have found and maintained their own strong national identity. And one way that they separate themselves from other cultures is through the yearly observance of rituals and customs that are uniquely Finnish. Through the celebration of festivals like Saint Juhannus Day and Midsummer Day, national and individual identities are strengthened, and primal fears weakened through the comfort of repetition and ceremony.

Recipes for the Midsummer Festival
Finland

Gravlax

Wild Mushroom Salad

Finnish Meatballs

Baby Potatoes with Dill

Strawberry Sour Cream Cake

Gravlax

Makes 8-10 servings

>3 tablespoons kosher salt
>
>2 tablespoons sugar
>
>2 teaspoons white peppercorns, crushed
>
>1 teaspoon whole allspice berries, crushed
>
>1 large bunch dill (about 3 ounces)
>
>Two ½-pound center-cut salmon fillets, in 2 equal pieces
>
>1 tablespoon cognac (optional)
>
>Black bread
>
>Mustard

1   IN A SMALL BOWL, mix together the salt, sugar, peppercorns, and allspice. Chop the stems and leaves of the dill. Lay a piece of the salmon, skin side down, on a piece of plastic wrap large enough to wrap both fillets. Sprinkle the fillet with half the spice mix, moisten with half of the cognac, if using, and cover with all the chopped dill. Cover the second fillet with the spice mix and cognac. Sandwich the 2 fillets together and tightly wrap in the plastic wrap. Make sure the fillets are held tightly closed with a good seal.

2   PLACE THE WRAPPED SALMON on a plate and weigh it down with a 1-pound can or weight. Place in the refrigerator. Every 12 hours or so, open the package and baste the fish with the liquid that has formed around it. Let the salmon cure for at least 24 or up to 36 hours.

3   WHEN THE SALMON IS READY, scrape the dill mixture off with a spoon and refrigerate the fish until ready to serve. To serve the gravlax; slice thin pieces at a 45° angle with a long, sharp narrow knife. Lay the gravlax out on a platter and serve it with black bread and a bit of mustard. The gravlax will stay fresh for a week wrapped in plastic in the refrigerator.

Wild Mushroom Salad

Makes 4 servings

¾ pound mixed wild mushrooms (chanterelles, shiitake, cremini, and oyster)

¼ pound white mushrooms

1 teaspoon fresh lemon juice

1 teaspoon salt

Freshly ground white pepper

⅛ teaspoon freshly grated nutmeg

⅓ - ½ cup sour cream

2 tablespoons snipped fresh chives

1   DEPENDING ON YOUR SELECTION of mushrooms, slice or quarter the mushrooms into bite-size pieces. For example, with shiitake mushrooms, discard the tough woody stem and quarter the caps. Chanterelles and oysters look best when you accent their natural shape by quartering them lengthwise. Slice cremini and the white mushrooms.

2   SET A VEGETABLE STEAMER BASKET over an inch of water in a pan. Bring the water to a boil and lay the mushrooms out in an even layer on the steamer. Cover and steam the mushrooms for 5 to 6 minutes or until tender. Transfer the cooked mushrooms to a bowl, toss with the lemon juice, salt, pepper to taste, and nutmeg. Cool, then mix the cooled mushrooms with the sour cream and chives. Serve in a bowl, chilled or at room temperature. This salad gets better over time; make it a couple of hours ahead and refrigerate it until ready to serve.

Finnish Meatballs

Makes 4-6 servings

½ cup dry bread crumbs

½ cup milk

⅔ pound ground top round beef

⅓ pound ground pork

1 teaspoon dried thyme, crushed

1 medium clove garlic, minced

1 small onion (about 4 ounces), grated

1 large egg, lightly beaten

2 tablespoons oil

½ cup water

Lingonberry or cranberry relish

1 MIX THE BREAD CRUMBS and milk together in a medium-size bowl. Set aside for 15 minutes to allow the bread crumbs to absorb the liquid. In a separate bowl, combine the ground meats, thyme, garlic, and grated onion. After the meat mixture is combined, form a well in the center of the meat. Pour the beaten egg in the well. Using a fork, mix the bread crumbs into the egg. With your hands, mix all the ingredients together until just combined; don't overwork the meat or the meatballs will be dense. For ease in forming the balls, chill the mixture for 30 minutes.

2 TO FORM THE MEAT BALLS, dip your hands into water, then roll the meat into balls about 1½ inch in diameter. This is a soft dough, so don't worry if the meatballs are not perfectly round.

3 HEAT A LARGE SKILLET, add the oil, and then add the meatballs to the skillet. Sear the meatballs over medium to high heat for about 3 to 4 minutes. When the meatballs are evenly browned on all sides, add the water to the pan and continue cooking over low heat, shaking the pan occasionally, for 10 minutes, or until the meat is cooked through. Serve warm or at room temperature, with a lingonberry or cranberry relish.

Baby Potatoes with Dill

1 pound small yellow boiling potatoes (about 1 inch in diameter)

3 tablespoons unsalted butter

1 teaspoon salt

2 tablespoons chopped fresh dill

1   PLACE THE POTATOES in a pan so they fit snugly in a single layer. Add water to come halfway up the potatoes. Add the butter and salt. Bring to a boil, then turn the heat down to a simmer. Cover the pan with the lid slightly ajar. This steams the potatoes, and at the same time the buttery water evaporates to a glaze.

2   WHEN THE POTATOES ARE FORK TENDER, about 15 minutes, remove the lid. If there is still a lot of water left in the pan, turn the heat up and boil it down. If there is no water left and the potatoes look greasy, add a tablespoon of water and heat to make a creamy-looking glaze. Toss with the dill and serve immediately.

Strawberry Sour Cream Cake

Makes 8 servings

For the Cake:

1⅔ cups cake flour

½ teaspoon baking powder

½ teaspoon baking soda

2 teaspoons ground cardamom

¼ teaspoon salt

8 tablespoons (1 stick) unsalted butter, softened

1 cup granulated sugar

2 large eggs

2 large egg yolks

1 cup sour cream

For the Filling:

1 cup heavy cream

½ cup ricotta cheese

⅓ cup confectioners' sugar

1 teaspoon vanilla extract

2 pints strawberries

2-4 tablespoons granulated sugar

1 TO MAKE THE CAKE: Preheat the oven to 350°F. Brush a 9-inch springform pan with butter or oil.

2 SIFT THE FLOUR, baking powder, baking soda, cardamom, and salt together in a bowl and set aside. In a standing electric mixer or with a hand-held beater, cream the butter and sugar together at medium speed until light and fluffy. One at a time, add the whole eggs, then the yolks, beating thoroughly after each addition. Alternate mixing in the dry ingredients with the sour cream, a third at a time. Pour the batter into the prepared cake pan. Bake for 45 minutes or until the cake is lightly browned and pulls away from the sides of the pan. It should be slightly springy to the touch. Cool on a rack for 5 minutes, remove the sides of the springform, and cool completely on the rack.

3   WHILE THE CAKE IS BAKING, make the filling: By hand or in a standing electric mixer, whip the cream and ricotta cheese to the consistency of stiffly whipped cream. It is very important to have the filling the right consistency. Sift and fold in the confectioners' sugar and the vanilla. Chill until ready to use. Set aside 1 to 3 nice-looking strawberries for garnishing the top of the cake. Stem and slice the remaining strawberries into thirds or halves, depending on their size. Place them in a bowl, sprinkle with the granulated sugar, and set aside to macerate.

4   TO ASSEMBLE THE CAKE: Using a serrated knife, cut the cake horizontally into 2 layers. Lay the layers, cut side up on a clean work surface. Drizzle any collected strawberry juice over both cake layers. Spread a third of the cream filling on the bottom layer, arrange strawberry slices over the cream, then cover with another third of the cream. Cover with the other layer of cake. Spread the remaining cream evenly over the top and place the garnishing strawberries in the center of the cake. Transfer the cake to a platter and chill until ready to serve.

L ike most of our gatherings and celebrations, picnics
illustrate our desire to bring together the opposites in
our lives. We like the idea of quitting our structured
civilization and traveling into the untamed wilderness
to cook our food over a fire. The ritual of the picnic
allows us to feel free and adventurous, while at the same time
maintaining a nice, safe structure in which we feel secure.

A PICNIC IN ABRUZZO

Abruzzo, to the east of Rome, is a region of Italy known for the natural beauty of its beaches and its mountains. Only recently connected to the rest of Italy by a highway, Abruzzo lies on the other side of the Apennine mountain range, which boasts the country's tallest peaks. Its *Gran Sasso d'Italia*, "the Great Rock of Italy," soars almost 10,000 feet above sea level. For thousands of years these mountains acted as a natural barrier. Rome was in the west, Abruzzo in the east, and the twain rarely met. The mountains protected the people of Abruzzo from some of the less attractive developments of modern life, and allowed them to hang on to their ancient traditions and unspoiled environment. The center of the region, now a major national park, protects over one thousand square miles of the most pristine terrain in Europe.

As you travel east through Abruzzo, you eventually come to a hundred-mile-wide strip of flat land that runs along the Adriatic Sea. The long bands of clean beach at the edge of this strip have become one of Italy's most popular seaside destinations.

The Picnic

Italians love to eat *al fresco*. In small towns, people simply carry their tables outside and have dinner near the street. During the warm weather, countrypeople take many of their meals under the trees near the house or under the grape arbor on the patio. If they feel the call of the wild, they go on a picnic.

Ancient Greeks held picnics over two thousand years ago. They had social clubs that regularly held meals to which all the diners contributed something—more like our contemporary potluck. The meals took place in a dining room, but there was no official host. No host meant that there was no need to return the invitation. It was a responsibility-free party.

The word *pique-nique* first appeared in print in a French text dated 1692; it was used to describe a meal to which diners were required to bring their own wine.

Lord Chesterfield first used the word in English in 1748. He called a book with contributions by different authors a "picnic."

During the late eighteenth and early nineteenth centuries, eating clubs became very popular in England. They offered "subscription" meals. A member decided on a menu and posted it in the club. If you wanted to participate, you wrote your name next to one of the dishes, indicating that you were coming, and that you were bringing that dish.

One of the English eating clubs, called The Picnic Club, became quite famous, or rather, infamous, for though the food was up to the highest standards, the behavior of the club's members most certainly was not. All the gossip about the club's antics, however, brought the word *picnic* into common use, though nobody knows how the word came to mean "a meal eaten outside."

One's idea of the proper place for a picnic has a lot to do with cultural heritage. The English, for instance, always tried to arrange a picnic so that it was facing a spectacular view. Heavily influenced by the Romantic and Victorian poets, these picnickers wanted to get a look at nature. Ruins were always a nice alternative if you couldn't find a roaring cataract, and the real or false remnants of earlier civilizations slowly decaying in the background made for nice picnic conversation.

In reality, the English preferred their *wild* in the distance. In the foreground, they preferred to see a few very large picnic hampers that contained everything they could possibly want for eating outdoors. At an elaborate picnic, there would be hampers for linens, porcelain, crystal, cutlery, and objects like nutmeg graters; the wine hamper; hampers filled with meats, cheeses, salad greens, desserts, and pastries; and, of course, the tea hamper. Every item had its own compartment, and, of course, nothing was disposable. The servants washed everything in a nearby stream.

Victorian sensibilities affected many other European nations, and the decorum of the society of the time resulted in a great interest in picnicking all over Europe. Only societies that regularly took their meals in the formal atmosphere of a strict dining room could fully enjoy the release of picnicking in an open field.

Like the Victorians, we love the idea of being one with nature. But the moment we get out there, the first thing we do is try to separate ourselves from it. We mark off our territory with a picnic cloth. We may even hold down the edges of the cloth with boundary stones. Then we take advantage of the gastro-nomic gifts of the countryside by covering the cloth with foods we cooked at home. Actually, we are trading the discomforts of our more formal, enclosed dining rooms and restaurants for the joys of prickly grass, pointy stones, flying insects, and unpredictable weather. There is much to the old saying "A change of aggravation is like a holiday."

Nobody wants to eat in a place that's really dangerous. We all like to have control of the wild during mealtimes. A touch of risk in getting to the picnic spot is acceptable, but the place itself must be secure. Today, we've added an even greater amount of control to the experience by creating "picnic areas," where you are provided with a table, a security patrol, and convenient trash cans.

The idea of a picnic being "free and wild" eventually turned into the idea of a picnic being easy. When something is simple to accomplish, we say, "Hey—it was a picnic." A difficult experience may be noted as "no picnic." And quite frankly, the work that goes into making a great picnic is no picnic!

The Regional Foods of Abruzzo

In much the same way that the geography of Abruzzo is divided between sea and land, the food of Abruzzo also falls into two separate categories: olives and seafood from the flat land, recipes for game and berries from the mountains. The forests produce over twenty varieties of mushrooms. Field and mountain flowers are visited by the local bees, resulting in many varieties of honey. The pastry chefs of the region use that honey in some of their most famous recipes. The region is also "pancake country"; *scrippelle 'mbusse* are delicate pancakes served in soup in place of noodles. Pigs are raised in the hills, for sausages, salami, and prosciutto. The region is also very serious about its cheeses—caciocavallo, mozzarella, smoked cheese, pecorino, and parmigiano. The cooks of the Abruzzo enjoy intense flavors and season their dishes with hot peppers, thyme, and saffron.

The Wine of Casal Thaulero

In the 1960s, a group of landowners began to realize that they would have to join the "real world" of twentieth-century business and marketing if they wanted to keep making wine in Abruzzo. So they established a consortium of agricultural producers. The group, which currently has over one hundred members, owns a total of twenty-five hundred acres in the area. They named their consortium Casal Thaulero after a castle in the neighborhood, and they put a bear on the label of the group's wine because the Abruzzo Regional Park is known for its bears. The bear, which symbolizes the love of and dedication to nature, reminds consumers that the vineyards all practice organic farming. Since they have adopted the bear as the consortium's mascot, the members of Casal Thaulero have done much to conserve its habitat, and have helped California parks set up exhibitions on bear safety.

Olives and Olive Oil at Colavita

When it comes to gatherings and celebrations, the olive tree and its products—olives and oil—are in the same mythic category as bread and wine. Olive trees can live for hundreds of years, and their roots are so deep that even if the tree is cut down, its roots will survive and send out new growth. When people noticed this trait, the olive tree became a symbol of regeneration, immortality, and dependability.

The technological skill necessary to cultivate an olive tree, make the olive edible, and produce olive oil is so complex that the ancient Greeks used "olive knowledge" as a criterion for judging a society's development. The cultivation and production of olive oil meant that the culture was living in a state of relative harmony, for the demands of processing were so intensive that they generally occurred in more or less peaceful times. For many centuries, olive harvesting and processing were done by sailors, in winter, when tough weather kept them on shore. Olive production became their winter work, and reinforced the symbol of olives representing home, safety, and the security of a smoothly running society. When one of the doves that Noah sent out to search for land returned with an olive branch in its beak, the signs of peace and eventual regeneration were blended in one symbol.

Olive oil, since it gave off very little smoke, became useful for the long-burning lamps of religious rituals. Olive oil began to symbolize the feeding of the body and the soul, and was used for an annointment in biblical times, and, later, in the coronation ceremonies of the kings and queens of Europe.

Italians use a considerable amount of olive oil in their cooking, and it is not surprising that Italy has some of the world's finest olive groves and is a leading olive oil producer. In the town of Campobasso, south of Abruzzo, olive oil is pressed by the most traditional means at the Colavita olive oil factory.

The olives are brought in from the fields, the leaves and stems are removed, and the olives are washed and transported to the press. The pressing is done by three stone wheels. Each stone, weighing a little over two thousand pounds, crushes

both the meat and the pits of the olives, making a thick paste. This paste is spread onto disks made of hemp, and the disks are placed on a spindle. When the pile of disks is about five feet high, it is moved over to a machine that applies an enormous amount of pressure to the stack, pressing out the olive's dark juice and oil. This mixture goes into a piece of equipment that separates the olive juice from the extra virgin olive oil. The filtered oil is then poured into bottles and corked.

Recipes for a Picnic
Abruzzo, Italy

Homemade Pasta

Giovanna's Tomato Sauce

Pasta Frittata

Chicken with Black Olives

Chocolate-Coated Almonds (Sassi d'Abruzzo)

Jam Tart (Crostada Marmalada)

Homemade Pasta

Makes about 1½ pounds

Mrs. Giovanna De Luca
Casal Thaulero Winery

> 3 cups unbleached all-purpose flour
> 4 large eggs, at room temperature
> Cornmeal
> 4 quarts water
> 1 tablespoon salt

1   MOUND THE FLOUR on a clean work surface and make a well about 6 inches wide in the center. Crack the eggs into the well. With a fork, break the eggs and gradually combine them with the flour. Do not let the eggs run out of the walls of the flour. When the eggs have mixed with the flour to make a loose paste, use the palms of your hands to bring the walls of flour and the eggs together to form a soft dough. The amount of flour the eggs will absorb will vary from batch to batch.

2   WHEN YOU HAVE A PLIABLE DOUGH, clean your hands and the work surface of any excess flour and egg. Knead the dough until it is smooth and elastic, about 5 to 7 minutes. Set the dough aside, covered with a towel or wrapped in plastic, and let it rest for at least 20 minutes or up to 2 hours. (Do not refrigerate the dough or it will get too wet.)

3   SET UP A PASTA MACHINE. Cut off a quarter of the dough (keep the rest covered while you work) and flatten it into a square that will fit through the widest setting of the machine. Feed the dough through the machine and then fold the flattened dough like a business letter. Pass the folded dough through the machine again and repeat this process until the dough is satiny smooth. Close the machine's rollers down a notch and feed the dough through the machine again. Repeat this process at each setting down to the thinnest. Lay the pasta sheet out to dry on a towel. Repeat this procedure with the rest of the dough. Before cutting, let the dough dry until it is leathery but still pliable, about 1 hour.

4   CUT THE DOUGH into foot-long pieces and pass the sheets through the small *tonnarelli* or wide *fettuccini* cutters. Lay the pasta out on a tray to dry and dust it with cornmeal to prevent the pasta from sticking together.

5   WHEN READY TO SERVE, bring the water to a boil, and add the salt. Add the pasta and cook at a rapid boil for 1 to 2 minutes, depending on the size and how long it has been drying. Drain and serve with the sauce of your choice.

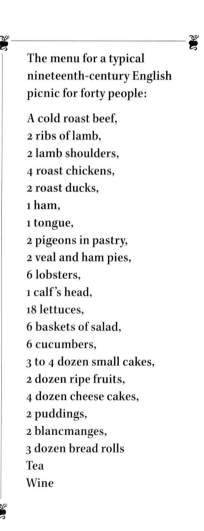

The menu for a typical nineteenth-century English picnic for forty people:

A cold roast beef,
2 ribs of lamb,
2 lamb shoulders,
4 roast chickens,
2 roast ducks,
1 ham,
1 tongue,
2 pigeons in pastry,
2 veal and ham pies,
6 lobsters,
1 calf's head,
18 lettuces,
6 baskets of salad,
6 cucumbers,
3 to 4 dozen small cakes,
2 dozen ripe fruits,
4 dozen cheese cakes,
2 puddings,
2 blancmanges,
3 dozen bread rolls
Tea
Wine

Giovanna's Tomato Sauce

Makes about 5 cups

Mrs. Giovanna De Luca
Casal Thaulero Winery

3 tablespoons olive oil

1½ pounds oxtails (or beef short ribs or beef shin), trimmed of excess fat

2 teaspoons kosher salt

¼ teaspoon freshly ground black pepper

1 medium onion, diced

1 carrot, sliced

1 tablespoon minced garlic

½-1 teaspoon crushed red pepper flakes

1½ cups dry red wine

4 cups tomato puree

¼ teaspoon freshly grated nutmeg

¾ teaspoon fresh sage (4 medium leaves) or ½ teaspoon dried sage, crushed

½ pound spicy Italian sausage

1 HEAT THE OIL IN A LARGE SAUCEPAN. Season the oxtails with some of the salt and pepper and brown them on all sides over medium-high heat. Remove the oxtails from the pan and sauté the onion, carrot, garlic, and pepper flakes until translucent, 4 to 5 minutes. Return the oxtails to the pan, add the red wine, tomato puree, nutmeg, and sage and bring to a simmer.

2 PRESS THE SAUSAGE out of its casing and break the meat apart. Fry the sausage meat in a small skillet for 5 minutes. Drain the excess fat and add the cooked sausage meat to the simmering sauce.

3 SEASON THE SAUCE to taste with the remaining salt and pepper and cook, covered, over low heat for 45 minutes. Remove the oxtails from the sauce before serving.

Pasta Frittata

Makes 4-6 servings

Mrs. Giovanna De Luca
Casal Thaulero Winery

1½ cups cooked pasta, spaghetti, linguini, or angel hair, cut in 3-inch lengths

1 cup Giovanna's Tomato Sauce or other tomato sauce

6 large eggs

⅔ cup grated Parmesan cheese

¾ teaspoon kosher salt

¼ teaspoon freshly ground black pepper, or less to taste

1 tablespoon olive oil, plus additional for brushing the pan lid

1   IN A SMALL BOWL, combine the cooked pasta with the sauce. In a medium bowl, whisk the eggs with the cheese, salt, and pepper. Add the pasta and sauce and whisk to mix thoroughly.

2   HEAT THE OIL in a large nonstick skillet. Add the egg-pasta mixture, and cook over moderate heat. With a spatula or fork, gently pull in the edges of the frittata from the sides of the skillet, and let the liquid of the uncooked egg mixture slide to the edges and cook. Repeat this procedure 2 or 3 times.

3   WHEN THE FRITTATA begins to hold its shape, after about 5 minutes, the center will be uncooked; shake the frittata to loosen it from the pan. Reduce the heat to very low and cover the pan. Cook until it is set and the center looks glossy, about 7 to 10 minutes. The frittata should hold firm when shaken in the pan.

4   LIGHTLY BRUSH A FLAT PAN LID WITH OIL, place the lid over the pan with the frittata. Then flip the frittata onto the lid, and slide the frittata back into the pan to cook the other side. Cook the other side of the frittata over medium-high heat until lightly browned, 1 to 2 minutes. Carefully transfer the frittata to a large plate and serve warm or at room temperature.

Chicken with Black Olives

Makes 4 servings

Mrs. Giovanna De Luca
Casal Thaulero Winery

One (3-pound) chicken, cut into 8 pieces
1 teaspoon kosher salt
½ teaspoon freshly ground black pepper
2 tablespoons extra virgin olive oil
¾ cup white wine
¾ cup chicken broth
3 cloves garlic, crushed
2 teaspoons minced fresh rosemary
2 teaspoons minced fresh oregano
2 teaspoons minced fresh thyme
1 cup black olives, Gaeta or nicoise, rinsed

1   SEASON THE CHICKEN PIECES with half the salt and pepper. Heat the oil in a large skillet or Dutch oven. Brown the chicken, skin side down, over high heat, about 5 minutes.

2   WHEN THE CHICKEN IS GOLDEN BROWN, turn it over, pour the wine and chicken broth into the pan, scatter the garlic, herbs, and olives over the chicken, and add the remaining salt and pepper. Shake the pan to distribute the olives and herbs evenly. Reduce the heat, and braise the chicken over medium-low heat for 25 to 30 minutes, basting with the pan juices while cooking.

3   HEAT THE BROILER. When the chicken is done, transfer the cooked chicken to an oven-proof platter. Cook the chicken under the broiler for 1 to 2 minutes to crisp the skin. Raise the heat under the braising pan and simmer the juices for 2 minutes to thicken. Spoon the olives and juices over the chicken and serve.

Chocolate-Coated Almonds (Sassi d'Abruzzo)

Makes 4 cups

Mrs. Giovanna De Luca
Casal Thaulero Winery

4 cups whole unblanched almonds
1½ cups sugar
⅓ cup water
½ cup unsweetened cocoa, sifted

1   PREHEAT THE OVEN TO 400°F. Spread the almonds out on a baking sheet and toast for 10 minutes, until lightly browned. Cool slightly.

2   IN A MEDIUM HEAVY-BOTTOMED saucepan, stir the sugar and water together with a wooden spoon. Bring the mixture to a boil, and cook until it turns clear, about 2 minutes. Add the cocoa, and stir well to dissolve. Add the nuts, and continue to stir constantly, turning the nuts over in the mix. Cook for 3 to 4 minutes, until the sugar recrystallizes to a sandy texture that coats the nuts. Be careful not to overwork the nuts or the sugar will fall off. Pour the nuts out onto a baking sheet and spread to cool.

3   PICK THE COOLED NUTS off the sheet to separate them from the excess sugar, and serve at room temperature. Store in a sealed plastic bag at room temperature.

Jam Tart (Crostata di Marmallata)

Makes 4 cups

For the Pastry Dough:

¼ cup sugar
8 tablespoons (1 stick) unsalted butter, diced
2 large eggs
1 teaspoon vanilla extract
1 teaspoon grated lemon zest
Pinch of salt
2 cups all-purpose flour

For the Filling:

1 cup strawberry, raspberry, or blueberry jam

For the Egg Wash:

1 large egg
1 teaspoon water
Pinch of salt

1   TO MAKE THE DOUGH IN AN ELECTRIC MIXER: In the bowl of a standing mixer or with a hand-held blender, cream the sugar and butter together. Mix in the eggs, vanilla, and lemon zest until smooth. Add the salt and flour, and mix until the dough comes together. Be careful not to overmix the dough or it will be tough.

TO MAKE THE DOUGH BY HAND: Place the flour, salt, and sugar in a bowl. With your finger–tips, work the butter into the dry ingredients until it resembles coarse meal. In a small bowl, lightly whisk together the eggs, vanilla, and lemon zest. Add the wet ingredients to the flour-butter combination and mix until the dough comes together. Form the dough into a disk, wrap it in plastic, and chill for at least 1 hour or overnight.

2   TO ROLL THE DOUGH: Cut off a third of the dough and set it aside for the lattice top of the tart. Press the remaining dough into a disk, and roll it out on a lightly floured surface into a 12-inch round about ¼-inch thick. Trim any rough edges, transfer the round to a parchment-lined cookie sheet, and chill while you roll out the other piece of dough into a 10-x-6-inch rectangle. To make the strips for the lattice top, cut 12 even 10-inch strips. Cut 2 strips in half to make 5-inch lengths. You will have a total of 14 pieces.

3 REMOVE THE PASTRY ROUND from the refrigerator and, with a spatula, spread the jam over the surface of the dough, leaving an inch border all around. Place 7 strips of pastry over the jam. Use 2 of the short strips at the ends. Trim off any excess dough that drapes over the edge of the tart. Turn the tart and repeat the procedure with the remaining strips of dough to form a lattice pattern. Fold the border of the tart over to cover the ends of the lattice, making a 1-inch rim.

4 TO MAKE THE EGG WASH: In a small bowl, whisk together the ingredients. With a pastry brush, lightly brush the dough with the egg wash. Press the tines of a fork into the edge of the crust to make a decorative pattern. Chill the tart for 1 hour before baking.

5 PREHEAT THE OVEN TO 350°F. Bake the tart for 30 to 35 minutes in the upper third of the oven, until the crust is lightly browned. Remove the tart from the oven and slide it onto a rack to cool. Chill for 1 hour and serve.

BEAR SAFETY TIPS

The members of the Casal Thaulero consortium have come up with three useful strategies for avoiding large, burly, picnic-crashers:

1 Always do your cooking at least 100 yards away from your campsite.

2 Bears love fatty foods, especially hamburgers and bacon.

3 Never sleep in the clothes that you did your cooking in; they will attract bears and repel everybody else.

The late 1940s saw the beginnings of an unusual American culinary phenomenon. Men, brandishing over-sized cooking implements and wearing funny chef hats and aprons, began grilling hot dogs and hamburgers in backyards all over America. At a time when the cultural roles of men and women had become blurred, the outdoor barbecue served as a testing and display ground. Of course, the history of barbecuing goes back much further than the 1940s. In Puerto Rico, in particular, the technique has been in use for at least four thousand years.

A BARBECUE IN
PUERTO RICO

A Short Introduction to Puerto Rico

Puerto Rico is an island—one hundred miles long and thirty-five miles wide—in the middle of a chain of islands that runs from just below Florida to just above Venezuela. The island's north coast faces the Atlantic Ocean and its south coast looks out over the Caribbean Sea.

San Juan, the island's capital city, was built by Spanish explorers during the early sixteenth century and is one of the oldest cities constructed by Europeans in the Western Hemisphere. Just to the south of San Juan, a ridge of high mountains runs the length of the island. As the rain clouds of the Atlantic pass across Puerto Rico, they are stopped by this mountain range. The summit, which is at the eastern end of the island, is capped with a dense rainforest that pulls over a hundred billion gallons of water from the passing clouds each year. Because most of the rain clouds are brought to a halt at the midpoint of the island, much of the southern area of Puerto Rico lies in a "rain shadow," an area that rarely gets moisture. As a result, the southern half of Puerto Rico is almost always warm and sunny.

The largest city in the south is Ponce, which likes to call itself "the pearl of the south." It is named after the great-grandson of Juan Ponce de Leon, who sailed with Christopher Columbus, became the first governor of Puerto Rico, and spent some time wandering around Florida, searching for the Fountain of Youth. In the late 1980s, Ponce underwent a giant restoration project in conjunction with its upcoming three hundredth birthday party. The government had a very straightforward objective—to make the city as beautiful as possible. It buried telephone and power cables, repaved the streets, and restored hundreds of buildings in the historic sections of the city.

Up in the hills to the west of Ponce is the town of San German. Also founded by the Spanish, it is the second-oldest town in Puerto Rico. San German was first built on the coast in 1508, but was moved inland in 1573. The original site was directly in the path of ocean storms, and was a difficult location to defend. The present San German contains some of the earliest structures built by Europeans in the New World. The town has two churches: Porta Coeli, which means "Heaven's Gate," built in 1606; and San German de Auxerre, which was constructed in honor of the town's patron saint.

The Origins of Barbecue

King Ferdinand and Queen Isabella of Spain were the venture capitalists behind Columbus' explorations. When Isabella died, Ferdinand married Germaine de Foix, and it is after the patron saint of his second wife that San German is named. For a number of years, a number of pirate clans, known as the "devils of the sea," called San German home. The town was a lovely spot if you were a pirate looking for a rental. It was far enough away from the central government of San Juan, yet a convenient commute to the ocean.

During the first few hundred years of European exploration in the Caribbean, piracy was a major occupation, and a lot of it was organized by the governments of Europe. The king of one of Europe's powers would give a pirate a letter that said something along the lines of, "Feel free to steal whatever you like from anyone you want, but not from the ships of my country." The pirates would then plunder along around the Caribbean, doing good by doing bad, always able to point out that they were "only following orders."

It is hard to find something nice to say about the pirates who sailed along the deserted coasts of the Caribbean during the sixteenth, seventeenth, and eighteenth centuries. They ravaged everything and everyone in their path. The one positive aspect of their history seems to be in the area of gastronomy. Like everything else, they looted the idea of barbecue from the native Arawak tribes.

The Arawaks had been living in the area for about 3,500 years. They made their beds by weaving together a rectangle of green bendable sticks. These look a lot like the metal frames we use under some mattresses today. They called such a bedframe a *barbacoa*, and the same word was used to describe frames they used for cooking. Meat was tied to the same kind of stick frame and placed close to a fire. The fire was confined, protected, and controlled by building it in a pit, over which lay the grid of the *barbacoa*, in a manner much like our present-day grill. The word came into the English language as *barbecue*.

One of the ways that the European explorers made sure that they would have enough to eat in the future was by dropping off a few animals on a deserted island and letting them go wild. The sailors would note the location of the island, then return, year after year, to hunt for meat. Having killed an animal and feasted upon it, the sailors would smoke the leftover meat in order to have provisions back on board. They took another native word— *boucan* or *buccan*—to describe the smoking process. In French, the word was *boucanée*, and soon those who lived on it were called *buccaneers*.

A modern remnant of this ancient form can be found along the roadsides in Puerto Rico where there are hundreds of *lechoneras,* or "places where the suckling pig is roasted." Each *lechonera* has its own slightly different recipe and its own slightly different cooking technique.

A fine piece of barbecued meat must have a well-defined smoke ring, and it must be pink at the bone. Originally, the beast was barbecued whole, even if it was as large as a steer. (The Acadians of Nova Scotia believed that the origin of the word *barbecue* was *barbe a queue*—"whiskers to tail," indicating the smoking of a whole animal.)

The Backyard Barbecue

Throughout history and all over the world, men have insisted that meat is *their* thing. *Men* do the hunting for meat. They get together in groups and incorporate ancient rituals and as much drama as possible. They go out for days at a time and, if they are successful, they return home in triumph to the women and children who were left at home. (The expression "bringing home the bacon," which now means making the money to buy the meat, is simply a modern-day metaphor for the same ritual.) Of course, the food supply produced by women, who gathered berries and edible plants, was much more dependable and fundamentally much more important to the overall diet.

Men respond to fire as if it is a male element. To this day, in most Western societies, men typically start the fire for any outdoor cookery. They light the coals, watch them glow, and, in this setting, feel comfortable in their role as cook.

During World War II, all the resources of the United States were mustered to provide equipment and supplies to the Armed Forces at home and abroad. In many cases, women stepped into the jobs that men had vacated in order to fill the needs of industry. "Rosie the Riveter" found herself outside the home, working at a job that had once belonged to a man. When the men came back to the States after the war, sociologists believe that one way they asserted their male role in family life was by barbecuing! Taking hold of their oversized cooking tools, wearing a chef's hat (which is a symbol of authority in a professional kitchen) and combining the primal elements of fire and meat were all attempts at reestablishing a male hierarchy at home.

The Crafts of Puerto Rico

Not all the great creative work of Puerto Rico takes place in the kitchen. The southern and western parts of the island have long traditions of craftwork. The town of Moca, just off the west coast, was never a wealthy town, and most of its children could afford to go to school only for a year or so. They learned to read and write, and then, by age seven or eight, the girls would be sent off to learn how to make lace. It was the fastest way for them to start earning a living.

The art of lacemaking originated in Italy during the fourteenth century. It evolved from embroidery, and handmade lace was prohibitively expensive until the early 1800s, when a lacemaking machine was developed in England. Since then, the art of making handmade lace has almost disappeared. Towns like Moca, and a nearby sister village named Isabela, are two of the last places left in the world where this art is still practiced.

The fine crochet-like lace of Puerto Rico is called *Mundillo*, but it is also known as "pillow lace" or "bobbin lace." Threads are wound on bobbins and worked in a

pattern that is held in place on a pillow. Baby dresses, handkerchiefs, and rolls of lace are all made completely by hand by the lacemakers of Puerto Rico.

A lacemaker will manipulate as many as thirty-eight bobbins at a time. This kind of lacemaking is found only in Spain and Puerto Rico, and the theory is that the skill was imported to Moca and Isabela about four hundred years ago.

Maskmaking is another craft that distinguishes the artisans of southern Puerto Rico. Most of them live near the city of Ponce and do their work at home. The imaginative masks are made of papier-mâché. Strips of newspaper are dipped in a paste of flour and water and then molded over a form to dry. The materials are inexpensive, and the final mask is light enough so that it can be worn in the heat of the tropical sun. The masks of Ponce were originally made for Carnival and traditionally present the face of the devil. Devil masks have always been a technique for trying to control the supernatural. Young men, their faces hidden by masks, move through the streets trying to terrify as many people as possible, under the theory that their own fears of life may be reduced in direct proportion to the fear they produce in others. It never really works that way, but people keep trying. Another craft tradition of Puerto Rico is the creation of the *santo*, or holy image used in a church or at home. In Puerto Rico, the *santo* is a wooden statue representing a saint or other figure from the Roman Catholic tradition, carved by a folk artist. (*Santo* means "saint" in Spanish.) Historians who have studied the *santo* tradition point out that the images are taken from religious works dating back to the Middle Ages in Europe. The artists work at home, helped by family members who are learning the art.

During the early history of Puerto Rico, many country people were cut off from the educational, medical, and religious facilities of the larger towns. Religion filled the void, and resulted in a belief that helpful saints protected the family. The *santos* were the physical representations of these saints, and focused and inspired prayers. After a priest blessed a statue, it became a vessel for the spirit of the saint. In every house, a special place was selected as the shrine. The dwelling place of holy energy, the chosen saint could now help the family with direct intervention and assistance.

Recipes for the Barbecue
Puerto Rico

Grilled Shrimp with Mango Salsa

Grilled Chicken Adobo

Tropical Barbecued Pork Ribs

Pineapple Tarts

Espresso Flan

Grilled Shrimp with Mango Salsa

Makes 4-6 servings

2 ripe medium mangoes

½-1 serrano chili, to taste, seeded and finely minced

¼ cup minced red onion

⅓ cup fresh lime juice

3 tablespoons minced fresh coriander leaves

1 teaspoon kosher salt, or more to taste

⅛ teaspoon freshly ground black pepper, plus more to taste

1¼ pounds raw medium shrimp, peeled and deveined

2 tablespoons vegetable oil

4-6 romaine lettuce leaves, washed and dried

1 lime, cut into 4-6 wedges

1 CUT THE SKIN FROM THE MANGO. Cut the flesh of the mango away from the broad oval pit. Dice the flesh and transfer it to a bowl. Squeeze the excess pulp from the mango pit into the bowl. Puree a third of the mango in a food processor or blender.

2 COMBINE THE DICED MANGO with the puree and the chili, onion, lime juice, coriander, and measured salt and pepper. Set aside while you grill the shrimp.

3 PREPARE AN OUTDOOR GRILL or heat a large ridged grill pan. In a bowl, toss the shrimp with the oil and lightly season with salt and pepper to taste. Grill the shrimp over medium-high heat for 2 to 3 minutes per side, or until the shrimp turn pink and begin to curl. Take care not to overcook the shrimp.

4 TO SERVE, lay the lettuce leaves on salad plates, and divide the fruit salsa onto the lettuce. Place the shrimp on the mango salsa along with the lime wedges. Serve the shrimp warm or at room temperature.

Grilled Chicken Adobo

Makes 4 servings

4 medium cloves garlic

1 medium onion

1 teaspoon dried oregano, crushed

2 teaspoons kosher salt

½ teaspoon freshly ground black pepper

⅛ teaspoon cayenne pepper

2 tablespoons tomato paste

¼ cup distilled white vinegar

¼ cup peanut oil

One (3-pound) chicken, cut into 8 pieces

1   PUREE ALL THE INGREDIENTS except the chicken in a blender to make the adobo marinade. Put the chicken in a bowl and cover with the marinade. Marinate the chicken in the refrigerator for at least 4 hours or overnight.

2   WHEN READY TO SERVE, prepare an outdoor grill or heat the broiler. Arrange the chicken pieces on the grill, or on a large pan, so the skin side will be away from the heat source. (Cooking the skin after the meat has cooked avoids burned chicken skin.) Cook the chicken for 20 minutes on the first side, and then turn to brown the skin gently for about another 8 minutes. Transfer the cooked chicken to a platter and serve warm.

Tropical Barbecued Pork Ribs

Makes 4 servings

2½ teaspoons kosher salt

1 teaspoon freshly ground black pepper

2 teaspoons ground allspice

3 pounds pork ribs

2 tablespoons vegetable oil

1 medium onion, sliced

4 medium cloves garlic, sliced

1 tablespoon minced fresh ginger

½ teaspoon crushed red pepper flakes

¾ cup pineapple juice

2 tablespoons molasses

2 tablespoons dark rum

2 cups canned tomatoes with their juice

1   PREHEAT THE OVEN TO 325°F, or build a small to medium fire on one side of a large outdoor grill.

2   MIX 2 TEASPOONS OF THE SALT, plus the pepper, and the allspice in a small bowl. Rub the ribs all over with this seasoning mix. Lay the ribs on a pan in the center of the oven or on the side of the grill away from the fire. Cover the ribs. The idea is to cook them with the gentle indirect heat of the fire. Cook the ribs for 1 hour, tending the fire as needed.

3   TO MAKE THE SAUCE: Heat the oil in a medium saucepan; add the onion, garlic, ginger, and pepper flakes, and cook over medium heat for 15 minutes, or until the onions are soft. Add the pineapple juice, molasses, rum, tomatoes, and the remaining ½ teaspoon salt, and simmer for 15 to 20 minutes. Puree the sauce in a blender or food processor until smooth.

4   AFTER THE RIBS HAVE COOKED for an hour, raise the heat of the oven to 450°F or stoke the coals for a hotter fire. Paint the ribs with the barbecue sauce and cook for 30 to 40 minutes, basting frequently and adding more sauce as needed. The ribs should have a dark golden glaze and the meat should be tender and completely cooked. Slice the ribs and serve warm.

Pineapple Tarts

Executive Chef Vijay Raghavan
Horned Dorset Primavera

½ pound prepared puff pastry
¾ cup sugar
3 tablespoons water
Four (½-inch-thick) fresh pineapple slices, tough inner core removed;
  or canned pineapple slices
Salt
Freshly ground black pepper

1   ON A LIGHTLY FLOURED SURFACE, roll the pastry into a square about ⅛ inch thick. Using a 4-inch plate as a guide, or a cutter, cut four disks of pastry. If you are using a plate, cut the pastry with a rolling pizza cutter or the tip of a small sharp knife. Transfer the cut pastry rounds to a baking sheet. Pierce the pastry 6 to 8 times with the tines of a fork. The punctures will help prevent the dough from rising unevenly during baking. Chill the pastry in the refrigerator while you prepare the sugar. The disks can be prepared up to this point and refrigerated for 1 day or frozen for up to a week.

2   PREHEAT THE OVEN TO 425°F. In a small, heavy-bottomed pan, dissolve the sugar with the water. Cook the sugar over medium-high heat until caramelized. Do not stir the sugar as it cooks or it may recrystallize. Swirl the pan when the sugar begins to brown. Carefully pour the caramelized sugar into four 4-inch, 10-ounce ramekins.

3   PLACE THE PINEAPPLE slices in the ramekins on top of the caramel and season lightly with salt and pepper. Lay a pastry disk on top of each pineapple and transfer the ramekins to a baking sheet. Bake the tarts for 15 to 20 minutes, or until the pastry is puffed and golden brown. Remove ramekins from the oven and cool for 5 minutes. Holding the ramekins carefully with a cooking mitt, twist the puff pastry to loosen the tart, caramel, and pineapple together. Carefully invert the ramekins to release the tarts onto individual serving plates. Serve the tarts warm or at room temperature.

Espresso Flan

Makes 4 servings

Executive Chef Vijay Raghavan
Horned Dorset Primavera

1½ cups milk
1½ cups heavy cream
⅓ cup coarsely ground espresso coffee beans
4 large eggs plus 2 large egg yolks
1½ cups sugar
3 tablespoons water

1   PREHEAT THE OVEN TO 325°F. Line a baking pan with a paper towel.

2   IN A SAUCEPAN, bring the milk and heavy cream to a boil. Turn off the heat, add the ground espresso beans, and steep, covered, for 15 minutes.

3   IN A BOWL, whisk the eggs and yolks with 1 cup of the sugar until smooth. Set aside.

4   IN A SMALL, heavy-bottomed pan, dissolve the remaining ½ cup of sugar in the water. Cook the sugar over medium-high heat until caramelized. Do not stir the sugar as it cooks or it may recrystallize. Swirl the pan when the sugar begins to brown. Carefully pour the caramelized sugar into four 10-ounce ramekins or oven-proof custard cups.

5   STRAIN THE ESPRESSO-infused milk mixture through a fine mesh strainer into the egg mixture. Whisk just to combine. Pour the espresso custard into the prepared ramekins, and gently spoon out any air bubbles off the surface of the custards. Transfer the custards to the baking pan. The towel will help keep the ramekins from shifting around when the pan is moved.

6 POUR BOILING WATER into the baking pan until it comes halfway up the sides of the ramekins. Carefully transfer the pan to the center shelf of the preheated oven and bake for 40 to 45 minutes. When making custards it is important to remember that cooking times vary; fresher eggs cook faster than older eggs. To check the custards, gently jiggle a ramekin. If the custards are set, they shake as a firm unit; if underdone, waves of custard will shiver in the center. If the custards need more time, continue cooking, checking every 5 minutes, until done. Remove the set custards from the oven and the water bath.

7 COOL THE RAMEKINS for 15 to 20 minutes before refrigerating for at least 2 hours or overnight. Unmold each custard by inverting the ramekin onto a serving dish. The caramel serves as its sauce. Serve chilled.

THREE GLORIOUS

DAYS AT THE HOSPICES DE BEAUNE

T he Great Schism, when the popes moved from the Vatican in Rome to Avignon in France, greatly expanded the Burgundian wine trade. In 1366, Petrarch, the Italian poet, wrote from Venice to Pope Urban V, who was then visiting Rome, and urged him not to go back to Avignon. He said he knew the pope would be pressured by his cardinals to go back to France "because they think of the Rhône as a river Paradise, that brings them the wine of Burgundy, which they regard as the fifth of the natural elements."

About Burgundy

People have been living in Burgundy, a district in the middle of France, since the Stone Age. The Celts once dominated the area, and the ancient Romans had a number of strongholds in the region. During the fifth century, people from the Baltic Sea came down and settled in the area. They were known as the Burgundians.

Charles the Bald was one of the first people to put Burgundy on the map. (The idea of adding a descriptive word to the name of a ruler was a big deal in Burgundy. Not only did they have Charles the Bald, they had Charles the Bold, Philip the Good, and James the Fearless.)

King Louis XI of France was not fond of the Burgundians, to put it mildly. When Charles the Bald was the Duke of Burgundy, the king let matters lie. But when Charles the Bold became duke, enough was enough. This Charles was too rich and too famous for King Louis to bear. So, in the middle of the 1400s, Louis forced Burgundy to become a part of France, and it has been a part ever since.

The political capital of Burgundy is the city of Dijon, but its gastronomic capital—and its real heart—is a strip of land that runs south from Dijon through the town of Beaune.

The Hospices de Beaune

During the 1400s, Nicolas Rolin, chancellor to Philip the Good, Duke of Burgundy, was one of the most powerful men in Europe. Rolin had been widowed twice when, in 1423, he married Guigone de Salins, a very pious and respectable woman who came from a very wealthy family. (*Salin* means "salt-marsh." For centuries her family had owned the most valuable salt mines in France.)

Times were good for Nicolas and Guigone, but not so good for almost everyone else. The Hundred Years' War had just ended, and bands of demobilized soldiers wandered around the countryside destroying everything and everyone they could get their hands on. Three years of devastating famine had begun, and ninety percent of the people who lived in Beaune were considered destitute. Nicolas saw these terrible times not as a problem, but as an opportunity to make up for a few past peccadilloes and perhaps rack up a few extra points in Heaven *en avance*. He built the *Hospices de Beaune*, also called the *Hotel-Dieu*, a great hospital for the needy of Burgundy. Today the magnificent Hospices is a tourist destination because of its art and architecture.

Upon entering the Hospices, patients were required to bathe, confess their sins, have their hair cut if it was necessary, give up their clothes (as we still do), and wear hospital gowns. They also had tablets affixed to their wrists that stated their names and addresses. There were separate wards for the extremely ill, for people awaiting operations, for people with fevers, for women having babies, and for convalescents. There was also space for the destitute, and for travelers like pilgrims, who had nowhere else to stay.

During the winter, one of the great comforts of the Hospices was its warmth. Big fires were built in its large fireplaces, and people who were cold could sleep near the fire, under fur blankets. The beds at Beaune held two people each, a common practice in both hospitals and hotels at the time. (Often a hotel bed would hold five people or more, and it was the custom to wear a cap in bed but nothing else.)

Much of the art created for the Hospices was commissioned by Rolin with the purpose of distracting the minds of the patients from their own problems and redirecting their thoughts to prayer and to requests for God's forgiveness. The great polyptych of Roger van der Weyden, now kept in a separate room of the Hospices, was originally painted to grace the altar in the *Grande Salle des Malades*, or "room of the sick." Each time Mass was said, or when someone was dying, the panels were opened out, showing their depiction of the Last Judgment and its promise of redemption. The outside of the polyptych, when closed, depicts Chancellor Rolin and his wife in a cozy grouping with the saints of healing: St. Sebastian, patron of plague victims, and St. Antony Abbot, patron of sufferers from skin diseases.

If a wealthy patient recovered and left the Hospices, it was expected that appreciation would be shown in the form of a generous gift to the hospital. Money and land were always nice, but in 1471, for the first time, someone donated the grapes from a vineyard. (Wine, a regular part of the patients' diet, was considered a health-giving liquid. Water, on the other hand, was known to often cause illness.) The gift of the grapes was a real boon. They could be turned into wine, annually. Some of that wine was used in the hospital and the rest was sold, year after year after year. This was a gift that kept on giving.

Over the centuries, many vineyards were designated for the Hospices. Today, the Hospices has holdings on over fifty estates, and they are on some of Burgundy's best land. Every year the grapes are gathered from these hills, and the Hospices' winemakers go to work on that year's vintage.

On the third Sunday in November, the results are sold at the world's largest charity wine auction. Buyers come from all over the world to bid on lots of the Hospices' wine, and many millions of dollars are raised to continue the upkeep of the building and art treasures within it.

Three Glorious Days of Eating and Drinking

Named in the 1950s, the *Trois Glorieuses* are three events organized around the wine auction. The first, a great feast, takes place in the cellars of the château Clos de Vougeot on the night before the wine auction. On Sunday, at 2:30 P.M. sharp, the auction begins in the market at Beaune. The auction is held *a la chandelle*—it's timed by candles. Monday evening brings a sumptuous dinner at the village of Meursault on the Côte de Beaune. Called *La Paulée de Meursault*, it is a harvest feast.

The Clos de Vougeot

Italy was the original home of the order of the Benedictine monks, yet the order's greatest monastery was at Cluny in Burgundy. Over the centuries, many of the Benedictines had become rich, powerful, and lovers of luxury. A few members, however, felt that too much of the good life was a bad thing, so they left the Benedictines and founded their own order. The Church eventually sainted the creator of this new order, calling him St. Bernard.

The order's first abbey was built on a marsh where only reeds grew. The monks were called Cistercians, because the French word for "reed" is *cistel*. The Cistercians withdrew into the solitude of the countryside, renouncing worldly pleasures—with one possible exception: they made great wine. The rules allowed the monks to have a little wine every day. Wine was also an important part of their religious services. But the monks really made an effort at developing their winemaking skills so they could sell their surplus and use the money to support the monastery. Of course, making great wine was applauded all around: it tasted better to the monks, showed their devotion to God, and made them financially stable. Eventually, the Cistercians were running a huge international operation dealing in fine wine.

In 1150, a man named Walo Gilles donated land to the Cistercians in exchange for a letter of recommendation that he could use to obtain better accommodations in the afterlife. Today that land is known as the Clos de Vougeot, where a half-million vines produce enough wine to fill about 300,000 bottles. By looking at the workings of Clos de Vougeot, it is still possible to get an idea of what the wine business

looked like about a thousand years ago. Carts, loaded with grapes, once passed into the central courtyard. Then, just as now, the grapes were piled in wooden trays to let the free-running juice pour out, and then emptied into huge press trays. The presses, powered by monks turning the enormous screws, crushed out the juice. Some presses still used today are over seven hundred years old, and each press has a name. (One such press is called *Têtu*, "the stubborn.") Tremendous barrels were used to ferment the grape juice and make wine.

The Cistercians did everything they could to make the best possible product. The people who built the Clos de Vougeot knew that a contented winemaker was a happy monk, so they laid out the place in a very efficient manner. All activities took place on one level—there was no running up and down staircases. The one-level plan was a good idea from the operation's viewpoint, but it also made sense in terms of construction. The land in the area is made up of very hard limestone. Digging a wine cellar would have been a murderous job. The builders covered all the walkways to protect the monks from the bad weather, dug a great well, and set up an ingenious system for getting the most water up to ground level with the least amount of effort.

Today the Clos de Vougeot is the home of an organization called the *Confrerie des Chevaliers du Tastevin*. Very loosely translated, this means "the bunch that likes to drink good wine." (A tastevin is a small, silver saucer-shaped dish used to taste wine. It has a number of irregularities on its inner surface that reflect and refract the light to show off a wine's color.) In this case the wine they like to drink comes from Burgundy. The society—a nonprofit association—was set up in 1934 to help promote the wines and the culture of the region.

Every year, during the last weekend of November, about six hundred people get together in the old wine storage area of Vougeot to celebrate the induction of new members to the Confrerie. The Confrerie wear elaborate costumes that seem vaguely academic: hats that look like crowns, tastevins hanging like medals from ribbons around their necks, and robes to their feet. They have a world-wide membership.

The Food of Burgundy

The food of Burgundy, like the food of most places, is the result of its history and geography. Burgundy is in the very center of France, and there are no important rivers connecting the area to the ocean. For this reason, it was left to itself, and developed its own culture, rather than adopting elements of other societies.

Basically, the food of Burgundy is farm food, but it is farm food *extraordinaire*. Its tastes are simple and direct, but fresh ingredients and blends of herbs and spices make it one of the great cuisines of France. The town of Dijon is the mustard capital of the world, and entire shops are devoted to the sale of various kinds of mustards. Local Charolais beef is the finest in France, and it's often found in the

Burgundian specialty *boeuf bourguignon*, a dark and flavorful beef stew made with red wine, onions, bits of bacon, and mushrooms. Burgundy is also the home of *escargots de Bourgogne*—the ultimate dish for snail-and-garlic lovers. There are remarkable fish and chicken dishes (many drenched in cream-based sauces) and delicious pork recipes, including suckling pig and country sausage. Burgundy has many cows, and they are responsible for some excellent cheeses, and many varieties of local mushrooms grow wild in the area. Various flowers and herbs indigenous to the region flavor its honey. Interestingly, Dijon, in addition to its reputation for mustard, has a league-leading position for its gingerbread. (The dough is made and then allowed to concentrate its flavor by resting for a couple of months before it is baked.)

During the seventeenth century, the chef to the Burgundian Count of Plessis-Praslin decided to roast some almonds and then coat them with sugar. They were offered to the ladies at the court of Louis XIII, were an immediate hit, and took the name of the Count. Today we call them "pralines."

The district also produces *créme de cassis*, a sweet liqueur made from currants. When a little of the currant liqueur is mixed into a glass of white wine, the wine turns a cool rose color, becoming a before-dinner aperitif called a Kir. The drink was named for Canon Felix Kir, the mayor of Dijon during the 1950s. (A little of the liqueur mixed into a glass of champagne is known as a Kir Royale.)

The Wine of Burgundy

The first known mention of the great vineyards of Burgundy is in a note sent to Emperor Constantine in the year 312, and describes the district as famous for the culture of its vines. The note goes on to complain about the lack of maintenance on the local drainage system and asks the Emperor to get it fixed as soon as possible. I suppose good drinking and eating and a direct and outspoken approach to life have always been part of the local character.

By the thirteenth century, the wine of Beaune was considered the best red wine in France, and it was certainly the most expensive. It was sent to Reims for the coronations of kings, and exported not only to the south, via the Rhône river, but also to Paris and to northern and eastern Europe. The wealthy dukes of Burgundy made much of their wines, presenting them as prestigious gifts to kings, queens, and popes. In 1395, Duke Philip the Bold wrote the great Burgundian Charter, laying down detailed laws for wine production in Burgundy that are still upheld today.

Each town along the road from Dijon to just below Beaune is famous for its wine, and the name of the village is inevitably on the label of the wine it produces. The most famous areas for wine lovers are Chablis, Côte d'Or, and Beaujolais. These areas don't produce a lot of wine, but the quality is extremely high.

During the French Revolution, the Church's monasteries were broken up and its lands confiscated. In Burgundy, the church lands were sold to local people. The Vougeot priory, for instance, went to a wood merchant, who later sold it to a banking family, who in turn sold it to a weapons manufacturer. In 1889, it was bought once more, split up by its owner into fifteen pieces, and sold to winegrowers. Today, the 90,000 acres of Burgundian vineyards are owned by over 46,000 different landholders. In many cases the actual parcel of earth owned by the grower is tiny. And each owner has a particular idea about how grapes should be grown. In general, the people who grow the grapes don't make the wine. But that is not the case at Bouchard Père & Fils.

The Château de Beaune

Built as a fortress during the fifteenth century, the Château de Beaune has only been home to the Bouchard name since the 1800s. The château, far from merely being the seat of a noble family, has also been the center of the family business ever since.

A series of underground caves was part of any respectable fifteenth-century fortress. They were important for supplies and troop movements. Today the caves of the château are used for the aging of over six million bottles of Burgundian wine, including a selection of very rare wines dating back to the 1800s. Wine-making starts in the vineyards, and Bouchard is the largest owner of the highest classifications in Burgundy—over two hundred and thirty acres in twenty-five different places around the Côte d'Or. The parcels are separated by rural hamlets, dirt roads, and ancient stone fences.

Bouchard is an old name in Burgundy—the family actually started making wine the year before George Washington was born—but some of its techniques are quite innovative. They were the first winemakers in Burgundy to initiate the practice of culling a "green harvest," which entails taking perfectly good bunches of grapes off the vines early in the season in order to concentrate the juices in the remaining grapes, thereby intensifying the flavor. They were also the first winemakers to spread pine tree bark on the ground as mulch, in order to help the earth hold moisture and warmth. Luckily, the bark also shielded the vines from harsh spring frosts.

Recipes for The Hospices de Beaune
France

Cheese Puffs (Gougères)

Beef Stew with Red Wine (Boeuf Bourguignon)

Buttered Noodles with Herbs

Chicken with Mustard Cream Sauce (Poulet Dijonnaise)

Glazed Carrots, Radishes, & Green Beans

Clafoutis

Cheese Puffs (Gougères)

Makes about 30 small puffs

⅔ cup water

3 tablespoons unsalted butter

¼ teaspoon kosher salt

¾ cup all-purpose flour

3 large eggs

½ cup finely grated Gruyère or Comté cheese

2 tablespoons Dijon-style mustard

⅛ teaspoon freshly grated nutmeg

Pinch of cayenne

1   PREHEAT THE OVEN TO 425°F. Line a baking sheet with parchment or brush it with butter and dust with flour.

2   IN A MEDIUM SAUCEPAN, bring the water, butter, and salt to a boil. When the butter is melted, remove the pan from the heat and sift in the flour. With a wooden spoon, stir the flour and liquid together to make a paste. Return the pan to the heat, and stir the paste to dry it out; in about 2 minutes it will form a smooth, shiny ball that pulls away from the sides of the pan.

3   TRANSFER THE PASTE TO A MIXING BOWL; stir with a wooden spoon for 1 minute to cool the paste.

4   WHISK 1 EGG in a small bowl and reserve 1 tablespoon of the whisked egg to use as a glaze for the puffs. Add the remainder of the whisked egg plus the other 2 eggs, one at a time, to the paste, making sure each egg is fully incorporated in the dough before adding the next egg. When doing this by hand, the egg may at first seem to resist mixing with the dough, but stay with it and the egg will bind with the paste to make a stiff dough. Once all the eggs are incorporated, mix in the cheese, mustard, nutmeg, and cayenne.

5 WITH A PASTRY BAG or 2 spoons, form the dough into plump 1-inch rounds, spaced 1½ inches apart on the prepared baking sheet. If using spoons, dip them in warm water after forming each round so the dough doesn't stick to the spoons. If you are using a pastry bag, gently squeeze the bag to form the rounds; release the pressure before you lift the bag to avoid lopsided tails.

6 LIGHTLY BRUSH THE ROUNDS with the reserved egg. Bake the cheese puffs for 20 minutes until they are puffed and golden brown. For crisp, light puffs, do not open the oven door while they are cooking. Serve warm. The gougères can be made a day ahead and frozen for future use, then reheated in a 350°F oven for 5 minutes.

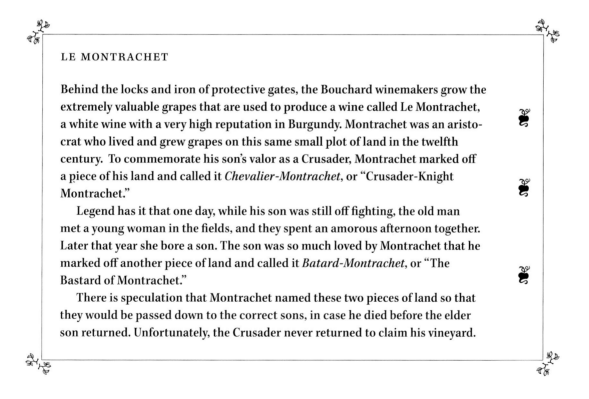

LE MONTRACHET

Behind the locks and iron of protective gates, the Bouchard winemakers grow the extremely valuable grapes that are used to produce a wine called Le Montrachet, a white wine with a very high reputation in Burgundy. Montrachet was an aristocrat who lived and grew grapes on this same small plot of land in the twelfth century. To commemorate his son's valor as a Crusader, Montrachet marked off a piece of his land and called it *Chevalier-Montrachet*, or "Crusader-Knight Montrachet."

Legend has it that one day, while his son was still off fighting, the old man met a young woman in the fields, and they spent an amorous afternoon together. Later that year she bore a son. The son was so much loved by Montrachet that he marked off another piece of land and called it *Batard-Montrachet*, or "The Bastard of Montrachet."

There is speculation that Montrachet named these two pieces of land so that they would be passed down to the correct sons, in case he died before the elder son returned. Unfortunately, the Crusader never returned to claim his vineyard.

Beef Stew with Red Wine (Boeuf Bourguignon)

Makes 4 servings

Executive Chef Christophe Crotet

Hostellerie de Levernois

3 tablespoons vegetable oil

1 medium onion, diced

1 medium carrot, peeled and diced

2 cloves garlic, diced

2 sprigs fresh thyme or 1 teaspoon dried, crushed

2 pounds cubed stewing beef (chuck or sirloin tip)

1½ teaspoons kosher salt

½ teaspoon freshly ground black pepper

2 tablespoons all-purpose flour

4 cups red wine

1 tomato, seeded and diced

2 cups pearl or white boiling onions

¼ pound bacon, cut into ½-inch strips

¼ pound mushrooms, quartered

2 tablespoons minced fresh flat-leaf parsley

Buttered Noodles with Herbs (recipe follows)

1   HEAT 1 TABLESPOON OF THE OIL in a Dutch oven or ovenproof stewpot, and sauté the onion, carrot, garlic, and thyme over medium heat until browned, 8 to 10 minutes. When the vegetables are nicely colored, transfer them to a bowl. Wipe out any little bits of vegetable clinging to the pan so they don't burn when you sear the beef.

2   PAT THE MEAT CUBES DRY and season them with ½ teaspoon of the salt and ¼ teaspoon of the pepper. Add ½ tablespoon of the oil to the pan and sear the beef in batches over high heat until it is a rich mahogany brown on all sides. This will take approximately 5 to 7 minutes depending on the thickness of the meat. Cubes tightly packed in the pan won't brown properly. Clean out any juices that are released before the next batch. Over high heat add ½ tablespoon of oil for each batch, then sauté the meat until browned on all sides.

3 PREHEAT THE OVEN TO 375°F. Return the vegetables and the meat to the pan, dust the meat and vegetables with the flour, and cook for 2 minutes over medium heat, stirring frequently. Toasting the flour helps to develop the overall flavor of the stew. Add 3 cups of the red wine to cover the beef and bring to a boil. Add the tomato and season the stew with the rest of the salt and pepper. Cover the stew with a round of parchment paper or the lid slightly ajar, place it in the oven; and cook for 1½ hours, or until the meat is tender. (If as the stew simmers the wine reduces below the meat, add a little water.)

4 WHILE THE STEW COOKS, bring a medium pot of water to a boil. To peel the pearl onions, trim the roots and make a small x with a paring knife in the other end. Boil the onions for 3 minutes, spoon them out, and set them aside to cool. Then squeeze the onions out of their skins. In the same water, blanch the bacon pieces for 3 to 4 minutes, and drain.

5 HEAT A MEDIUM SKILLET, add the remaining oil, and brown the bacon and onions. Add the mushrooms and cook over high heat until golden brown. Pour off any excess fat, add the final cup of red wine to the vegetables, and simmer until the onions are tender, about 10 minutes.

6 WHEN THE BEEF IS TENDER, remove the stew from the oven, stir in the vegetables, and simmer for 10 more minutes. Pour the stew into a warm bowl, dust with the minced parsley, and serve with buttered noodles.

Buttered Noodles with Herbs

Makes 4 servings

4 quarts water

8 ounces wide egg noodles

2 tablespoons unsalted butter

1 tablespoon mixed minced fresh herbs, such as sage, parsley, chives, thyme,
  savory, or chervil

¼ teaspoon kosher salt

⅛ teaspoon freshly ground black pepper

1   IN A POT, bring the water to a boil and salt generously. Cook the noodles according to package directions until tender but not mushy. Reserve ¾ cup of the water the pasta was cooked in.

2   WITH A SLOTTED SPOON or a strainer, transfer the noodles to a medium-size skillet and mix with the butter, herbs, and the cup of reserved cooking water. Toss the noodles over medium heat until all the water is evaporated and the noodles are lightly glazed. Season with the salt and pepper. Serve immediately.

Chicken with Mustard Cream Sauce (Poulet Dijonnaise)

Makes 4 servings

Executive Chef Christophe Crotet
Hostellerie de Levernois

1½ tablespoons vegetable oil

One (3½-pound) chicken, cut into 8 pieces

2 teaspoons kosher salt

¼ teaspoon freshly ground black pepper

1 small onion, diced

1 shallot, diced

1 carrot, diced

2 sprigs fresh thyme, or 2 teaspoons dried thyme, crushed

1 cup white wine

1 cup heavy cream or *crème fraîche*

3 tablespoons Dijon-style mustard

1   PREHEAT THE OVEN TO 375°F. Heat the oil in a Dutch oven or ovenproof skillet. Season the chicken pieces with half the salt and all the pepper, and brown the chicken in batches over high heat on all sides. Transfer the chicken to a plate, and add the onion, shallot, carrot, and thyme to the pan. Cook the vegetables over medium heat, until the onions are lightly browned. Return the chicken to the pan, cover with a round piece of parchment or the lid slightly ajar, place the pan in the oven, and bake for 15 minutes.

2   REMOVE THE CHICKEN from the pan to a warm spot while you make the sauce. Pour the wine into the pan and, with a wooden spoon, scrape up any browned bits clinging to the pan. Simmer the wine and reduce to about ⅓ cup. Add the cream and simmer gently until thickened and the satiny sauce coats the back of a spoon. Whisk in the mustard, and season with the remaining salt. Return the chicken to the sauce to heat through, and serve immediately.

Glazed Carrots, Radishes, & Green Beans

Makes 4 servings

> 2 medium carrots, peeled and cut lengthwise into quarters and then
> into 1½-inch-long pieces
> 1 bunch radishes, trimmed and quartered (about 1 cup)
> ⅔ cup water
> 2 tablespoons unsalted butter
> ¼ teaspoon kosher salt
> Pinch of sugar
> 1 pound green beans, trimmed and cut into 1½-inch-long pieces
> 2 teaspoons minced fresh flat-leaf parsley
> Salt and freshly ground black pepper, to taste

1   IN A SKILLET, combine the carrots, radishes, water, butter, salt, and sugar. Bring to a gentle simmer, and cover with a round of parchment or a lid slightly ajar. This moderates the evaporation of the cooking liquid to make a light glaze. Cook the vegetables for 10 to 15 minutes, or until tender. (The vegetables can be cooked to this point up to 2 hours ahead.)

2   WHILE THE ROOT VEGETABLES ARE SIMMERING, bring a pot of water to a boil. Salt the water and cook the green beans, uncovered, until tender but not mushy, about 10 minutes. (If not serving the vegetables right away, rinse the beans under cold water to stop the cooking and set the color.) In the skillet toss the beans with the carrots and radishes until heated through, add the parsley, salt, and pepper, and serve immediately.

Clafoutis

Makes 6 servings

Executive Chef Christophe Crotet
Hostellerie de Levernois

2 teaspoons unsalted butter
1 cup cake flour
1 cup granulated sugar
2 eggs
½ cup milk
2 tablespoons brandy
1 pound pitted cherries or blueberries or a combination (if using frozen or canned,
    drain well before using)
Confectioners' sugar

1   PREHEAT THE OVEN TO 375°F. Brush an 8-inch cake pan, skillet, or casserole with
the butter.

2   IN A BOWL, mix together the flour and sugar. Make a well in the center of the dry ingredients and using a hand-held beater whisk in the eggs, milk, and brandy. Whisk the batter
until thick and aerated. Pour half the batter (1 cup) into the prepared pan, sprinkle the fruit
over the batter, and cover with the rest of the batter.

3   BAKE FOR 45 TO 50 MINUTES, or until the clafouti is set. The clafouti will be the texture
of a moist pound cake. Serve warm, with a dusting of confectioners' sugar on top.

BORDEAUX'S HARVEST FESTIVAL

Every year, at the end of September or the beginning of October, the vineyards of Bordeaux see one of the most ancient rituals in Europe —the festival of the grape harvest.

A Very Short History of Bordeaux

France's Bordeaux region lies in the southwest part of the country, and borders on the Atlantic Ocean. The Gironde is an estuary that cuts in from the Atlantic, and is wide and deep enough to make the city of Bordeaux a port, though it is fifty miles from the coast. During the third century, the Romans appeared in the area, and by the fourth century it was a major commercial center.

In 1152, King Henry II of England married Eleanor of Aquitaine. The lands of Bordeaux were in her dowry, so this vast territory became part of England, and remained under English control for over three centuries. During this period, the English discovered the great wines of Bordeaux, and began an export business that changed the culture of the region, while making its wines well known throughout the world.

The Festival of the Harvest

Most gatherings and celebrations occur on specific dates. That date can be the same every year—Christmas, for example, is always on December 25—or it can move in relation to another date. Many celebrations take place a certain number of days before or after Easter, for instance, and Easter itself may fall anytime between March 22nd and April 25th, depending on the vernal equinox. But harvest celebrations can take place only after the crop has been brought in. So the time for a harvest festival changes from crop to crop and from place to place.

Autumn's first full moon stays in the sky longer than any other full moon of the year. It also seems to give more light, pausing, huge and golden, just above the horizon as it rises. And since that light is used by farmers who are busy bringing in their crops, it is known as the Harvest Moon. Generally, the fall harvest is a happy time. People who live on what they grow are satisfied, because they can see that they will have plenty to eat. They feel a sense of control over destiny because their plans for winter provisions have been realized.

Yet harvesting is a two-edged scythe. Farmers cannot help but equate the act of harvesting with the destruction of life—in this case, the life of plants. Of course, they had to kill the plants in order to feed their families, but the taking of life in

any form is always frightening. In the past, many farmers believed that plants had a spirit inside—a kind of soul. They felt that the spirit suffered when the plant was cut down. And they worried that if the spirit wasn't honored and thanked properly, it wouldn't come back the next year with a new crop. The farmers suspected that, as the harvest went on, the spirit jumped from plant to plant to avoid the reapers—until it ended up in the last plant to be cut down. At the end of the harvest season, the soul of the plant was hiding inside this last stand. Each farmer tried hard not to be the one who did the final cutting. Sometimes a whole group would stand around the last plants and throw their tools at the remaining stand. In that way they would be unable to tell who actually administered the final blow.

But harvesting a vineyard was different. The vines that gave the grapes stayed alive. The grapes were a gift: if you cared for the vine and honored the gift, everything would go well in the future. Perhaps that's why there's not a plant in the world more cared for than the grapevine of a vineyard. Proof of that honor becomes apparent every time wine is served in a restaurant. Wine gets its own list, separate from the rest of the menu. Often, a special waiter will deal only with uncorking and serving the wine. Nothing at the table gets more attention.

Harvest is also a time for "first fruits," the first "fruit" of everyone's work throughout the growing season. (The ritual should really be called "first bites.") Before anyone started eating at an ancient harvest feast, a piece of food from the harvest was offered to the gods, as a way of giving thanks for the good season. The ritual of reserving the first bite of the harvested food for the gods is actually how taxation got started. In the beginning, you offered a little bit of what you had to the Great Spirit. Then the first portion was taken by the ancient priesthood. Eventually the right to an opening share of everything harvested was taken over by government, in the form of taxation.

Harvest celebrations, and the feasts that accompanied them, were an opportunity for a society to relax from the intense physical labor of field work. They allowed people to take time to reflect on the ending of the yearly cycle of growth, and quelled fears associated with the bringing of death to plants, by allowing the populace to blow off a little steam. The hot, difficult work of reaping and picking and threshing was replaced, in many societies, with a fun-filled, frenzied party of eating, drinking, and romancing. Bruegel's tumult-filled paintings of harvest festivities capture the spirit of the moment.

The Grape Harvest at Château Mouton-Rothschild

In 1853, the English branch of the Rothschild family bought a winemaking property in the Bordeaux region of France and renamed it Château Mouton-Rothschild. Although it was an excellent vineyard, no one in the family showed any real interest in it until 1922, when Baron Philippe de Rothschild decided on winemaking as his life's work.

In 1924, the baron introduced a new and rather revolutionary practice. He had all the wine he produced that year put into bottles at the château. Until then, wine was shipped in barrels and the wholesale buyer bottled it any way he wanted. Some wholesalers did a fine job, but some were less than skilled. (It was a little like a chef cooking a fine dinner and having some of it served by impeccable waiters

while the rest came to the table in the hands of The Three Stooges.) Bottling the wine at the château gave the baron complete control of the entire process.

The system eventually became an important aspect of production for all the great winemakers of Bordeaux. Every bottle of wine bottled at the château where the grapes were grown now displays a line on the label that says *mis en bouteille au château* —"put in the bottle at the château." The grower suddenly became responsible for the quality of the wine from grape to presentation.

Baron Rothschild realized that this new association between the winemaker and the final bottle made the label a kind of birth certificate, a producer's guarantee. So he decided to make his labels as distinctive and interesting as possible. Every year he commissioned a well-known artist to produce an original work of art for his label. Famous artists like Miró, Chagall, Braque, Picasso, and Warhol all made labels for Château Mouton-Rothschild.

The baron also decided that he could use the distinctive grapes of Bordeaux to produce a moderately priced wine, which he called Mouton Cadet. Mouton Cadet, which means "Mouton, Junior," is one of the best-known Bordeaux in the world, and annual consumption is about 15 million bottles a year.

The plateau of Mouton-Rothschild is considered an ideal piece of land for the area. The Cabernet Sauvignon grape is grown there, along with some Merlot, which is used in the final blend of Mouton Rothschild.

Good-tasting and nourishing food is essential to keep the grape harvesters going. Each day, during the Rothschild harvest, lunch is served to more than three hundred people. It takes place in a large covered "dining shed" at the edge of the fields, and it is always a hot meal. A typical lunch might include a thick vegetable soup, grilled veal chops and noodles, cheeses, oranges, and wine from Château d'Armailhac. (Château d'Armailhac is an adjoining estate bought by the baron in 1933.) Harvesting these grapes can take between ten days and three weeks, depending on the weather. It is best if the grapes are perfectly dry before they are picked, so if it rains, the harvest is delayed.

The Foods of the Bordeaux Harvest

For hundreds of years, Bordeaux had two (admittedly interrelated) advantages going for it: great wine and great wealth. Together, they made the area one of France's most important places for eating. Bordeaux is the home of the black truffle—and of foie gras, the liver of specially raised geese. From late summer until the end of fall, the forests are filled with wild mushrooms; shallots are a flavorful ingredient in many dishes, and oil is the preferred cooking medium. In Bordeaux, steaks are often barbecued over a bed of grapevine prunings.

Goose is one of the traditional foods at harvest time. In the past, as the harvest came to an end, geese were let loose on the fields to fatten on the corn left by the harvesters. These were geese that had hatched in the spring to be eaten in the fall, making them a symbolic link between the two seasons of the year. The festal goose was used to help foretell the future—the custom of breaking the wishbone of a chicken started as a reading of a goose's bone. People believed that the bird's bone would foretell the winter weather—a dark bone meant that a severe winter was coming up; a light one forecasted a mild season. No bone at all meant that you were already in trouble.

Recipes for the Harvest Festival
Bordeaux, France

Potato & Leek Soup with Cod

Crispy Potato & Celery Root Cake

Beefsteak Bordelaise

Mushrooms with Garlic & Parsley

Onion Confit

Warm Goat Cheese Salad with Walnuts

Individual Apple Tarts

Potato & Leek Soup with Cod

Makes 4 servings

Executive Chef Francis Garcia

Le Chapon Fin Restaurant

4 cups water

1 pound boiling potatoes, peeled and diced

1 medium onion, diced

1½ teaspoons kosher salt, more to taste

2 leeks, white and light green parts, washed and diced

⅓ pound cod fillet, diced

⅓ cup chilled unsalted butter, diced

2 tablespoons minced fresh chives

4 teaspoons cognac or brandy (optional)

¼ teaspoon freshly ground black pepper

1   IN A MEDIUM SAUCEPAN, boil the water and add the potatoes, onion, and salt. Reduce the heat, and simmer for 3 to 4 minutes until the potatoes are just cooked. Be careful not to overcook the potatoes, or they will get mushy as the soup finishes. Skim off any foam that forms on the surface of the cooking water.

2   ADD THE LEEKS and simmer until tender, 2 to 3 minutes. Add the cod and simmer for 2 more minutes, or until cooked. Reduce the heat to low, and gently whisk in the butter. This will enrich the soup and give it a creamy finish. Stir in the chives and add a splash of cognac or brandy, if desired. Season with fresh pepper and more salt if needed. Serve in warmed soup bowls.

Crispy Potato & Celery Root Cake

Makes 4 servings

1 pound boiling potatoes, peeled

1 small celery root, peeled (about ½ pound)

1½ teaspoons kosher salt

½ teaspoon freshly ground black pepper

1½ tablespoons vegetable oil

1½ tablespoons unsalted butter

1   IN A FOOD PROCESSOR or with a hand grater, shred the potatoes. Rinse the potatoes in cold water until the water runs clear. Shred the celery root, but do not rinse.

2   DRAIN THE POTATOES and wrap them in a clean kitchen towel. Squeeze out the excess water, or spin-dry in a salad spinner. It is very important that the potatoes be dry or the cake will be soggy. Mix the celery root with the potatoes, and season with the salt and pepper.

3   HEAT A HEAVY-BOTTOMED or non-stick medium skillet with sloping sides. Add 1 tablespoon each of the oil and butter and heat. Add the potato mixture to the pan. Using a spatula, press the mixture into a neat cake about 1½ inches thick. Lightly brown the cake over medium-high heat for 4 to 5 minutes. Shake the pan to loosen the cake, reduce the heat to low, and continue to cook the cake, loosely covered, for 10 to 12 minutes.

4   TO FLIP THE CAKE, brush a flat lid, smaller than the cake, with oil, invert the cake onto the lid, and hold it aside for a moment. Raise the heat to medium-high and add the remaining butter and oil to the pan. Carefully slide the cake back into the pan, and cook, uncovered, until the bottom is golden brown, about 5 more minutes. Invert the cake onto the lid again and re-crisp the first side for about 1 minute. Slide the cake from the pan onto a cutting board, cut into wedges, and serve.

Beefsteak Bordelaise

Makes 4 servings

Executive Chef Francis Garcia
Le Chapon Fin Restaurant

For the Sauce:

2 cups red Bordeaux wine

1 shallot, minced

¼ teaspoon dried thyme

1 bay leaf

2 cups beef broth

1 teaspoon arrowroot, or 1½ teaspoons cornstarch

1 teaspoon warm water

2 tablespoons chilled unsalted butter, diced

½ teaspoon kosher salt

¼ teaspoon freshly ground black pepper

For the Steaks:

2 tablespoons vegetable oil

Four (6-ounce) fillets of beef (tenderloin) steaks, about 1½ inches thick,
   at room temperature

½ teaspoon kosher salt

½ teaspoon freshly ground black pepper

1   TO MAKE THE SAUCE: In a saucepan, combine the wine, shallot, thyme, and bay leaf. Boil gently, until the wine is reduced to ¼ cup of loose syrup that coats the shallot. It will take about 20 minutes to reach this point.

2   POUR THE BEEF BROTH into the wine and reduce over a high flame by about a third. The mixture wil thicken slightly. Dissolve the arrowroot or cornstarch in the water, and whisk it into the sauce. Bring to a boil and allow it to thicken to a point where it will coat the back of a spoon. Lower the heat, whisk in the butter, and season with salt and pepper. The sauce can be kept warm in a double boiler for an hour before serving. Remove the bay leaf before serving.

3   TO MAKE THE STEAKS: When ready to serve, heat a heavy-bottomed skillet. Add the oil. Pat the steaks dry with paper towels, and season one side of the meat with half the salt and pepper. Lay the steaks seasoned side down, in the pan, and cook over high heat until the steaks are a rich burnished brown, 2 to 4 minutes. Season the remaining side with the rest of the salt and pepper, turn the steaks, and brown the other sides, 2 to 3 minutes. Brown the sides of the steaks by holding them with tongs and searing the edges in the hot oil. Transfer the steaks to a warmed platter or individual plates. To add an extra beefy flavor to the sauce, pour off the residual oil left in the sauté pan, then pour the sauce into the pan and scrape up the brown drippings and bits. Pour the sauce over the steaks and serve.

Mushrooms with Garlic & Parsley

Makes 4 servings

8 large white mushrooms, wiped clean

2 tablespoons olive oil

½ teaspoon kosher salt

1 shallot, minced

1 medium clove garlic

2 tablespoons minced fresh flat-leaf parsley

1   POP THE STEMS from the mushroom caps, and dice the stems. Heat the oil in a medium skillet and brown the mushroom caps, rounded side down, over high heat, for 2 to 3 minutes. Turn the caps over and brown the other side. If the mushrooms are still firm, reduce the heat, cover the mushrooms, and cook for 3 to 4 minutes, or until tender. Add the diced stems to the pan and brown for 3 to 4 minutes.

2   SEASON THE MUSHROOMS WITH THE SALT. Add the shallot and garlic and sauté over medium heat until translucent, 1 to 2 minutes. Add the parsley and toss to coat the mushrooms. To serve, place the mushrooms on a warmed plate and spoon the diced stems into the caps.

Onion Confit

Makes 4 servings

4 tablespoons unsalted butter

1½ pounds onions, sliced (about 8 medium onions)

2 teaspoons kosher salt

1 cup red wine

2 tablespoons honey

½ teaspoon freshly ground black pepper

⅓ cup golden raisins

2 tablespoons red wine vinegar

1 IN A LARGE SKILLET OR Dutch oven, melt the butter and sauté the onions, adding the salt over 3 to 5 minutes, until the onions are slightly wilted. Then cover the onions and cook over low heat for 20 minutes. Check and stir the onions occasionally, making sure not to brown them. The long, slow cooking of the onions brings out their natural sweetness.

2 ADD THE RED WINE, honey, and pepper, and simmer uncovered over low heat for 30 minutes, or until most of the wine is reduced. Add the raisins and red wine vinegar, and simmer covered for 5 minutes more to thicken. Serve warm or at room temperature.

Warm Goat Cheese Salad with Walnuts

Makes 4 servings

For the Vinaigrette:

1 tablespoon whole-grain mustard

2 teaspoons red wine vinegar

½ teaspoon kosher salt

⅛ teaspoon freshly ground black pepper

½ cup walnut oil

3 tablespoons extra virgin olive oil

1 minced shallot

For the Salad:

½ cup shelled unsalted walnuts

8 ounces goat cheese, cut into 8 equal pieces (a log works well)

3 cups washed and dried arugula

3 cups washed and dried escarole, romaine or bibb

2 cups washed and dried chicory or frisee

1   TO MAKE THE VINAIGRETTE: Mix the mustard, vinegar, salt, and pepper together in a bowl. Slowly whisk in the oils. Stir in the shallot and set aside.

2   TO MAKE THE SALAD: Heat the oven to 350°F. Toast the walnuts on a baking sheet for about 10 minutes, or until lightly browned. Cool and chop fine. Roll the pieces of goat cheese in the walnuts to coat the cheese. Put the cheese in an ovenproof dish and heat until the cheese is warmed and soft, but not runny, about 5 minutes.

3   WHILE THE CHEESE IS WARMING, toss the greens in a bowl with the vinaigrette. Divide the greens onto 4 plates, place the warmed goat cheese on the salads, and serve immediately.

Individual Apple Tarts

Makes 4 servings

Executive Chef Francis Garcia
Le Chapon Fin Restaurant

Flour
1 pound prepared puff pastry, defrosted
4 Golden Delicious apples or other baking apples
2 tablespoons unsalted butter, cut into small pieces
4 tablespoons granulated sugar
Confectioners' sugar
Whipped cream or crème fraîche for serving

1   ON A LIGHTLY FLOURED SURFACE, roll the pastry out to a thickness of about ⅛ inch. If the dough gets warm and too soft to handle, slide it onto a cookie sheet and refrigerate for half an hour or until firm.

2   USING A PLATE OR A BOWL as a guide, measure four 6-inch disks of pastry, cutting the rounds with the tip of a small, sharp knife. Transfer the cut pastry to 2 parchment-lined cookie sheets. Pierce the pastry with the tines of a fork 6 to 8 times; this will help prevent the dough from rising unevenly during the baking. Chill the dough in the refrigerator while you prepare the apples. The disks can be prepared up to this point and refrigerated for 1 day or frozen for up to a week.

3   HEAT THE OVEN TO 425°F. Peel, core, and halve the apples lengthwise. Lay the cut side down and slice the apple halves in pieces ⅛-inch thick. Remove one sheet of disks from the refrigerator. Lay half the apple slices on the pastry in concentric circles, leaving a ½-inch border. Evenly dot the tarts with half the butter, and sprinkle a tablespoon of granulated sugar on each tart. Repeat with the other tray.

4   BAKE THE TARTS in the oven for 30 to 40 minutes, until the apples are browned at the edges and the pastry has turned a rich golden brown. Remove the finished tarts from the oven and cool them on a rack. Serve warm or at room temperature, dusted with confectioners' sugar and topped with a dollop of whipped cream or crème fraîche.

A FORMAL DINNER IN

During the last one hundred and fifty years, we have begun acting far less formally in social situations. These days, even when we are "being formal," we are much less formal than we used to be. Today, perhaps because of the in-roads of democracy, we believe that the old social rules kept people apart, and we behave informally, hoping that "being casual" will help bring us together.

THE LOIRE VALLEY

A Short History of the Loire

The Loire is the longest river in France, and people have been living on its banks since the beginning of recorded history. The Romans, in typical fashion, had a number of settlements in the area. During the fifth century, when the Roman army had pulled back and things were getting much less civilized, powerful local lords began turning the old Roman buildings into fortified strongholds. The lord's family lived inside the structure, but there was room within the walls to provide a safe haven for peasants, should the stronghold be attacked. Since it was the only defense system available, people tended to live near the castle, pledging fealty to its lord. During peaceful times, the peasants worked the land, and each fortification slowly became an agricultural center.

The Vikings, who came through the Loire Valley during the ninth century, were the most aggressive and terrifying invaders these strongholds had ever encountered. Instead of the feudal system of Church, kings, lords, and peasants, which everyone in the Loire Valley understood perfectly, the Vikings worked in raiding

parties, and were subject only to their ship's leader. These attacking forces, who had no king, Christian religion, or paperwork to deal with, burned, pillaged, and raped their way through every country they came into. Until the appearance of Viking boats, which was enough to bring total panic to a riverside community, building a defensive tower was a right that had belonged only to the French king. After a few Viking confrontations, the lords of the Loire decided to skip over that particular legality and began constructing the most strongly fortified towers possible. Stone walls with reinforced turrets and towers were very fashionable. A great hall was important, as were quarters for servants and soldiers. Stables and storerooms came in handy. But, of course, the most crucial requirement was a building that was hard to attack yet easy to defend.

During the fourteenth century, however, the political situation began to change. The Vikings had eased up, and construction for conflict was becoming less important to the average lord. Elements of comfort were becoming more valued. Fewer wars meant more windows. By the 1500s, sieges were out and sofas were in, and the fortified castle became the French château. Of course, you still built a moat now and then, but only to reflect the beauty and elegance of your towers. By that point in French history, what kept people out of your castle was not a stone wall or a moat, but their lack of entrée to your social milieu.

The Château Sully-sur-Loire is an interesting building because this shift from conflict to comfort is clearly reflected in its architecture. The original structure dates from the 1300s and was built as a fortress. It consists of three huge rooms that give you an idea of what life was like in the Middle Ages. Chests, used for storage as well as seating, are the basic furniture. When it was time to eat, planks of wood were put on top of trestles, covered with a cloth, and set. When it was time to sleep, the trestle tables were taken down and sleeping pallets were laid. The lord and his lady might use a private room, but the rest of the court slept together, as many as twelve to a bed. Tapestries were hung to keep out the cold and to add a degree of privacy.

The wing that was added to the château in the seventeenth century was clearly designed for pleasure and shows the influence of an early decorator. The ceilings are nicely painted, there's no exposed construction, and the floors are parquet.

The roof of the Château Sully-sur-Loire is considered one of the most valuable architectural elements of the period. It is over six hundred years old, and was made in the shape of a boat's keel. The timbers used to make the roof were soaked for several months, then slowly bent, heated, and dried. The roof took fifty years to complete.

In 1429, Joan of Arc appeared at Sully to convince Charles VII to get himself crowned as King of France, so that he could rally the populace and try to throw the English off his land. (He became king, but had a lot of trouble with the English.) For many years the Loire was the center of the royal court, and when the court moved to Paris, it maintained the châteaux along the river as country residences. When most people think about the romantic beauty of a French village or the French countryside, the images that come to mind are scenes from the Loire Valley.

Formality at the Table

The French royal court of the 1500s was a difficult, political and smelly place, in which the king, while trying not to get poisoned, was constantly making an effort to clean up the act of his nobles. Having finally gathered all of them into court life, the king was able to turn up the heat on manners, or *politesse*. Through the power of one-upmanship, this new code of politeness had a real impact on the way people lived. In the same way that the designers of the châteaux shifted their interest from armies to amenities, the route to power among the nobles shifted from muscles to manners. Combat was out; courtliness was in.

The king made table manners a political issue—if he liked your manners, you could sit next to him. This indicated to the rest of the court that you were in favor and had a great share of power and influence. The importance of the new table manners spread throughout the noble houses of France, and eventually throughout the aristocratic houses of all Europe.

The French Influence on Dining

Wherever you look during a formal dinner, you see the influence of the French. The host or hostess, for instance, is expected to have a seating plan, and the precise position of each guest at the table is marked with a card. Like the French kings, the host is expected to have particular reasons for wanting one person to sit next to another, and to show favor by "ranking" the guests' seating. The honored female guest sits to the host's right.

It is to the French Cardinal Richelieu, (archenemy of the Three Musketeers) that we owe the blunt-ended table knife. Richelieu, a punctilious sort, once saw a guest at one of his dinner parties picking his teeth with the point of a knife, and was so revolted by the display that he ordered all the knives in his household to have their points ground down to a round end. Eventually, a law was passed making it illegal for French knife manufacturers to produce dinner knives with points, except for steak knives.

Until the nineteenth century, formal dinners were served *a la francaise* or "in the French style." This method was based on the system that had been used during the Middle Ages and the Renaissance. When you arrived at the table the first course was already in place: the table was covered with different delicacies from which the guests could choose. After this first course, the platters were removed and the table was covered with new platters for the second course. The same thing happened again for the third.

In the early years of the 1800s, a Russian aristocrat named Prince Kourakin introduced an entirely new way of serving a formal dinner. Everyone sat down at the table and the food was served, one course at a time. This was known as dining *a la russe,* or "in the Russian style." We still use this arrangement. Service *a la russe* required many servants to handle the last-minute preparation and presentation. The rich liked showing off all their servants, but they felt deprived of their opportunity to display their great collections of china. They solved this problem by displaying the pieces in cabinets around the walls of the dining room.

The French word *desservir* means "to clear the table," and that is where our word *dessert* comes from. We clear the table to serve our sweets. The French were also responsible for raising napkin folding to professional status. Specialists were hired to come in and fold the napkins before an important meal. Fishes, boats, and swans were popular choices. (The folded napkins were left standing and less complex versions were actually used.)

We now use fewer implements at formal dinners than we did in the nineteenth century, but there are still so many of them that correct table manners are often described as "knowing which fork to use." At a correctly laid table there should really be no problem in choosing the right utensil. The diner starts with the outermost knives and forks and moves inward, the innermost pieces being the last ones needed. There may never be more than three knives laid at any one place; if there are more than three courses, a servant will supply the remaining knives.

Anglo-Saxon table manners allow a diner to place her left hand in her lap when she is not actively using that hand to feed herself. On the European continent, however, diners are supposed to sit with both hands in full view of the company. The unused hand should rest on the table's edge, visible only from the wrist. (Some people believe that, in the days of the early court, hands were kept in sight to keep people from scratching themselves at the table.)

Every European country has its own method for arranging knives and forks to indicate that the diner has finished eating. Americans are reminded by Emily Post never to push the plate away or to lean back and say "I'm through"; they must lay their knives and forks parallel on the plate's surface, tines up, with the sharp edge of the blade facing in.

These days, when we rise from the table at the end of dinner, we are supposed to leave our napkins loosely folded on the table—never on the chair. An old European superstition holds that a guest who leaves his napkin on the chair will never come to dinner again. The slightly unfolded napkin shows that you know that your host is going to wash the napkin before it is used by anyone else. If the napkin is folded very neatly, the diner intends to stay for another meal.

Foods of the Loire

The Loire is where great French cooking began. The most classic of French dishes got their start here, became part of the national cuisine, and were eventually adopted by many of the most respected restaurants around the world. When you look at the menu of a traditional French restaurant in Paris or London or New York, very often the dishes that are being described are dishes that began in the Loire Valley.

For the most part, the recipes of this region produce straightforward, down-to-earth home cooking. The talent of the cooks, however, is what has made the dishes famous. One of the most traditional of recipes, called *noisettes de porc aux pruneax*, or roast pork with prunes, is a simple idea, but, when done well, a remarkable dish.

For centuries, the noble families of France have come to the Loire to hunt. The woods are filled with wildlife: deer, hares, and rabbits; wild ducks, pheasants, partridges, and quail. The river and its tributaries supply pike, shad, freshwater salmon, carp, trout, eels—even crawfish. The area is also prime mushroom territory. In some shops there are large charts for tourists providing knowledgeable advice about which mushrooms are safe to eat. During the season, many pharmacies offer a safety-checking service to wild-mushroom-pickers, and both locals and tourists bring in their finds, just to be on the safe side.

The poultry is excellent and is often fricasseed: the chicken is cut into parts and sautéed with an assortment of vegetables. The baked specialties are fruit tarts and macaroons. And the Loire is also well known for its charcuterie. (*Charcuterie* is a word that traditionally refers to prepared pork products, but here it is used to describe all sorts of sausages, cured meat recipes, and pâtés.) One of the best known pâté-like dishes is called *rillettes*. Made from lean pieces of shredded cooked pork or duck mixed with fat, rillettes comes to the table in a crock, is spread on pieces of toasted bread, and served as an appetizer. *Jambonneaux de volaille* are chicken legs that have been cooked in wine, boned, stuffed, and served at room temperature.

Many of the recipes of the Loire include wine as an essential ingredient. *Coq au vin*, chicken cooked in wine, which may well be the most widely exported French recipe, is a specialty of the Loire.

Winemaking in the Loire Valley

The Loire river runs through France from east to west in a long, winding path that covers over six hundred miles. From one end to the other, wine grapes grow along the hills that come up from the river. They are generally used in making white wine. In the middle district, in Touraine and Anjou, the winemakers produce sweet wine, while at both ends of the region the winemakers make dry wines— Muscadet in the west, Sancerre and Pouilly in the east.

The Loire may, in fact, be responsible for the high quality of France's great wines. Legend tells us that one night, all the leaves of a monastery's grapevines were eaten by farm animals that had broken out of their stable. The monks were sure that their vineyard had been destroyed, but the following year, the vines that had lost the largest number of leaves produced the best grapes. The monks had inadvertently discovered the art of pruning—or was it divine intervention?

Dining at the Château du Nozet

In the eastern winemaking area of Pouilly-sur-Loire stands the magnificent and lavish Château du Nozet. The château, which boasts seventy rooms, intricate gardens, several fountains, many tapestries, and a convenient portrait gallery, is built on a parcel of land where wine grapes have been grown for over six hundred years. The family of Baron Patrick de Ladoucette has owned the castle since 1792. Known as "the Lord of the Loire," the Baron de Ladoucette also makes wine, including the crisp and elegant Baron de Ladoucette Pouilly-Fumé. His winery, which is the region's most modern facility, produces wines from only one kind of grape: Sauvignon Blanc.

This does not mean that the wines are simple. In fact, the sophisticated blending of grapes grown on different sites, where the vines produce flavors with very different characteristics, guarantees complexity in the final product.

The baron's ancestors settled in this part of France at about the time that noble families were beginning to adopt the rituals that are now considered to be the standard for appropriate etiquette at table.

In the last one hundred and fifty years, formality has taken some heavy blows, and in many societies has now been reduced to a bare minimum. Philosophical views of equality have made many people feel uncomfortable at the thought of eating with a footman in attendance at every chair. The prohibitive cost of servants, fast pace of modern life, and sixties revolt against class-consciousness and arrogance all made for an end to the ritual-rich customs associated with affluence. After World War II, the "casual" American style made the most of its cultural rootlessness. Americans wore blue jeans, ate fast-food, and entertained in the kitchen. This style began to take hold in many countries. It even made inroads in France.

People who dislike being formal often believe that formality sets them apart, and that they would rather bury those false divisions and establish closer contact with other people. But the human being will always find a way to show status—whether it is by wearing a particular brand of jeans, or by eating "alfresco" in an expensive new "trattoria."

Formality at dinner, aside from its political aspects, created a safety zone of comfort for all the people at the table. They all spoke the same language of politeness. They all knew all the rules. Freed from the distraction of having to think

Château du Nozet

Dîner du 14 Septembre 1995

Amuse-Bouche
Laurent Perrier Grand Siècle

Saumon mariné
Pouilly-Fumé de Ladoucette 1993 en Magnum

*Compotée d'Agneau de Loire Cuite en Blanquette
et Ses Coco Demi-Sec aux Herbes Fraîches*
Baron de L 1992 en Magnum

*Poitrine de Volaille de Nevers, Cloutée au Citron Vert
Tapinaude Morvandelle*
Sancerre Comte Lafond Rouge 1993

Fromages de la Loire

Parfait aux Framboises et son Coulis
Liqueur de Framboise Philippe de Bourgogne

about forks (because it was second nature), they relaxed and talked about culture, art, and politics, knowing that no one was suddenly going to start scratching or picking his teeth with a knife.

Dinner at the Château du Nozet progresses according to the tried-and-true rules of formality. That doesn't mean that the evening is stiff, or that the guests behave in a stilted manner. On the contrary, the comfort of manners leads to having a great time. When the party assembles, the baron offers an aperitif in one of the sitting rooms. When dinner is announced, the gentlemen escort the ladies (by rank) into the dining room, where place cards show the seating arrangement. After the ladies are seated, beginning with the hostess, the gentlemen take their seats.

At a truly formal meal, it was the custom to talk to the guest on your right as long as the hostess was talking to the guest on her right, then change speaking partners when she began to talk to the guest on her left. This rule kept the conversation flowing at large gatherings, and made sure that no one was ever left out of the conversation for too long. But it *did* result in some rather abrupt conversation-enders.

After a dinner served *a la russe*, accompanied by some excellent wines, the hostess announces the "withdrawal of the ladies," who then excuse themselves from the table to relax in a nearby boudoir. The men are invited to a study, where they are offered a glass of cognac and a cigar. After twenty minutes or so, the women rejoin the men in a nearby drawing room. (The term *drawing room* is a corruption of "withdrawing room," where people "withdrew" after dinner.)

The division of the sexes for a brief period allows a certain single-sex permissiveness to reign just long enough to allow relaxation. Withdrawing from the table gives women the chance to engage in topics not, perhaps, of interest to the men of the company. A similar relaxation comes over the men.

After reconvening, the party has coffee and a liqueur in the drawing room, and, after another round of conversation, people begin to thank their hosts and depart. Generally, a formal dinner begins at 8:00 and concludes around 10:30 P.M.

Recipes for a Formal Dinner
Loire Valley, France

Watercress & Parsnip Soup

Glazed Brussels Sprouts with Lemon & Pepper

Chicken with Red Wine (Coq au Vin)

Roast Veal with Tarragon & Onion Sauce

Vanilla & Spice Babas

Watercress & Parsnip Soup

Makes 4 servings

> 3 bunches watercress (about ¾ pound)
>
> 4 tablespoons unsalted butter
>
> 3 leeks, white and light green parts, sliced and rinsed well
>
> 1 pound parsnips, peeled and thinly sliced
>
> 4 cups milk
>
> 2 teaspoons kosher salt
>
> ¼ teaspoon freshly ground black pepper
>
> 1 tablespoon dry vermouth

1 TRIM AND SEPARATE the watercress leaves from the stems and set them aside.

2 IN A LARGE NONREACTIVE SOUP POT set over medium-low heat, melt the butter and sauté the leeks and watercress stems until tender and sweet, about 7 minutes. Add the parsnips, milk, salt, and pepper. Bring to a boil, reduce the heat, and simmer uncovered for 25 to 30 minutes, or until the parsnips are very soft.

3 WHILE THE SOUP IS SIMMERING, bring a small pot of water to a boil. Set aside a couple of watercress leaves for the garnish. Boil the rest of the watercress leaves for 3 to 4 minutes, or until tender. Drain and rinse them under cold water to set the color of the leaves.

4 FOR A SMOOTH RESULT, pass the soup through a food mill to puree and strain out the fibrous parts of the watercress stems. For a thicker texture, leave the stems in. To get a creamy texture and bright green color, puree the soup with the watercress leaves and stems in a blender or with an immersion blender. Return the soup to the pan, add the vermouth, and reheat gently. Serve the soup in warmed bowls with the watercress leaves as a garnish.

Glazed Brussels Sprouts with Lemon & Pepper

Makes 4 servings

1 pound small brussels sprouts, outer leaves and bases trimmed

1½ teaspoons kosher salt

2 tablespoons unsalted butter

1 tablespoon fresh lemon juice

3 tablespoons water

Pinch of sugar

¼ teaspoon freshly ground black pepper

1 CUT THE SPROUTS IN HALF through their base, keeping the leaves intact. Bring a pot of water to a boil and add 1 teaspoon of the salt. Boil the sprouts until tender but not mushy, about 5 minutes. Drain and rinse the sprouts under cold water to stop the cooking and set their color.

2 WHEN READY TO SERVE, heat the brussels sprouts in a medium pan with the butter, lemon juice, water, sugar, remaining salt, and the pepper. Cook for 3 to 4 minutes, turning gently, until the sprouts are lightly glazed and heated through. Serve immediately.

Chicken with Red Wine (*Coq au Vin*)

Makes 4 servings

Executive Chef Gérard Sallé
Hotel Plaza Atheneé, Paris

For the Marinade:

4 each chicken drumsticks and thighs

3 cups red wine

1 tablespoon minced fresh rosemary, or 2 teaspoons dried rosemary, crushed

2 bay leaves

¼ cup celery leaves

For the Preparation:

1½ teaspoons kosher salt

2 tablespoons vegetable oil

2 tablespoons all-purpose flour

¼ teaspoon freshly ground black pepper

2 cups pearl or small boiling onions

1 tablespoon unsalted butter

⅓ pound mushrooms, quartered

4 slices white bread

1 large clove garlic

1 tablespoon vegetable oil for dipping the toast edges

2 tablespoons minced fresh flat-leaf parsley

1   IN A MEDIUM BOWL OR CASSEROLE, marinate the chicken pieces with the wine, rosemary, bay, and celery leaves. Refrigerate overnight or for up to 24 hours.

2   THE NEXT DAY, preheat the oven to 375°F. Drain and reserve the wine and herbs from the chicken. Pat the chicken pieces dry and season them with ½ teaspoon of the salt. In a large ovenproof skillet or Dutch oven, heat the oil and brown the chicken pieces on all sides. Sprinkle the flour over the chicken pieces, and stir for 2 minutes to toast the flour. Pour the reserved wine over the chicken and, with a wooden spoon, scrape up any browned bits that cling to the bottom of the pan. Season the stew with the remaining salt and the pepper, cover it with parchment paper or the lid slightly ajar, bring to a simmer, and cook in the oven for 30 minutes.

3   TO PEEL THE PEARL ONIONS, bring a pot of water to a boil, trim the ends of the onions and then, with a paring knife, make a small x in the root end. Boil the onions for 3 minutes to loosen the skins, then drain and set aside. When cool, press the onions out of their skins.

4   IN A MEDIUM SKILLET over medium heat, melt the butter and sauté the onions and mushrooms until golden brown. Add the browned vegetables to the stew and simmer for 20 minutes, or until the onions are tender.

5   TRIM THE CRUST OFF THE BREAD and cut the bread into decorative triangles or heart shapes. Bake on a cookie sheet for 10 to 12 minutes, or until golden brown. While the toasts are still warm, rub them with the garlic clove. Set aside the toast for garnishing the stew.

6   TO SERVE, transfer the stew to a serving casserole. Dip the garlic toast edges in oil very lightly and then in the parsley and garnish the stew with the toasts. Serve with extra parsley sprinkled on top.

Roast Veal with Tarragon & Onion Sauce

Makes 4 servings

For the Veal:

> One (3½-pound) veal shoulder roast, boned and tied
> 1 tablespoon olive oil
> ½ teaspoon kosher salt
> ¼ teaspoon freshly ground black pepper
> ½ cup dry white wine

For the Sauce:

> 1 tablespoon unsalted butter
> 2 medium onions, thinly sliced
> 1 teaspoon kosher salt
> 2 tablespoons long grain white rice
> 1 tablespoon dried tarragon, crushed
> 1½ cups chicken broth
> ¼ teaspoon freshly ground black pepper
> ½ cup water

1   TO ROAST THE VEAL: Preheat the oven to 500°F. Brush the veal with the oil and season it with the salt and pepper. Place the roast on a rack in a roasting pan. Cook the roast for 20 minutes.

2   REDUCE THE OVEN TEMPERATURE TO 350°F. After 1 hour of cooking at the lower temperature, add the white wine to the pan. Continue to cook for another 40 to 60 minutes, or until the internal temperature of the veal roast is 150°F.

3   WHILE THE ROAST COOKS, make the sauce: In a medium saucepan over low heat, melt the butter and cook the onions with ½ teaspoon salt, covered, for 15 minutes. Stir the onions occasionally so they don't brown during the cooking. Add the rice, tarragon, and chicken broth; cover and simmer for 20 minutes, or until the rice is completely soft. Puree the sauce in a blender with the remaining salt and the pepper. Set aside.

4   WHEN THE ROAST IS FINISHED, remove it from the oven and let the meat rest in a warm spot, loosely covered with foil, for 10 minutes. To deglaze the pan juices, heat the roasting pan on a burner. Add ½ cup water and scrape up any browned bits and juices with a wooden spoon. Add the sauce to the pan juices and bring to a boil.

5   TO SERVE, remove the string from the roast and, with a carving knife, slice the veal against the grain into thin pieces. Pour some of the sauce onto a heated platter and lay the sliced veal down the center of the platter. Garnish the dish with vegetables. Serve the extra sauce on the side.

Vanilla & Spice Babas

Makes a dozen small cakes

Executive Chef Gérard Sallé

Hotel Plaza Atheneé, Paris

For the Babas:

⅔ cup milk

1 package active dry yeast (2 teaspoons)

2 cups all-purpose flour

2 tablespoons sugar

¼ teaspoon salt

2 large eggs

5 tablespoons unsalted butter, softened

For the Syrup:

1 vanilla bean

3 cups water

1 cup sugar

Zest of 1 lemon

Zest of 1 orange

¼ teaspoon cracked coriander seeds

½ teaspoon cracked cardamom pods

5 star anise

3 cinnamon sticks

For the Garnish:

Whipped cream or vanilla ice cream

1   TO MAKE THE BABAS: In a small saucepan, warm the milk slightly, 110° to 115° F.
Pour the milk into a small bowl and sprinkle the yeast over the surface. After about
5 minutes the yeast will expand and start to bubble.

2   IN THE BOWL OF A FOOD PROCESSOR fitted with the metal blade, mix the flour, sugar, and
salt together. With the machine running, add the eggs and the yeast mixture. Run the
machine until you have a smooth dough, about 1 minute. The dough will be loose and wet.

3   TRANSFER THE DOUGH to a lightly buttered bowl. Cover the dough with plastic wrap and
set it aside in a warm spot until the dough doubles in size, about 50 minutes.

4   BUTTER A 12-CUP MUFFIN TIN, or two 6-cup muffin tins. After the dough has doubled,
work the remaining softened butter into the dough with a spatula. The dough will resist the
butter at first, but continue working it in and the dough will accept the butter. The dough
will be fully incorporated and have a slightly glossy appearance.

5   POUR THE DOUGH OUT onto a clean work surface. With a pastry scraper or knife, divide the dough into 12 equal pieces. (To prevent the dough from sticking to your fingers, lightly dust your hands with flour.) Place the dough in the muffin cups about one third full. Set the muffin tray aside until the dough has risen to the top of the cups. That should take about 30 minutes. Preheat the oven to 350°F.

6   BAKE THE BABAS FOR 30 MINUTES, or until golden brown. Remove them from the oven and cool the tin on a rack.

7   TO MAKE THE SYRUP: Split the vanilla bean lengthwise to expose the vanilla "tar." Cut the vanilla bean into 4 even pieces. In a medium saucepan, combine the vanilla bean with the rest of the syrup ingredients and bring to a boil. Reduce the heat and simmer for 5 minutes to infuse the flavor of the spices into the syrup. Strain the syrup through a mesh strainer into a clean bowl.

8   WHEN READY TO SERVE, dunk the babas in the syrup to absorb but not be saturated with the syrup. Cut each baba in half, and place it in an individual bowl with some of the syrup. Garnish each serving with a dollop of whipped cream or a scoop of vanilla ice cream.

THANKSGIVING
IN COLONIAL
WILLIAMSBURG

When Abraham Lincoln called for the institution of an annual national holiday called Thanksgiving, he was hoping to remind North and South that the Pilgrims had lived in harmony with the Native Americans they encountered on these shores. His message of reconciliation is one we can still benefit from today.

A Short History of Williamsburg

Virginia was England's largest and most important colony in North America for well over one hundred years. By 1699, however, Virginia had outgrown its old capital in Jamestown, and had built itself a new one called Williamsburg, in honor of the King of England. The plan for the city was probably the work of Francis Nicholson, the governor of the time. Williamsburg was planned to be a center for learning, religion, and government, and that's what it became.

The College of William and Mary took up one side of the city, and was chartered in 1693. (The college's Wren Building is the oldest academic building still in use in the United States.) The Capitol stood on the other side, underscoring the belief that democratic government was only possible with an educated population.

Things began to change, however, just as they began to build the city. The philosophical ideal of the perfect city was suddenly expected to also be a center for manufacturing and retailing. One of the first changes was the addition of a large open area at the center of town to be used as a marketplace and fairground.

The training field for the Williamsburg militia was right next to the courthouse, and the militia mustered there a number of times each year, bringing together people from different levels of society and reminding everyone just who was in charge. Being a landowner generally meant that you got to be an officer.

The Duke of Gloucester Street runs from one end of Williamsburg to the other, and during the 1700s it was one of the busiest parts of the city—America's early prototype for Fifth Avenue and Rodeo Drive. The street was a bustling complex of general stores, specialty shops, and taverns. Prentis & Company, a small shop that is still standing, is a good example of what a store was like in the eighteenth century. When the patriots of Virginia decided to stage their own version of the

Boston Tea Party, the tea that they tossed into the York River was selected from a consignment belonging to Prentis. Dubois' Store was a grocery, and still offers products that were staples of Virginia's colonial diet: hams, fruit preserves, and relishes.

If you were interested in fashion's latest hats and clothes, the place to go was Margaret Hunter's Millinery Shop. Margaret imported clothing for women and children and sometimes made dresses for her customers. She was an important member of the business community and was officially known as a milliner, or maker of hats. (People who study the origins of words think that *milliner* comes from a phrase that meant someone who immigrated from the Italian city of Milan or who imported goods from Milan.)

A golden ball hanging outside a shop was a sign commonly used by jewelers, and today the jewelers of Williamsburg continue to make various objects in the style of the eighteenth century. The shoemaker's shop uses the same tools and techniques as those used in the 1700s and turns shoes out at the rate of one pair a day. Some shoes of the colonial period were made on a "straight last," which meant there was no difference between the left shoe and the right.

Red and white stripes on a pole indicated a barbershop. The red bands signified blood, the white stripes, bandages. For hundreds of years, doctors were actually members of the clergy. They could examine the patient and decide what should be done, but they were not allowed to cause bleeding, leaving that detail to local barbers.

During the 1700s, it was fashionable for men to wear wigs, which were also available at the barbershop. The eighteenth-century barbershop certainly offered an unusual collection of services—trim your beard, fit your wig, and have your appendix removed, and all at the same convenient location.

The Duke of Gloucester Street was home to the Raleigh Tavern—the most famous tavern of the time. It was a center for social, political, and business meetings. The Phi Beta Kappa Society, founded in Williamsburg in 1776, met at the Raleigh Tavern to slake its thirst for knowledge. George Washington ate there, and so did Thomas Jefferson.

At the time of its construction in the early 1700s, the Governor's Palace was considered one of the finest buildings in North America. The entry hall displayed weapons that proved the power and authority of the king's representative in the Virginia colony. Gardens and lands around the palace were designed to give the property and its inhabitants a feeling of dominance and importance.

During the early years of this century, the Reverend Dr. William Archer Rutherford Goodwin was the rector of Bruton Parish, which included the town of Williamsburg. Goodwin was fascinated with the role that Williamsburg had played in the American Revolution, and he wanted to restore the area and make it look and feel the way it had during the seventeenth and eighteenth centuries. He was able to communicate the value and importance of this dream to John D. Rockefeller, Jr., who provided funds to buy the land, research the history, and reconstruct the town.

Today Historic Williamsburg is called the "World's Largest Living Museum," but it is also home to hundreds of people who live and work there. The work is funded by the Colonial Williamsburg Foundation, a nonprofit educational institution. Over three million people visit Colonial Williamsburg every year.

A Short History of Thanksgiving

T he most well known day of Thanksgiving was held by the Pilgrims who had survived the voyage of their ship, the Mayflower, from England. Of the one hundred and eleven men who started the trip, fifty-five survived—and this was considered an act of God. Squanto, a Native American from the Pawtucket tribe, had shown the settlers how to plant corn and beans, which ensured their survival. In the middle of October, their governor declared a day of Thanksgiving, to be held at the beginning of December. It appears there were originally two feasts: the party in October with the Indians and the Pilgrims, which was a harvest feast, and the official Thanksgiving celebration that occurred a couple of months later and included many additional "thank yous" besides the one for the harvest. Our present Thanksgiving Day story combines these two historical events.

How Thanksgiving got onto the federal calendar is another story. In May of 1776, a group of Virginia delegates met in Williamsburg and took the lead in creating the plan for a union of all the colonies. Their actions resulted in the Declaration of Independence and the subsequent war of revolution. At the end of the Revolution, the people of the newly forming United States of America celebrated their victory with a Thanksgiving Day, proclaimed by General Washington on Thursday, November 26, 1789. Prayers of thanks may have been offered to the Almighty, but it was not a predominantly religious event; in fact, it was a very political holiday.

The history of America's Thanksgiving Day took a turn toward legalization when, in the middle of the War Between the States, a woman named Sarah Josepha Hale persuaded Abraham Lincoln that a Thanksgiving Day could help bring the country together. For thirty-six years, Sarah Hale had been the editor of *The Ladies' Magazine* in Boston, and had written editorials and letters to successive presidents and to the governors of all the states urging observation of an annual day that would express thanks to God for the blessings of the year. During these years she decided that the holiday should be held on the last

Thursday of November, remembering General Washington's 1789 Thanksgiving. Finally, Lincoln proclaimed the last Thursday of November 1863 as a day of national prayerful thanks. The president entreated Northerners and Southerners alike to remember the importance of the freedoms their country had achieved, and expressed his hope that everyone would pray for a swift end to the two-year-old war. Americans have been celebrating Thanksgiving Day every year since.

During the 1930s, business lobbyists pressured President Franklin Roosevelt to change the date of Thanksgiving to the third Thursday of November, so that the Christmas shopping season would be extended. It was too late. Everyone had already decided that the last Thursday of the month was part of the tradition. Roosevelt got so much grief for even considering the change that he recognized the old date legally just to calm people down.

The Rituals and Foods of Thanksgiving

Traditionally, the Thanksgiving meal was hosted by grandparents, or by the eldest members of a family. But in recent years the dinner is often given by a middle-aged couple who invite both old and young to join them. The meal brings the family together, and people are reminded of its history. The family photo albums are taken out, the old stories are repeated, and the members of the group refresh their memories of the past. Very often people tell stories about the cooking disasters or near-disasters of previous Thanksgiving meals. The stories tell how the family has weathered difficulties, forgiven each other for problems in the past, and come through it all healthily, and with good humor.

Sociologists say that Thanksgiving also celebrates the wholeness of the family even if the family is actually no longer whole. The occasion is often used to commemorate the links that are left. It has become commonplace for the children of divorced parents to attend more than one Thanksgiving dinner, eating the main meal with one part of their family and going to another part for dessert.

When families immigrate to the United States, they often keep to the foods of their native country. They also tend to continue celebrating their traditional holidays. The one American event that gets incorporated into the holiday cycle of just about

every new arrival is Thanksgiving, complete with all the traditional foods—turkey, stuffing, pumpkin pie, sweet potatoes, and cranberries.

The Native American tribes held their own harvest feasts, so it was not hard for the Pawtucket to join in for a little partying with the Pilgrims. An eyewitness report on Thanksgiving with the Pilgrims makes no mention of turkey, stuffing, cranberry sauce, sweet potatoes, or Jell-O molds. On the other hand, it does mention that there was exercise and perhaps a period dedicated to sports, which may be the reason that millions of Americans spend some part of Thanksgiving Day watching football.

Traditionally, people prefer to eat special dishes at an annual feast and like to taste those foods only in connection with that particular event. The food becomes part of what makes the festival noteworthy, and Thanksgiving is no exception. For many years, cranberries were exclusive to the Thanksgiving meal. Some people made their cranberry relish from fresh cranberries, but most people bought cranberry jelly in a can and served it in disks. The shape and dark red color of the berries were very distinctive. Giving food a distinctive shape, and serving it only in connection with a particular celebration, is an old technique for making a food unique to a specific festival.

Some historians believe that the traditional Thanksgiving sweet potato recipe was created as a symbol of unification. A Southern vegetable, the sweet potato was candied with maple syrup, a Northern ingredient. Thanksgiving is a time for stuffing. Stuffing a food has always been an important part of festival recipes. It's a way of making a dish "fancy" without necessarily making it expensive. The work that goes into the stuffing of the turkey is clearly visible to everyone at the table. A stuffed turkey is more satisfactory than an unstuffed bird because it shows more work, adds more food, and extends the number of flavors. It also sends a very clear message that life is plump, full, and bursting with abundance.

Sociologists point out that at any feast or festival we try to do two things: we make an effort to show that we are united, while also making an effort to show our individuality. The turkey and the stuffing symbolize both at Thanksgiving. The turkey is a universal container into which each family stuffs its "particular" stuffing. The stuffing shows a family's regional and individual history, and in some cases its wealth, but it is usually made according to The Family Recipe.

Recipes for Thanksgiving
Colonial Williamsburg, Virginia

Ginger Peach Glazed Turkey

Cornbread & Dried Fruit Dressing

Wild Mushroom & Rice Soup

Stuffed Acorn Squash with Apple, Onion, & Spinach

Lemon Almond Tart

Ginger Peach Glazed Turkey

Makes 6-8 servings

Executive Chef Hans Schadler

The Williamsburg Inn

For the Compound Butter:

8 tablespoons (1 stick) unsalted butter, at room temperature

1½ tablespoons minced fresh thyme leaves, or 2 teaspoons dried, crushed

2 teaspoons minced fresh sage leaves, or ½ teaspoon dried, crushed

1½ teaspoons minced fresh oregano, or ½ teaspoon dried, crushed

⅛ teaspoon kosher salt

Pinch freshly ground black pepper

For the Turkey:

One (10-12 pound) turkey

3½ cups chicken or turkey broth

2 sprigs fresh thyme

2 sprigs fresh sage

2 sprigs fresh oregano

2 teaspoons kosher salt

¾ teaspoon freshly ground black pepper

2 carrots, sliced

2 ribs celery, sliced

1 large onion, sliced

1 cup water

1 tablespoon arrowroot mixed with 3 tablespoons water

For the Glaze:

¼ cup peach slices, pureed

¼ cup peach preserves

1 tablespoon honey

2 tablespoons maple syrup

2 teaspoons minced fresh ginger

⅛-¼ teaspoon crushed red pepper flakes

1   TO MAKE THE COMPOUND BUTTER: Cream the butter and herbs together in a small bowl, and season with the salt and pepper.

2   TO MAKE THE TURKEY: Preheat the oven to 350°F. Remove the giblets from inside the turkey. Place the neck and all the giblets except the liver in a saucepan with the broth. Cover and simmer gently for 1 hour. Rinse the bird with cool water and pat it dry with paper towels. Stuff the cavity with the herb sprigs, ½ teaspoon salt, and ⅛ teaspoon pepper.

3   TO LOOSEN THE BREAST SKIN OF THE BIRD: poke the end of a small spoon between the breast meat and skin, starting at the open cavity of the turkey. Move the spoon over the breast to separate the skin from the meat; take care not to rip the skin. Do this on both sides of the breastbone. Place a spoonful of the compound butter under the skin, and press it out to distribute it evenly over the breast. Do this with half the compound butter, covering both sides of the turkey breast. Melt the rest of the butter and brush it over the skin of the turkey and season with the remaining salt and pepper. Truss the turkey with kitchen string.

4   PLACE THE SLICED VEGETABLES and the water in a large roasting pan. Set the turkey, breast side up, on top of the vegetables. Put the turkey in the preheated oven and roast for 15 minutes per pound, about 3 hours, basting the bird every half hour with the pan drippings.

5   TO MAKE THE GLAZE: While the turkey roasts, heat all the ingredients for the glaze in a small pan. Whisk the glaze together until it is a smooth liquid, but don't heat the glaze for too long or it will get too thick; a minute or two will be fine. During the last 45 minutes of roasting the turkey, brush the glaze on the bird with a pastry brush. Paint the turkey 2 or 3 times with the glaze, letting each application brown before adding the next.

6   WHEN THE BIRD IS DONE, check the internal temperature at the thickest part of the thigh. It should be 165° to 170°F. When the breast is pierced, the juices should run clear. Remove the bird from the oven and set it in a warm spot to rest for 20 minutes.

7   TO MAKE THE GRAVY: Place the roasting pan over a medium flame and pour in the prepared giblet broth. With a wooden spoon, scrape up all the browned bits from the pan. Degrease the sauce, either by skimming it with a large spoon or by pouring the sauce into a degreasing cup. Return the sauce to the pan and bring to a simmer. Thicken the sauce with the arrowroot mixture by whisking it into the sauce, boiling to thicken, and seasoning to taste. Carve the turkey and serve with the gravy.

Cornbread & Dried Fruit Dressing

Makes 6-8 servings

Executive Chef Hans Schadler

The Williamsburg Inn

6 cups finely crumbled cornbread (about one 8- to 10-inch bread)

⅓ cup dried cherries

⅓ cup dried cranberries

⅓ cup minced dried apricots

⅓ cup port

8 tablespoons (1 stick) unsalted butter

2 ribs celery, diced

1 medium onion, diced

1 tart apple (Granny Smith or Greening), peeled and diced

2 tablespoons minced fresh thyme leaves, or 2 teaspoons dried and crushed

1 tablespoon minced fresh sage leaves, or 1 teaspoon dried and crushed

2 cups dried white bread croutons

¼ cup minced fresh flat-leaf parsley

3 large eggs, lightly beaten

⅔ cup milk

1½ cups chicken or turkey broth

8 ounces country-style sausage (optional)

1 tablespoon kosher salt

¾ teaspoon freshly ground black pepper

1   HEAT THE OVEN TO 350°F. Spread the cornbread out on a roasting pan and toast in the oven until lightly browned, about 10 minutes.

2   IN A SMALL SAUCEPAN, simmer the dried fruit in the port over medium-high heat for 1 minute. Set the fruit aside to plump in the port while you prepare the dressing.

3   IN A MEDIUM SKILLET OVER MEDIUM HEAT, melt 6 tablespoons of the butter and sauté the celery and onion until soft, about 5 minutes. Add the diced apple, thyme, and sage, and cook for 2 minutes more.

4 IN A LARGE BOWL, stir together the cornbread, fruits, sautéed vegetables, and croutons. Mix in the parsley, eggs, milk, and broth.

5 IF USING SAUSAGE, break the meat out of the casing. Cook the sausage meat in a small skillet over medium heat for 3 to 4 minutes, until browned. Add the sausage to the dressing. Season the moist dressing with the salt and pepper and mix it well with a big spoon.

6 BRUSH A MEDIUM CASSEROLE with butter and add the dressing to the pan. Dot the top of the dressing with any leftover butter, cover with a piece of parchment paper or the lid slightly ajar, and bake in the oven for 50 minutes. Then remove the parchment and continue baking for 15 to 20 minutes, until the top of the dressing is crisp and brown. For a real burnished crust, run the dressing under the broiler for a couple of minutes. Serve the dressing warm, with the turkey.

ALL ABOUT MUSHROOMS

The six most popular mushrooms produced in the United States are in the white mushroom family. They are great all-purpose mushrooms, used in salads, sauces, vegetable dishes—even on pizza.

The crimini mushroom is related to the white mushroom but is a little darker, with a denser texture and earthier flavor, and it is used in the same ways that we use white mushrooms. Portobello mushrooms have very large caps and a rich, meaty flavor. They are often sautéed or grilled and served alone, or in stir-fried recipes. Enoki mushrooms, on the other end of the spectrum, have tiny button caps and long, thin stems. They grow in clusters and are used raw in salads or as garnishes. The oyster mushroom has a fluted shell shape, and is a good all-purpose mushroom with a very unusual texture. The shiitake is best when cooked. It can be served by itself or as an ingredient in a pasta sauce or an Asian dish.

When you are buying mushrooms at the market, look for those with a smooth, generally unblemished skin, and a firm cap. The surface should be dry—never moist or slick. A freshly picked white mushroom has a cap that comes around all the way to the stem and covers the membrane inside. When the cap has pulled back it means that the mushroom has begun to lose moisture. This is perhaps less attractive from an aesthetic point of view, but the reduced moisture will have concentrated the flavor, which makes these more interesting as a cooking ingredient.

Fresh mushrooms don't store well, so you should use them as soon after you buy them as possible, and keep them in the refrigerator until you are ready to start cooking. Either clean mushrooms with a moist cloth or give them a very fast wash in a colander. Mushrooms are highly porous and can absorb lots of water, which is not good for their taste or texture, so clean them quickly.

Wild Mushroom & Rice Soup

Makes 6-8 servings

Executive Chef Hans Schadler

The Williamsburg Inn

Bouquet garni: 2 sprigs thyme, 3 sprigs parsley, 2 bay leaves, green part of 1 leek

4 slices bacon, diced

2 medium leeks, white and light green parts, sliced and rinsed thoroughly

2 medium carrots, peeled and sliced

1 medium red onion, sliced

1 clove garlic, minced

1 pound mixed wild mushrooms (portobello, cremini, shiitake, oyster, or enoki), stems trimmed and caps coarsely chopped

1 teaspoon kosher salt, or more to taste

½ teaspoon freshly ground black pepper

½ cup dry sherry

7 cups chicken broth

⅔ cup wild rice

2 scallions, white and green parts, thinly sliced

1   TUCK THE INGREDIENTS for the bouquet garni into the fold of the green part of the leek and wrap it closed with kitchen string. Set aside.

2   IN A SOUP POT, sauté the bacon over medium heat until brown and crisp. Transfer to a paper towel to drain. Set the crisp bacon aside to sprinkle on the finished soup.

3   IN THE RENDERED BACON DRIPPINGS, sauté the leeks, carrots, and red onion over medium-high heat until wilted, 7 to 10 minutes. Add the garlic and sauté for 1 more minute. Add the sliced mushrooms, salt, and pepper. Add the sherry and simmer for a few minutes to flavor the mushrooms. Add the chicken broth, the bouquet garni, and wild rice; bring to a boil, then reduce to a simmer and cook, uncovered, for 35 to 45 minutes, until the rice is tender.

4   WHEN READY TO SERVE, remove the bouquet garni, ladle the finished soup into bowls, and garnish with the crisped bacon and sliced scallions.

Stuffed Acorn Squash with Apple, Onion, & Spinach

Makes 8 servings

2 cups pearl or small boiling onions

2 acorn squash

1¼ teaspoons kosher salt

⅓ teaspoon freshly ground black pepper

½ teaspoon ground coriander

½ cup apple cider

½ cup water

3 tablespoons unsalted butter

1 Golden Delicious apple, peeled and diced

1½ pounds spinach, stems trimmed, washed and drained

1 PREHEAT THE OVEN TO 350°F.

2 TO PEEL THE PEARL ONIONS: Bring a medium pot of water to a boil, trim the ends of the onions and, with a paring knife, make a small **x** in the root end. Boil the onions for 5 minutes to loosen the skins and partially cook them; drain and set aside. When cool, press the onions out of their skins.

3 CUT THE ACORN SQUASH INTO QUARTERS, and scrape out the seeds with a spoon. Season the flesh of the squash with ½ teaspoon salt, ⅛ teaspoon pepper, and the coriander. Pour the cider and water into a roasting pan. Place the squash, cut side down, in the pan and scatter the onions around the squash. Dot with 1½ tablespoons of the butter. Cover the pan with foil and bake in the oven for 40 minutes. Remove the foil and continue to bake, basting the squash with the pan juices, for 30 to 40 minutes, until the onions and squash are tender.

4 WHEN READY TO SERVE, heat the remaining butter in a skillet and sauté the diced apple until golden brown, about 5 minutes. Add the pan juices from the squash, the spinach leaves, and the remaining salt and pepper. Cook over medium-high heat for 3 to 4 minutes, until the spinach is wilted and tender.

5 TO SERVE, arrange the squash on a platter and spoon equal portions of the spinach mixture into each section of squash. Top with the roasted onions and serve immediately.

Lemon Almond Tart

Makes 6-8 servings

For the Almond Crust:

6 tablespoons unsalted butter

⅓ cup granulated sugar

1 cup all-purpose flour

⅔ cup sliced almonds, finely ground

Pinch of salt

1 large egg

1 tablespoon dark rum or bourbon

For the Lemon Curd:

¾ cup fresh lemon juice (4-5 lemons)

¾ cup granulated sugar

2 large eggs plus 3 egg yolks

6 tablespoons unsalted butter, diced

For the Garnish:

½ cup chilled heavy cream

2-3 tablespoons confectioners' sugar

2 teaspoons rum (optional)

1   TO MAKE THE CRUST: In a food processor, cream the butter and sugar together. Scrape down the sides of the bowl and add the flour, almonds, and salt. Run the machine for 30 seconds until the flour is evenly mixed with the butter. With the motor running, add the egg and rum or bourbon. Keep the machine running until the ingredients form a cookie-like dough. Turn the dough out of the machine and with lightly floured hands, press it into a 10-inch tart pan with a removable bottom. Make sure the dough is evenly distributed over the bottom and sides of the pan. Refrigerate the crust for at least 1 hour before baking.

2   TO MAKE THE LEMON CURD: Combine the lemon juice, sugar, eggs, yolks, and diced butter in a medium saucepan. Place the pan over medium heat and whisk constantly for about 5 minutes, or until the curd thickens. (The mixture should reach a temperature of 160°F.) Be careful not to boil the lemon mixture or the eggs will curdle. Transfer the lemon curd to a small bowl, press a piece of plastic wrap onto the surface, and poke a couple of holes in the surface of the plastic. Set aside to cool. Refrigerate the lemon curd when it is cool. The refrigerated curd will keep for 1 week.

3   PREHEAT THE OVEN TO 400°F. Pierce the crust 4 or 5 times with the tines of a fork to prevent the dough from rising unevenly during baking. Line the tart shell with foil or parchment paper, and weigh it down with pastry weights or dried beans. Bake the tart for 12 to 15 minutes, until the shell is set and firm. Lift the foil and beans from the tart, and bake for 15 minutes more, or until the crust is golden brown. Set the crust on a rack to cool.

4   FOR THE GARNISH: When the crust is cool, spread the cooled lemon curd into the shell. Place the tart in the refrigerator until ready to serve. Whip the cream in a chilled bowl to soft peaks, sift in the confectioners' sugar, and stir in the rum. Pipe or spoon small dollops of the cream around the edge of the crust. Slice and serve.

MEETING FOR COFFEE

Most of our gatherings and celebrations have their origins in the heavens, or in annual occurrences that alter our natural surroundings. Often these cosmic events are coupled with a religious occasion. The gatherings came first, then particular foods and drinks were associated with them. There is, however, one famous exception. Coffee is the drink that has created a gathering of its own, a gathering that for hundreds of years has been associated with creativity and with the exchange of new and often revolutionary ideas.

IN EUROPE

& AMERICA

A Short History of Coffee

Of the many stories about the discovery of coffee, the most famous tells the tale of a goat herder in Abyssinia who noticed that his goats became very bouncy and playful after eating the berries of a certain bush. He tried a few himself, and soon felt quite nimble. A local monk joined in the experiment and found himself in the same excited state. The berries became a regular part of the diet at the local monastery and were considered a gift from heaven, since they helped keep the brothers awake during their evening prayers.

The word *coffee* comes from an Arabic word for wine. Islamic law forbids wine's consumption, and in many ways the Islamic world has chosen coffee to take its place. As early as the fifth century, Arabian doctors were using coffee as a medicine, but its first serious cultivation as a cash crop took place in Yemen during the 1400s. Religious pilgrims visiting Mecca spread the news about coffee throughout the Arab world, and the coffeehouse soon became part of every Islamic community.

A Dutch traveler by the name of Carstens Niebuhr describes a typical Middle Eastern coffeehouse:

> *Coffee houses are commonly large halls, with floors that are covered with straw mats. At night they are illuminated by many lamps. The customers are served with smoking pipes and cups of coffee. Scholars sit in these establishments and tell tales, deliver speeches on various subjects and receive small contributions from the audience for their efforts.*

The caffeine in coffee is a stimulant, and in these ancient Arab coffeehouses it stimulated original thought, a sense of freedom, and a desire to discuss politics and social change. But the ruling class was threatened by this development, and in 1656, the Grand Vizier of the Ottoman Empire outlawed the coffeehouse. Yet the idea that coffeehouses were gathering places for revolutionaries and centers of social unrest stayed around for hundreds of years. In fact, plans for the French revolution, as well as for the American Revolution, were discussed and planned during meetings held in coffeehouses.

The first coffeehouse in Great Britain was opened in Oxford in 1650 by a Turkish immigrant. In England, coffeehouses were the perfect setting for proposing new business plans, and the first stock exchange in England got started in a coffee-house, as did the world's most famous insurance company, Lloyds of London. People who were interested in a specific kind of business would congregate in a particular coffeehouse. Industry grew up around them.

In 1674, a Women's Petition Against Coffee was published in London. It claimed that coffeehouses kept men from their homes and made them sexually impotent. The following year, King Charles tried to close the coffeehouses with a proclamation that read:

> *Whereas it is most apparent that the multitude of Coffee Houses of late years set up and kept within this kingdom, and the great resort of idle and disaffected persons to them, have produced very evil and dangerous effects; and that many tradesmen and others, do herein misspend much of their time, which might and probably would be employed in and about their Lawful Calling and Affairs; and that in such houses...divers false, malicious and scandalous reports are devised and spread abroad to the Defamation of his Majesty's Government, and to the Disturbance of the Peace and Quiet of the Realm; his Majesty hath thought fit and necessary, that the said Coffee Houses be put down, and suppressed.*

The public outcry in response to this proclamation was so great that it was withdrawn in eleven days. Coffee and free speech won the day.

In 1683, the city of Vienna was attacked and surrounded by a Turkish army. Eventually, the siege was broken and the Turks retreated, leaving behind hundreds of sacks filled with coffee beans. Coffee was a regular part of the Turkish diet, but it was almost unknown to the Viennese. A war hero named Franz Kolschitsky was in the know, however, and he gathered up the beans, brewed them, and sold the city its first taste. As a reward for his wartime efforts, he was given a building, which he turned into the city's first coffeehouse—a model for what is today a distinctive gastronomic landmark. By the middle of the 1700s, there were tens of thousands of coffeehouses throughout the great cities of Europe.

The coffeehouse played its part in the Age of Enlightenment, the 1700s, a time when philosophers believed in the reasonable mind of man, in natural law, and in universal order. They promoted a rational and scientific approach to religious, political, and economic issues, and attacked the social restraints and censorship of the time. The idea of man as an essentially rational being set the stage for the economic policies of Adam Smith and the political ideas of Thomas Jefferson and Benjamin Franklin. It was in coffeehouses that many of these social, financial, and political concepts were first presented and discussed.

The English brought coffee to their American colonies, but it was expensive in comparison to tea, which is why the early settlers were great tea drinkers. When King George's tax on tea caused the patriots of Boston to stage the Boston Tea Party, the event was more financial than political, and totally unrelated to gastronomy. (The history of how people really eat and drink shows that politics play a very small role in our food selections. Prices, on the other hand, constantly alter the way we eat.) During the Revolutionary War, the American colonists drank coffee because tea was not readily available. But when the war was over they went right back to drinking tea, which was cheaper. When the newly formed United States of America went into battle with England for a second time during the War of 1812, the supply of English tea was once again greatly reduced. Americans returned to drinking coffee, but this time the coffee came from Latin America rather than from Africa or Asia. It was inexpensive, and of the best quality.

After the war, Americans stopped purchasing their tea from the great English tea companies, buying it instead from American shipping companies. The quality of the tea significantly declined, which caused most people to continue drinking coffee. The choice was very simple: terrible tea or excellent, inexpensive coffee. Today, the United States is a nation of coffee drinkers, and we drink over half a billion cups every day.

Since the 1950s, Americans have been in pursuit of better quality coffee and more sophisticated coffee-making methods. The percolator, deemed by many coffee experts considerably less than an ideal method, was replaced by a French drip pot, or a Napoletana, or the Moka, or the Melitta filter pot. In his search for a liquid of perfect purity, a New York chemist named Morris Slumbom invented the Chemex. Dozens of other methods soon followed, including the plunger-driven Melior. Finally, the electric espresso and cappuccino maker became the wedding present of the 1990s. Espresso and cappuccino have taken America by storm, a storm that started in Italy.

Illy Caffe

Francesco Illy, one of the founding fathers of espresso, began the Illy Caffe company in 1933. In 1935, he built and patented the Illetta, which is considered to be the forerunner of most modern espresso machines. Today, the company is run by his son, Ernesto Illy, a chemist by training, who has applied all of his skill to the technology involved in making a better cup of espresso. The Illy roasting facility is in the Italian city of Trieste.

The process begins with the arrival of nine different varieties of the Arabica coffee bean. They come from Ethiopia, Kenya, Columbia, and Brazil—areas that are considered to be ideal for growing the beans that make espresso. The first task undertaken at the roasting company is ridding the new shipment of any defective beans. The most accurate and sophisticated technology for doing the job uses photoelectric cells and a set of color codes to spot a bean that is not up to standard. If the bean is the wrong color, it is taken out of the stream at a rate no human eye or hand could match. Such a machine sorts 400 beans per second. The process is critical—a single bad bean can affect the taste of hundreds of other beans. It takes about 50 beans to make a cup of espresso.

Once the beans are sorted, the blending begins. In order to have a great cup of espresso, three major characteristics must be balanced: the taste, the aroma, and the body of the liquid. It is almost impossible to get this balance in one shipment of coffee beans. (Which is where the nine varieties and the blender come in.)

When a brand name is on a coffee (or any other food product for that matter), we expect it to taste the same all the time. But the elements that go into making up that brand are constantly changing. Crops vary from year to year. But the consumer always expects the same taste from the same product. Coffee blenders sample every batch of beans that comes into the plant, and constantly revise the formula for the brand so that the final product always has the same taste, body, and aroma.

When the experts choose their coffee beans, they also pay attention to the way that particular coffee acts when it is ground. Some beans will grind well for espresso; others are better for filter coffee or for a plunger system.

The most important stage in the production of coffee is the roasting, which is done in huge rotating cylinders. The temperature inside the cylinder rises slowly, and the beans begin to give up their moisture and plump. The cell walls, however, can only take a certain amount of pressure before they explode. Temperature is critical: the bean must be roasted, not blown up. Once the beans are done, they are cooled in one of two ways: Water is the fastest way to cool them down, but it reduces the quality of the product. Streams of cool air are the preferred coolant for the best coffee beans.

Once a bean is perfectly roasted, however, the process is far from over. If the coffee is not adequately stored on the way to brewing, the taste will be ruined. Air is the enemy of roasted coffee and will steal the coffee's flavor within a few weeks. One system of preserving the flavor is to put the coffee into a can, then hermetically seal or vacuum-pack it. But this solution will work only for about three months, and coffee loses much of its flavor in the process.

A second system is "the valve release" method. Coffee goes into a bag, the air is taken out, and the bag is sealed. The gases given off by the coffee escape through the valve, which slows the deterioration process down to a year.

The best results come from a system of pressurization. The beans go into airtight metal containers, the air is removed, and low-pressure inert gases like nitrogen or carbon dioxide take its place. The can is sealed, holding the beans inside under pressure without loss of aroma for three years.

Espresso coffee can be bought ground or as whole beans. Dr. Illy feels that if the coffee is held under pressure, it can be bought in the ground form and will be perfect. Otherwise, it is better to buy the whole bean and grind it at home.

In order to make a cup of espresso, the ever-precise Dr. Illy recommends using 7 grams of Arabica blend ground into 1 millimeter grains plus 30 ccs of pure bottled spring water heated to exactly 90 degrees Centigrade. The water should be sent through the ground beans at 9 atmospheres of pressure for no longer than 30 seconds.

If this method is just a tad too complicated for your kitchen, Dr. Illy has invented a "pod," a pre-measured individual serving of espresso, tamped and sealed in filter paper. Put the disc into the espresso machine. Make the espresso. Throw the disk into the garbage, or into a handy composter. With this method, one hops from pod to pod. Something is always brewing with Ernesto, who could easily be called the Edison of Espresso.

AMARETTI DI SARONNO

In 1789, the bishop of Milan decided to pay a visit to the Italian town of Saronno. The bishop gave the town very little notice about his arrival, and the town had no time to prepare a suitable celebration. Giuseppe and Osolina, who were madly in love, decided to mark the occasion by quickly inventing a cookie using the ingredients at hand—egg whites, sugar, and the kernels of apricots. The result was an extraordinarily light, crisp confection. Osolina decided to wrap them in pairs as a symbol of the love she and Giuseppe shared.

Today, these cookies are called Amaretti di Saronno, and are shipped all over the world. They are still wrapped in pairs, and in the same kind of square paper that Osolina originally used almost three hundred years ago. The design on the paper, however, illustrates the ship that first brought Amaretti cookies to America.

When the bishop visited Saronno, he tasted the Amaretti and gave them his gastronomic blessing. He also performed the marriage of Giuseppe and Osolina, who lived happily ever after, and whose children and children's children have continued to bake the cookies his unheralded arrival inspired.

Recipes for Coffee
Europe & America

Lemon Curd Tart

Tiramisu

Gingerbread Loaf

Lemon Curd Tart

Makes 6-8 servings

Chef Monique Barbeau
Fullers Restaurant, Sheraton Hotel, Seattle, Washington

For the Lemon Curd Tart:

- 7 eggs
- 2 tablespoons grated lemon
  zest (about 2 lemons)
- 6 lemons, juiced
- 1½ cup granulated sugar
- 1 deep dish 9-inch prebaked pie shell

For the Candied Lemon Zest Garnish:

- 4 lemons, rind peeled, julienned,
  and blanched
- 4 tablespoons granulated sugar
- 4 tablespoons water

For the Lemon Curd Tart:

1   IN A LARGE SKILLET bring 1 to 2 inches of water to a boil.

2   IN A LARGE HEAT-PROOF MIXING BOWL, that will fit snugly in the skillet to form a bain marie, combine the eggs, lemon zest, lemon juice, and sugar. Whisk together until well combined. Transfer the bowl to the skillet and whisk the mixture continually at a fairly vigorous rate until it thickens to the consistency of a thick hollandaise sauce. This should take 10 to 15 minutes. You know it's ready when the whisk is removed from the custard and holds soft folds on its surface.

3   POUR THE CURD in the prebaked pie shell, cover with plastic wrap, and place in the refrigerator to chill and set for 40 minutes.

To Make the Candied Lemon Zest Garnish:

1   PLACE THE JULIENNED LEMON ZEST, the sugar, and the water into a small saucepan and bring to a boil. Reduce to a simmer and cook until the water evaporates completely. Set aside.

2   WHEN THE TART COMES OUT of the refrigerator, garnish the rim with the candied lemon zest and serve.

Tiramisu

½ cup warm espresso or strong coffee

½ cup granulated sugar

2 tablespoons brandy or rum

12 crisp classic Italian ladyfingers (one sleeve of a two-sleeve, 7-ounce package)

3 large egg yolks

¼ cup orange juice

8 ounces mascarpone cheese, at room temperature

1 teaspoon minced orange zest

1 tablespoon orange liqueur

½ cup heavy cream

¼ cup chopped chocolate-covered espresso beans or chocolate chips

1 teaspoon ground cinnamon

1   IN A MEDIUM BOWL, mix together the espresso, ¼ cup of the sugar, and the brandy or rum. Cool. Briefly dip 8 of the ladyfingers into the coffee and then lay them in the bottom of a 4-cup shallow serving dish. Do not soak the ladyfingers. Reserve the coffee mixture.

2   IN A MEDIUM HEAT-PROOF BOWL, whisk the egg yolks together, and then whisk in the remaining sugar and the orange juice. Set the bowl over a pot of simmering water, and with a hand-held mixer or a whisk, whip for 3 to 4 minutes, or until the eggs are thick and light yellow in color. Remove from the heat and whip until cool.

3   CREAM THE MASCARPONE UNTIL SOFTENED, and mix with the eggs. Add the orange zest and orange liqueur. In another bowl, whip the cream to soft peaks and then fold it into the mascarpone mousse. Fold in the chopped espresso beans or chocolate chips.

4   SPREAD TWO-THIRDS of the mascarpone mousse over the ladyfingers. Break up the last 4 ladyfingers and briefly soak them in the coffee-brandy mixture. Scatter them over the mousse and then cover with a smooth layer of the remaining mousse. Chill for 2 hours, dust the tiramisu with the cinnamon, and serve.

Gingerbread Loaf

Makes 6 servings

Chef Genevieve Harris
The Bathers Pavilion, Balmoral, Australia

For the Gingerbread Loaf:

7 ounces butter, softened

1 cup dark brown sugar

1 egg

2½ cups all purpose flour

1½ teaspoons baking soda

2 tablespoons ground cinnamon

1 tablespoon ground ginger

¾ cup boiling water

¾ cup dark corn syrup

For the Caramelized Apple Sauce:

3 cups water

2 cups granulated sugar

1-inch piece fresh ginger, peeled

5 Granny Smith apples, peeled, cored,
  and sliced

1½ cups dark brown sugar

1½ cups water

Vanilla ice cream for serving

To Prepare the Gingerbread:

1 PREHEAT THE OVEN TO 375°F. Grease a 4½ x 8½-inch loaf pan with butter and place a 3½ x 14-inch strip of parchment paper lengthwise on the bottom with the excess folded over the two short edges.

2 IN A LARGE MIXING BOWL, combine the butter and brown sugar and whisk well. The mixture will look grainy at first; keep whisking until the butter and sugar are smooth. Add the egg and whisk it into the mixture until it's fluffy and smooth in appearance.

3 IN A SEPARATE BOWL mix together the flour, baking soda, cinnamon, and ginger.

4 IN ANOTHER BOWL or heat-proof measuring cup, stir together the boiling water and corn syrup.

5   SIFT ⅓ OF THE FLOUR MIXTURE OVER THE BUTTER, sugar, and egg mixture. Whisk to combine completely. Pour ⅓ of the corn syrup water into the batter and whisk to combine completely. Repeat this procedure 2 more times to combine all the dry and wet ingredients.

6   POUR THE BATTER into the prepared loaf pan and bake for 45 to 55 minutes until a wooden toothpick inserted in the gingerbread comes out clean.

7   COOL THE CAKE FOR 10 MINUTES ON A RACK. Loosen the loaf by running a knife down the long edges of the pan. Using the parchment handles, lift the loaf from the pan. Remove the parchment and allow the loaf to cool on the rack.

To Make the Caramelized Apple Sauce:

1   WHILE THE LOAF IS BAKING, place the 3 cups of water, the granulated sugar, and the ginger in a saucepan and bring to a boil, then reduce the heat and simmer for about 1 minute until the syrup gets clear. Add the apples and continue to simmer for 1 minute until the apples are tender but not soft. With a slotted spoon remove the fruit from the poaching syrup and set aside. Discard the poaching liquid.

2   AFTER THE LOAF IS SET ON THE RACK TO COOL, in a saucepan bring the brown sugar and water to a boil. Cook until the liquid is reduced by a third. Reduce to a simmer and carefully place the poached apples in the syrup. Shake the pan gently to agitate the apples in the syrup and glaze them. Cook for 5 minutes. With a slotted spoon remove the apples from the syrup and set aside.

To Serve:

1   SLICE THE LOAF INTO 1-INCH PIECES. Pile several apple slices on the pieces and spoon several tablespoons of syrup over the apples and around the loaf. Garnish with a generous dollop of vanilla ice cream and serve immediately.

CHRISTMAS IN GERMANY

O f all the gatherings and celebrations in the Western world, none is more festive than Christmas. Originally, the holiday was a purely religious occasion celebrating the birth of Christ. But the commercial elements in our contemporary society have made a great effort to usurp the event. Thankfully, the strongest message of Christmas still manages to outshine consumerist fantasy, and reminds us every year that the greatest gifts of life are beyond the material. The light that shines from the candles of Christmas is a reminder that the greatest light is within us.

A Short History of Christmas: Religion and Traditions

During the fourth century, Constantine the Great made Christianity the official religion of the Roman Empire. Often, when a new religion is adopted by a culture, the dates for the new festivals remain on or near the dates used by the old religion. (Governments find that the transition is easier that way.) Christmas is a good example of this policy.

On December 25, four days after the longest night of the year, the Romans celebrated the Feast of the Unconquered Sun, proclaiming their belief that the sun would return. The idea of light coming back in spite of the power of darkness was a symbol that translated well into the new religion, and became a symbol for the coming of Christ. In fact, for many centuries, Christ was often called the "Unconquered Sun." Straw radiating like rays of light from around the baby Jesus in the manger is a graphic representation of this idea.

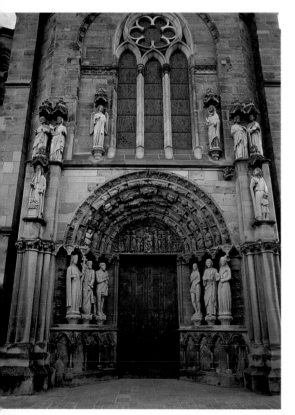

There are two important periods of abstinence in the Christian year. The greatest is Lent, which takes place during the six weeks before Easter. The second is Advent, which occurs during the four weeks before Christmas. (The four weeks symbolize the time covered in the Old Testament—the world was once thought to have lasted four thousand years from creation to Christ.) One idea behind both Lent and Advent is anticipation: get ready for a great feast by not eating. The word *advent* means "coming," and the period is marked by a sense of expectation—a sense that is heightened by fasting as the event approaches.

Today, Advent calendars are found all over the Christian world, but the custom began in Germany. The Advent calendar has a miniature door for each day from the first day of Advent until Christmas. Each day, one of the doors is opened and inside is a picture or a saying or a little present.

Many of the Christmas rituals that are now practiced all over the world actually originated in Germany. In some German houses you will also see a "Star of Seven," a seven-branched candlestick inherited from Jewish tradition. The candles are lit every evening during Advent, and are eventually carried to the midnight service on Christmas Eve. This custom was one of the rituals that eventually led to lights on the Christmas tree.

Germany is also the home of the *Christkindlemarkt*, an ancient market or fair that is thought to have originated in the Middle Ages. The fair, traditionally held in the old marketplaces, begins around December 4th and continues until Christmas. Before the Protestant Reformation, there was a ceremony in which the Christ Child was given to the people of the city. The figure of the baby Jesus was taken out of the Christmas crib and presented to a crowd of children. After the Reformation, the crib ceremony was abolished and a child dressed as a "golden angel" welcomed visitors to the fair. Toy reproductions of these angels are sold at the market and used to decorate the home.

One of the most important rules in any festival is that the festival itself and most of the objects within it must be temporary. A festival, by definition, is something out of the ordinary, different from everyday life. If it stays around too long it loses its impact. Food is always a mainstay at festivals because it doesn't last, and at the Christmas market, food—or anything made of edible materials—is the most important product for sale.

At the market, stands are loaded with *Pfefferkuchen,* or "peppernuts" (a medieval recipe for spice cakes made with pepper); *Lebkuchen,* or honey cakes, frosted cookies with elaborate designs; grilled herring, and sausages. In parts of Germany you will find a hard gingerbread called *Spekulatius,* which is often prepared in a mold that depicts St. Nicholas. Other gingerbreads are shaped into Christmas tree ornaments. Using pepper and strong spices in cakes goes all the way back to the time of the ancient Romans and the birth of Christ.

The idea of gift-giving is actually a major part of the story of Christmas. The Christ Child is seen as a Christmas present from God to humanity. The Magi, later known as the Three Kings, brought presents to the Christ Child in the manger. Human beings are expected to respond to God's generosity by continuing the giving of gifts.

In Germany, the feast of St. Nicholas officially begins on December 6th. St. Nicholas was a bishop in Turkey during the fourth century A.D. He was famous for giving gifts to children and dowries to poor girls so that they could get married. The three bags of gold he gave to each girl eventually became the three gold balls that are often on display in front of pawnbroker shops.

On the night before his feast begins, St. Nicholas appears dressed in bishop's vestments. He walks about the town accompanied by his "dark side," a fellow called *Knecht Ruprecht*, a frightening masked figure who is sometimes dressed in furs with antlers.

In many towns, St. Nicholas actually comes to people's houses and meets the children. The parents often slip him a note with information about each child. He then announces what each child has done throughout the past year, both good and bad. The children have no idea how he knows.

In parts of Germany where St. Nicholas does not actually appear but passes in the night like Santa Claus (whose name, by the way, comes from the Dutch for St. Nicholas), children will leave a shoe or a stocking beside the bed or outside the door. If the child has been good, St. Nicholas will leave a present, but bad children get a stick, a piece of coal, or a potato.

The Christmas tree, a Protestant idea invented to take the place of saints and human figures, was already a well-established tradition in Germany when Prince Albert, the German husband of Britain's Queen Victoria, introduced it to England during the 1840s. The Christmas tree then made its way from England to North America, but it also took a more direct route from Germany, coming over with the great immigrations of the nineteenth century. Families often have homemade Christmas tree decorations that have been passed down from one generation to the next. Each has its own story: who made it, when, and how. The decorations and the stories are a way of keeping the family's history alive.

In obedience to the rule that festivals are only temporary, the Christmas tree must be taken down right after Epiphany, on the 6th of January. Most Germans are very strict about this rule, and it is believed that bad luck will haunt a house that has kept a tree up too long.

The Foods of Christmas

Every country in Europe has its own Christmas foods and Christmas Eve dinner customs. In Poland, people put pieces of straw under the tablecloth so the dishes will sit on a slant to remind the diners of Christ's poverty. In Russia, an empty chair is left for a passing stranger, or a foreigner is invited to the meal. Christmas Eve is the night when animals were supposed to be able to speak and to understand human language. Germans still remember this belief, and animals, especially house pets, are often treated with special respect on this night by being given special foods.

The traditional pre-Christmas meal is rather simple. The main dish is usually fish, most often carp. In Germany it is lucky to receive the roe with your portion, for a common belief holds that a lot of little eggs means a lot of good fortune. The vegetable dishes often include beets and cabbage—red and green are always the colors of Christmas. Red is for warmth and brightness; green is a promise that the leaves will return to the bare trees.

At the Christmas feast, which takes place around midday in Germany, the meal may begin with *Griessknudel*, a clear broth served with semolina dumplings. A roast goose is traditionally served as the main course. (Every family has its own stuffing recipe, which may include sauerkraut, dried fruits, apples or chestnuts.) Roast hare is another traditional Christmas main dish. Whether goose or hare, roast potatoes will be served. No German meal can take place without potatoes in some form.

There are also many German Christmas breads and cakes. One of the most typical is the *Christstollen*, which is filled with nuts, raisins, lemon peel, and other dried fruits. It is almost the German version of the English Christmas pudding. And there are dozens of different baked sweet cakes and cookies, like marzipan, anise cakes, almond cookies, hazelnut macaroons, and chocolate pretzels. Nuts are always left in convenient bowls around the house, and represent the puzzle of life. You must open them up to find your destiny. *Gluhwein,* or mulled wine, and mulled cider might accompany dessert.

Apples are hung on the tree and represent the Tree of Knowledge in the Garden of Eden. They are bright and shiny and very appealing. Germans have been putting them on the tree for many hundreds of years. The apple is another symbol of hope and light during a dark time.

People learned to preserve apples for the long winter months, and they serve as an example of human intelligence and resourcefulness.

Wines of the Mosel Region

Making wine in the Mosel is not an easy job; the area contains some of the hilliest country in Germany. The slopes along the riverbanks are nearly vertical, and the cultivation and harvesting is work for mountaineers. The wines of the Mosel are naturally low in alcohol content, yet high in acidity, which makes them a good companion to food.

Barbara Rundquist-Müller and her husband, Erik, help manage a family winery that is named after her grandfather, Rudolf Müller. The Müllers have been making wine since the twelfth century, and today are among the most traditional winemakers in the Mosel valley. The family produces a number of wines, one of which is the *Berncasteler Doctor*, an estate wine. Some of the Müller family's wines are classics from the Mosel and Rhine regions and are made primarily from the Riesling grape. The *Rudolf Müller Piesporter Treppfchen* is one of these. But their most famous is a wine called The Bishop of Riesling.

This wine is named after the eighteenth-century Archbishop of Trier. During the 1700s, the bishop published a decree saying that only the Riesling grape variety could be grown in the Mosel region. He also created the basic structure for the Mosel wine industry and set up a plan to raise the quality of local wines and the standing of his community. The wine that bears his name is made completely from Riesling grapes that come from the Bernkasteler area, and has become one of the most widely distributed Rieslings in the world.

Recipes for Christmas
Germany

Beef Roulades

Roast Christmas Goose

Riesling Soup

Red Wine Spiced Cabbage

Stollen

Ginger Spice Cookies

Beef Roulades

Makes about 20 small roulades (4-5 servings)

Mrs. Barbara Rundquist-Müller

Rudolf Müller Winery

For the Roulades:

> 2 pounds sirloin of beef, sliced into ½-inch-thick slices approximately 9 x 4 inches
>
> ½ teaspoon kosher salt
>
> Freshly ground black pepper to taste
>
> 3 medium cloves garlic, minced
>
> ½ pound Westphalian or Black Forest ham, thinly sliced into pieces to fit over the sirloin slices
>
> 25-30 basil leaves, washed and dried
>
> 1 tablespoon vegetable oil
>
> 1 tablespoon unsalted butter

For the Sauce:

> 2 tablespoons sugar
>
> 2 tablespoons unsalted butter
>
> 2 cups Riesling or other white wine
>
> ½ cup raisins
>
> ½ cup heavy cream
>
> 1 teaspoon arrowroot dissolved in 1 tablespoon water
>
> ¼ teaspoon kosher salt
>
> Pinch of freshly ground black pepper
>
> ⅛ teaspoon freshly grated nutmeg

1   TO PREPARE THE ROULADES: On a clean work surface, lay a slice of the beef with a long edge facing you. Season each slice of the meat with salt, pepper, and the garlic. Cover the beef with pieces of ham (cut the ham to cover the meat evenly). Lay 3 or 4 basil leaves on top. Roll the beef up to make a long, tight package. Slice the roulade into pieces about 3 inches long. Secure each roulade closed with a toothpick. Repeat this with the rest of the beef. Set the roulades aside while you make the sauce. The roulades can be made a day ahead and refrigerated until ready to cook.

2   TO MAKE THE SAUCE: In a saucepan over medium-high heat, whisk the sugar and butter together, then cook, undisturbed, until the sugar begins to caramelize to a light toffee color. Remove the pan from the heat and carefully add the wine; when you add the liquid the sugar will splatter at first and then solidify. Return the pan to the heat and stir the sauce until the sugar liquefies. This will take about 5 to 7 minutes. Add the raisins and simmer until the wine reduces by about a third. Add the cream to the sauce and bring to a boil. To thicken the sauce, whisk the disolved arrowroot into the sauce and bring the sauce to a boil. Boil for about 1 minute. Season with salt, pepper, and nutmeg. Set aside while you cook the roulades.

3   TO COOK THE ROULADES: Heat a large skillet, add the oil and butter and, when the foam begins to subside, add the roulades to the pan. Don't overcrowd the pan or the roulades won't brown. If necessary, cook the beef in batches. Brown the roulades over high heat on all sides, about 5 minutes. Transfer the cooked roulades to a warmed platter and remove the toothpicks. Add the sauce to the skillet. Increase the heat to high and scrape the bottom of the pan with a wooden spoon to collect any browned bits. Serve the roulades with the sauce on top.

Roast Christmas Goose

Makes 4-5 servings

Executive Chef Andreas Hauk

Hotel Nassauer Hof

One (8-9 pound) fresh goose

3 cups beef broth

1 large onion, outer skin removed, ends trimmed, cut into 1-inch pieces

1 Granny Smith apple, cut into 1-inch pieces

1 navel orange, cut into 1-inch pieces

4 sprigs fresh thyme, coarsely chopped

2¼ teaspoons kosher salt

¼ teaspoon freshly ground black pepper

1 tablespoon vegetable oil

1 cup white wine

1 tablespoon arrowroot dissolved in a few tablespoons of water

1   REMOVE THE GIBLETS and neck from the cavity of the bird. Discard the liver, but reserve the gizzards and neck. Trim the neck flap, tail, and inside cavity of excess fat. Reserve the fat for rendering, and use in the Red Wine Spiced Cabbage, if desired (see Note). Cut the wing tips at the joint and reserve the tips for a goose broth. With a boning or paring knife remove the wishbone by cutting underneath both sides of the bone to free it from the flesh. Cut through the bottom of the wishbone where it meets the neck, and then pull until it comes free.

2   IN A POT, make a goose broth by simmering the gizzards, neck, wing tips, and wishbone in the beef broth for 1½ hours. Strain into a saucepan and reserve for making the gravy.

3   PREHEAT THE OVEN TO 350˚F. Mix the onion, apple, and orange together in a bowl with the thyme, ½ teaspoon salt, and ⅛ teaspoon pepper. Stuff the goose with this mixture, and sew the cavity shut with kitchen string. Tie the legs of the bird together. Prick the skin all over with a fork and rub with 1½ teaspoons salt.

4   HEAT A LARGE ROASTING PAN on top of the stove and add the oil. Carefully sear the goose on each side of the breast and the back for 3 to 4 minutes or until lightly browned. Transfer the bird to a plate and pour off the excess fat from the pan. Add ½ inch of water and return the goose to the pan, laying it on one side. Place the pan in the oven and roast for 45 minutes. Check the bird while it is roasting to make sure the water doesn't evaporate, or the goose fat will burn. Carefully pour off the excess fat. Prick the goose with the fork again, rotate the bird to the other side, add ½ inch of water to the pan, and continue to roast for another 45 minutes. Pour off the excess fat, turn the goose so the breast is up, add ½ inch of water to the pan, and continue to roast for another hour.

5   WHEN THE BIRD IS DONE, the juices will run clear from the breast and the thigh will move easily in its joint. To brown the skin of the bird, raise the heat to 500° and cook for 10 to 12 minutes. Remove the bird from the oven and let it rest in a warm spot for 20 minutes while you make the gravy.

6   TO MAKE THE GRAVY, discard all the excess fat from the roasting pan. Put the roasting pan over a medium flame and pour the wine into the pan. With a wooden spoon scrape up all the browned bits from the pan and cook the wine to reduce by about half. Add the wine and pan juices to the goose broth, and bring to a simmer. To thicken the sauce, whisk the disolved arrowroot into the sauce and bring it to a boil. Season with the remaining salt and pepper.

7   TO SERVE THE GOOSE, discard the stuffing, which is used only to perfume the bird during roasting. Carve the breast, leg, and thigh into thin slices. Arrange on a warmed platter and serve with the gravy.

NOTE

To render goose fat, place the goose fat in a heavy-bottomed pan with about ¾ to 1 cup water. Bring to a low simmer and cook slowly to evaporate the water and extract the fat. The key to rendering is to moderate the heat so the fat doesn't brown. When the fat is rendered, all the water should be evaporated, all the fat will be liquid, and any skin will have cooked down to small pieces. If desired, separate the fat from the skin and chill the fat for future use.

Riesling Soup

Makes 4-6 servings

Mrs. Barbara Rundquist-Müller
Rudolf Müller Winery

4 tablespoons unsalted butter

1 pound turnips, peeled and grated

3 medium leeks, white and light green parts, sliced and washed

1 medium onion, peeled and diced

2 teaspoons kosher salt

¼ teaspoon freshly ground black pepper

2 cups Riesling wine

2 cups beef or chicken broth

½ cup heavy cream

2 tablespoons minced fresh flat-leaf parsley

1 MELT THE BUTTER IN A SOUP POT; add the turnips, leeks, and onion, and season with the salt and pepper. Cover and cook the vegetables over medium heat until soft and tender, about 20 minutes, stirring occasionally to make sure they do not brown.

2 ADD THE WINE TO THE VEGETABLES and simmer over medium heat to reduce by about one half. This will take about 10 minutes. In a blender, process the soup to a coarsely textured puree.

3 RETURN THE SOUP TO THE PAN, add the broth, and simmer for 3 to 4 minutes. Add the cream and continue to simmer for 3 to 4 minutes more to thicken slightly. Serve the soup in warmed bowls with a sprinkling of parsley on top.

Red Wine Spiced Cabbage

Makes 4 servings

Executive Chef Andreas Hauk

Hotel Nassauer Hof

½ head red cabbage

3 cups red wine

2 bay leaves

1 teaspoon juniper berries (optional)

1 cinnamon stick

2 teaspoons kosher salt

⅛ teaspoon freshly ground black pepper

1 tablespoon vegetable oil, or rendered goose fat

1 medium onion, sliced

2 teaspoons sugar

1 apple

1 USING A MANDOLINE OR A KNIFE, slice the cabbage into very thin long strips. In a non-reactive bowl, marinate the cabbage in the red wine, along with the bay leaves, juniper berries, cinnamon stick, salt, and black pepper. Refrigerate the cabbage overnight.

2 THE NEXT DAY, drain and reserve the cabbage marinade. In a large skillet, heat the oil or goose fat and sauté the onion over high heat for 3 to 4 minutes, until translucent. Add the cabbage and cook for 3 to 4 minutes more, until wilted. Add the marinade and sugar, reduce the heat to low, cover the pan, and braise the cabbage for about 1 hour or until it is tender.

3 PEEL AND CORE THE APPLE. Grate the apple into the cabbage, and continue to cook for 10 minutes more.

Stollen

Makes 1 large loaf

Executive Chef Andreas Hauk
Hotel Nassauer Hof

½ cup dark rum
1 cup currants
⅔ cup milk
Two (¼ ounce each) packages active dry yeast
⅓ cup granulated sugar
2¼ cups all-purpose flour
1 teaspoon kosher salt
½ cup ground almonds
9 tablespoons unsalted butter, softened
2 tablespoons diced candied orange peel
2 tablespoons diced citron or other candied fruit
½ cup confectioners' sugar, plus more for dusting

1   HEAT THE RUM in a small saucepan, remove from the heat, add the currants, and set aside to plump.

2   IN ANOTHER SMALL SAUCEPAN warm the milk slightly. Pour the milk into the bowl of a standing mixer, sprinkle the yeast over the surface, and add a tablespoon of the granulated sugar. Let the yeast proof. After about 5 minutes, the yeast will expand and start to bubble.

3   WITH THE DOUGH HOOK ATTACHMENT and the machine on medium speed, add 1½ cups of flour and the salt to the milk to make a wet dough; mix for 2 to 3 minutes, until smooth.

4   CONTINUE MIXING ON MEDIUM SPEED, and add the almonds and the remaining sugar. Reserve a tablespoon of butter, break the rest into 4 or 5 pieces, and add it to the dough. The dough will be very wet and sticky. Add enough of the remaining flour to make a soft, elastic dough, and continue to mix at medium speed for 4 to 5 minutes.

5   DRAIN AND RESERVE THE RUM from the currants. Add all the dried fruit to the dough and mix for 2 to 3 minutes more, or until evenly incorporated.

6   COAT THE INSIDE OF A BOWL with the reserved tablespoon of butter. Turn the dough out of the mixing bowl, dust your hands with flour, and form the dough into a ball. Roll the dough in the bowl until it is covered with the butter. Cover the bowl with plastic wrap and set the bowl aside in a warm spot until the dough doubles in size, 1 to 1½ hours.

7   WHEN THE DOUGH HAS DOUBLED, carefully turn it out onto a parchment-lined baking sheet, lightly dust with flour, and press it out into a large oval, about 15 inches long. Fold the dough over lengthwise like a clam shell, with the top covering four-fifths of the bottom. It's like a very long Parker House roll. Straighten the long edges of the loaf. Cover the dough with a kitchen towel. Let it rest for 30 minutes. Preheat the oven to 400°F.

8   BAKE THE STOLLEN in the middle of the oven for 10 minutes. After 10 minutes rotate the baking sheet to ensure even cooking. Reduce the temperature to 350°F. Continue to bake the stollen for 25 to 35 minutes until it is golden brown and sounds hollow when thumped. If the bottom of the loaf is browning too quickly, slip a cool baking sheet underneath to control the heat. Transfer the finished loaf to a rack to cool.

9   AS THE LOAF COOLS, make the glaze. In a small pan whisk 2 tablespoons of the reserved rum or water with the confectioners' sugar. Cook over low heat until the mixture is dissolved and slightly thickened, about 30 seconds to 1 minute. Paint the top of the warm stollen with the glaze. Cool. Wrap in plastic wrap until ready to serve. Dust with the confectioners' sugar for a finished look before serving.

Ginger Spice Cookies

Makes about 3 dozen cookies

2 cups all-purpose flour

2 tablespoons cocoa powder

1 teaspoon baking powder

1¼ teaspoons ground ginger

¾ teaspoon ground cinnamon

¼ teaspoon ground allspice

⅛ teaspoon freshly ground black pepper

¼ teaspoon kosher salt

8 tablespoons (1 stick) unsalted butter, softened

½ cup light brown sugar

⅓ cup pureed candied ginger

1 large egg

½ cup honey

Confectioners' sugar for dusting

1 IN A BOWL, sift together the flour, cocoa, baking powder, spices, pepper, and salt.

2 IN A SECOND BOWL, using a hand-held mixer, cream the butter and brown sugar. Add the pureed candied ginger and the egg; mix until smooth.

3 ADD HALF THE FLOUR MIXTURE to make a soft dough. Then mix in the honey and follow with the remaining flour mixture. The dough will be very soft. Dampen your fingers to prevent them from sticking while you work. Divide the dough into 3 rectangular pieces; lightly dust each piece of dough with flour and press between 2 sheets of plastic wrap. Refrigerate until well chilled, at least a couple of hours or overnight.

4 PREHEAT THE OVEN TO 350°F.

5 USING A ROLLING PIN, roll each piece of dough between the sheets of plastic wrap until it is about ¼ inch thick. If the dough gets very soft, which it can, return it to the refrigerator for 10 to 15 minutes before cutting. Lightly dust a clean work space with flour, peel off the top sheet of plastic, and invert the dough onto the work space. Then peel off the other piece of plastic. Make sure the dough is not sticking to the counter before cutting it into cookies. Cut the dough into 2-inch stars, circles, or other medium-size cookies.

6 LINE 2 COOKIE SHEETS with parchment or dust with flour. Transfer the cookies with a spatula to the sheets. Bake the cookies for 15 minutes, or until the edges are lightly browned. Cool the cookies on a rack. When the cookies are cool, dust them with confectioners' sugar. Store in a well-sealed container.

Index

Photo Credits

page:

2	© Bettmann Newsphotos UPI	88	© Phillip Ruth 1996	172	© Portuguese Office of Tourism
3	© Laurent-Perrier 1996	89	© Burt Wolf 1996	173	© Burt Wolf 1996 (upper)
4	© Phillip Ruth 1996	90	© Burt Wolf 1996	173	© Burt Wolf 1996 (lower)
7	© San Francisco Examiner Archive	92	© Burt Wolf 1996	175	© Burt Wolf 1996
8	© San Francisco Examiner Archive	93	© Burt Wolf 1996	179	© Burt Wolf 1996
10	© Burt Wolf 1996	95	© Burt Wolf 1996	186	© Burt Wolf 1996
11	© Burt Wolf 1996	104	© Burt Wolf 1996	187	© Burt Wolf 1996
12	© Phillip Ruth 1996	105	© Burt Wolf 1996	189	© Burt Wolf 1996
13	© Burt Wolf 1996	106	© Burt Wolf 1996	190	© Burt Wolf 1996
22	© Phillip Ruth 1996	108	© Burt Wolf 1996	191	© Burt Wolf 1996
23	© The Bettmann Archive	109	© Burt Wolf 1996	192	© Burt Wolf 1996
24	© Phillip Ruth 1996	110	© Burt Wolf 1996	193	© Burt Wolf 1996
26	© STB/Still Moving	111	© Burt Wolf 1996	194	© Burt Wolf 1996
27	© STB/Still Moving	113	© Burt Wolf 1996	195	© Zoomi Oy/ Finnish Tourist Board
28	© Phillip Ruth 1996	120	© Burt Wolf 1996	202	© Phillip Ruth 1996
29	© Phillip Ruth 1996	121	© Seville Office of Tourism	203	© Phillip Ruth 1996
30	© STB/Still Moving	122	© Burt Wolf 1996	204	© Burt Wolf 1996
31	© Burt Wolf 1996	125	© Archive Photos	205	© Phillip Ruth 1996
38	© Burt Wolf 1996	126	© Burt Wolf 1996	206	© NY Public Library
39	© Burt Wolf 1996	127	© Seville Office of Tourism	208	© Burt Wolf 1996
40	© Burt Wolf 1996	129	© Burt Wolf 1996	209	© Burt Wolf 1996
41	© Burt Wolf 1996	136	© Burt Wolf 1996	218	© Bob Krist/ Puerto Rico Office of Tourism
42	© Burt Wolf 1996		Used by permission from Disney Enterprises, Inc.	219	© Phillip Ruth 1996
45	© Burt Wolf 1996	137	© Natalia Ilyin 1996	220	© Burt Wolf 1996
52	© Burt Wolf 1996	138	© Burt Wolf 1996	221	© Bob Krist/ Puerto Rico Office of Tourism
53	© Burt Wolf 1996	140	© Burt Wolf 1996	222	© Burt Wolf 1996
54	© Taiwan Office of Tourism		Disney character © Disney Enterprises, Inc.	224	© Burt Wolf 1996
56	© Taiwan Office of Tourism	141	© Burt Wolf 1996	225	© Bob Krist/ Puerto Rico Office of Tourism
57	© Burt Wolf 1996		Disney character © Disney Enterprises, Inc.	226	© Bob Krist/ Puerto Rico Office of Tourism
58	© Burt Wolf 1996	143	© Burt Wolf 1996	227	© Burt Wolf 1996
59	© Burt Wolf 1996	154	© Burt Wolf 1996	234	© Beaune Office of Tourism
61	© Burt Wolf 1996	155	© Burt Wolf 1996	235	© Beaune Office of Tourism
70	© William Tucker	156	© Taiwan Office of Tourism	237	© Beaune Office of Tourism
71	© Phillip Ruth 1996	157	© Burt Wolf 1996	238	© Phillip Ruth 1996
72	© Mariano Advertising	158	© Taiwan Office of Tourism	239	© Burt Wolf 1996
73	© Michael Terranova	160	© Burt Wolf 1996	240	© Burt Wolf 1996
74	© W. Bartsch	161	© Burt Wolf 1996	241	© Beaune Office of Tourism
76	© Wally Porter	170	© Joao Paulo	242	© Burt Wolf 1996
78	© Ron Calmia	171	© Joao Paulo		
79	© Burt Wolf 1996				
86	© Burt Wolf 1996				
87	© Burt Wolf 1996				